DANGEROUS GROUND

The Inside Story of
Britain's Leading Investigative Journalist

DANGEROUS GROUND

The Inside Story of
Britain's Leading Investigative Journalist

ROGER COOK

With Howard Foster

HarperCollins*Entertainment*
An Imprint of HarperCollins*Publishers*

HarperCollins*Entertainment*
An Imprint of HarperCollins*Publishers*
77–85 Fulham Palace Road,
Hammersmith, London w6 8jb

www.**fire**and**water**.com

Published by HarperCollins*Publishers* 1999
1 3 5 7 9 8 6 4 2

A catalogue record for this book
is available from the British Library

ISBN 0 00 257210 9

Set in Linotype PostScript Janson by
Rowland Phototypesetting Ltd,
Bury St Edmunds, Suffolk
Printed and bound in Great Britain by
Caledonian International Book Manufacturing Ltd, Glasgow

CONTENTS

To my long-suffering wife and daughter,
and the hardworking team
without whom 'The Cook Report'
would not have been possible.

ACKNOWLEDGEMENTS

I didn't really want to write this book. A documentary script is about my endurance limit. That it happened at all is largely due to my friend and former producer, Howard Foster, who did most of the keyboard pounding and who also tells me we've only scratched the surface so far . . .

Thanks also to Carlton Television for use of video stills from 'Cook Report' programmes, and to all those whose own recollections helped jog or amend my overloaded memory.

FOREWORD

I have never kept a proper diary. Script notes from time to time, but never a diary. So, although 'The Cook Report' stories herein are accurately retold from filmed records and programme files, background anecdotes and other incidental details are only as reliable as the collective memories of self, friends and colleagues will allow. And, remember, I have been hit over the head a few times . . .

DANGEROUS
GROUND

The Inside Story of
Britain's Leading Investigative Journalist

PREFACE

At the height of the South African summer the Low Veldt is covered in dense foliage. I wiped the sweat out of my eyes and looked to my left and to my right in the hope of seeing some landmark I could use to guide me when the time came to make a run for it. Nothing – just the same unending pattern of tall grass and dark clumps of thorn trees. Unless you knew the territory, you could drive through the red dust of these dirt tracks for days and never find your way out.

I looked across at my unsuspecting companions. Perched next to me, high up on the observation bench at the back of the customised hunting wagon, was one of the biggest men I had ever seen. Well over six feet tall with a grizzled, blond beard, Sandy McDonald must have weighed in excess of twenty stone. A Remington hunting rifle with telescopic sights rested across his enormous thighs.

In the canvas-covered driving seat, Mossie Mostert struggled with the wheel, the late-morning sun forcing him to pull his peaked hunting cap low over his eyes. As we bounced across the rough terrain, he steered us closer to our quarry. He stared fixedly past a pair of large-bore rifles and a long, wooden gun rest which were clipped across the folded windshield in front of him. A small, wiry figure with a notoriously short temper, his family owned the property we were hunting on.

On the bonnet of the Land Cruiser sat the tracker, a fit, muscular Afrikaner in standard-issue hunting greens and the obligatory camou-flaged cap. He gripped the sides of his lookout seat perched over the front bumper. The butt of a Browning 9mm pistol poked out of a holster at his hip.

At my back stood two colossal Africans known in the big game world as 'skinners'. Their job was to use the fearsome array of knives which they carried strapped to their belts as soon as I had done what their bosses expected of me – to shoot and kill a North Transvaal male lion in the most inhumane and illegal way. Once they had removed the animal's skin and cut off its magnificent head and mane, it would be time for me to pay the white hunters their extortionate fee. Then I'd wait for my trophy to arrive a few months later, impressively mounted by a South African taxidermist.

But I wasn't about to do what was expected of me. In a few minutes' time the cosy atmosphere aboard this bouncing, dust-streaked wagon would be destroyed when I told them exactly who I was and that the cameraman who was filming them was not simply making a vanity video for me. I was there to blow apart a huge conspiracy within the worldwide big game hunting industry.

CHAPTER 1

The Man Behind the Microphone

My clearest memory of New Zealand is of my father trying to move us out of it as fast as he possibly could. It was the cold, wet June of 1944 and while his fellow countrymen were busy fighting the Japanese, Dad, who was a teacher and therefore in a protected occupation, was growing daily more obsessed with the idea that the enemy was about to launch an invasion in midget submarines.

Every evening he would draw a dining chair up to the sideboard, switch on our ancient Ekco valve-radio and tune in to the news. Although the Japanese had been stalled for months in the Far East by the Allies, Dad refused to believe that this was anything other than propaganda to keep the Kiwi population from mass panic.

'We've got to find a flight to Sydney. If we try to sail there the Japs will sink us with one of their torpedoes,' he announced solemnly to my mother as he twisted the radio's big Bakelite switch to the off position.

Mum had long since given up arguing with him. Most of her time was taken up looking after me, rising two, and my sister Jane who was a babe in arms. We had already had two failed airborne escape attempts – one terminated by a mechanical failure and the other by the weather – but she reckoned that we might as well be a poor and struggling family in Australia as in New Zealand. If Dad was happy pestering the civil and military flight schedulers each and every day for seats on a plane to Sydney, then that was fine by her.

After weeks of telephone calls and personal visits to friends in the RNZAF, Dad came home early one day in a state of high excitement from the art college at which he taught. He told my mother to pack

only the most essential belongings and be ready with Jane and me
for him to collect that evening. With that he strode out of the house,
happy for the first time in months.

Full of misgivings – and not a little fear – my mother did as she'd
been asked, and crammed clothes, food, toys, kitchen and cleaning
utensils and important personal papers into a variety of bags and
cases. She had just finished when Dad pulled up outside the house
in a borrowed utility truck.

He managed to load everything in the back, including a huge,
white bassinet that had been my first pram and was now Jane's. We
set off from Auckland's southern suburbs for the harbour. It turned
out that a contact of his in the air force – probably just to get Dad
out of his hair – had come up with a one-way ticket for four to
Sydney in a Shorts Sunderland flying boat. Mum groaned when she
heard what our means of escape was going to be. Jane and I sat
happily in the bassinet, unaware of what was about to happen.

The weather was worsening as we left the harbour road for the
small quay allocated to air force and naval aircraft. The Sunderland
– once a civil airliner now stripped of creature comforts and pressed
into military service – was tied up to a wooden pontoon and was
bobbing up and down alarmingly, waves foaming over the floats.

My mother later told me that she would have turned round there
and then and abandoned our third escape bid if she hadn't already
handed the keys of our rented house back to the landlord's agent so
that we had nowhere to sleep that night.

With the help of the pilot and engineer Mum and Dad loaded our
meagre belongings into the back of the fuselage and, finally, Jane
and I were passed by our increasingly-fretful mother across a narrow
stretch of choppy water to Dad and the comparative safety of the
flying boat cabin. That journey from Auckland to Sydney has gone
down in Cook family history as an adventure unparalleled in foolish-
ness. My sister and I were strapped into the bassinet which Dad
wedged in the gangway between the seats. Whenever we started to
show signs of fear we were given large, red apples to eat.

The captain wound up the four engines of the seaplane and it
bucketed off across the white horses and slowly pulled itself clear of
the angry, grey swell. It headed out across the darkening Auckland
Bay and then turned westwards for Australia – leaving New Zealand

to the mercy of the advancing Japanese hordes, to the eternal, unspoken relief of my father.

But there was still plenty of drama to come en route to the longed-for safety of New South Wales. The bad weather that had been brewing as we left Auckland developed into a full-blown Pacific storm with low, black masses of cloud, tearing winds and horizontal rain.

Eventually, the cockpit door opened and the flight engineer motioned Dad over. With a series of sharp, pointing motions of the hands upwards and, ominously, downwards, he conveyed his inability to maintain the plane's altitude. He needed a sacrifice, Dad told Mum as he eased himself grimly back into his seat. We were going to have to jettison our cargo – some military supplies, and the Cook family luggage.

My parents conferred frantically. Mum had already left behind many treasured belongings. Now she was being asked to sub-divide again what she already considered to be our bare essentials. The flight engineer slid open the side door of the flying boat and tipped out the official cargo. He turned to Dad who, with a terse nod from his wife, passed through three heavy cases of her clothes. By common consent, he kept the tools of his trade – his paint box and easel. Mum scooped out her few pieces of jewellery from a large, inlaid mahogany box her grandmother had brought from England and handed the empty box to the engineer. The heirloom was whipped away by the wind to join the rest of our lost baggage, scattered over the Tasman Sea a very few thousand feet below.

Whether the storm chose that moment to abate or whether our sacrifice had actually made a difference, the aircraft's nose slowly started to lift and the wings levelled. We were gaining height and after what seemed an eternity to my parents but was probably no more than five or six hours, we banked steeply downwards in bright, evening sunshine to land on the smooth, blue waters of Rose Bay in Sydney Harbour.

We went to stay with Dad's relatives for a few days while we recovered from the journey and he found us a place to live. He had already fixed himself up with a job as a peripatetic teacher of lettering and illustration at Sydney Art School. This wasn't going to bring in much money but he planned to supplement his income with commissions for paintings, as he had done back in New Zealand.

Our lack of funds meant we couldn't afford much in the way of accommodation. We moved from run-down place to run-down place with my mother making the most of what was available to us until my aunt found us a rambling stone-built house to rent, complete with leaking roof, in Hunter's Hill, a pleasant and leafy, northern suburb of Sydney. The decor was uniformly cream over brown, with embossed wallpaper. The linoleum was worn at the joins of the floorboards underneath and the lights were still powered by gas. Gas also fuelled the capacious copper cauldron in which the family washing was done. But whatever the house lacked in looks and amenities, it made up for in size. We children were happy and well-fed for the years that we were there but it was pretty primitive and Dad was always talking about 'moving on'.

My father had a gift for spotting houses that 'had potential'. The trouble was that in his hands that potential was never realised. Our next family home was extraordinary, even by his standards. He'd been out house-hunting for weeks, to my mother's exasperation. She was quite content where we were but he was determined to buy property and leave the rental market behind.

One evening he took us all out to see the property he said had the 'biggest potential' he'd ever seen. In the twilight it certainly looked impressive – large, colonial-style with wooden verandas all around it, giving it the air of a miniature plantation-owner's spread in America's Deep South.

Daylight brought a more realistic appraisal. The house certainly had a good position, on a small hill in semi-rural Dundas, but the roof was corrugated iron and badly-rusted, the verandas were collapsing, there was no mains drainage and the house hadn't received any maintenance since the 1920s – hence the affordable price.

If the neighbours were looking for the new owners to restore the house to its former dignity, they were in for a big disappointment. The attraction of the Dundas house for my father was its very dilapidation. All he cared about was his painting; the rest of the world, including his family, barely existed.

The house was surrounded on three sides by the crumbling veranda, but my sister and I were forbidden to set foot on any of its rotten wooden boards, except to reach and leave the front door, where it was still comparatively safe. As children, we didn't give a second thought to the danger. We loved the place. It was full of interesting nooks and crannies and, though my mother slaved to keep it clean, its general structural and decorative condition meant that kids could do no lasting damage. The scars of tricycle collisions in the hall merely added to the patina.

To Dad, the family home was also, perversely, a heaven-sent refuge from the family. A week after we moved in he laid two planks across the collapsing floor and used them to escape to the side of the house where, out of sight, he set up his easel and carefully laid out his paints. There he would sit, sketching and painting and drifting off into his dream world without being bothered by Mum, Jane or me.

Dad was one of those people you could pass in the street and never notice. He was five feet nine inches tall with receding, ginger hair and a goatee beard. He was slightly gnome-like and had an absent-minded manner that drove my mother to despair. The result was that she became a de facto single parent – a job she did pretty well.

His absent-mindedness became well known in the neighbourhood. A few months after we moved in, he bought an ancient Austin Seven. With everything he needed in life stowed safely on the back seat, or strapped to the rear-mounted spare tyre – his easels, paints and palette – he would drive off into the Blue Mountains to spend uncounted days painting landscapes, sleeping in a small tent he carried with him and only returning home when he ran out of provisions.

One day Dad walked into the house and announced that the Austin had been stolen: 'I'm off to the police station to report this. We'll soon catch the beggars,' he huffed as he trudged off down the road.

He returned two hours later – in his car.

A police patrol had already spotted it before Dad arrived at the station. It was exactly where he had left it – in the art college car park. He'd gone in there to pick up some water-colour paper on his way back from a day's painting. When he failed to find any he wandered out of the front of the college, his exasperation obliterating the memory of leaving his car round the back.

When I was seventeen years old and living in digs near my part-time job at the Sydney Daily Telegraph, I called in at home to find Dad sitting alone in his veranda studio. Without looking up he said quietly, 'You were home late last night.'

I hadn't the heart to point out that I had left home more than three months before.

His desire to be left in peace influenced even his most generous acts. For my fifth birthday he made me a toy soldier's drum and hand-painted it blue with intricate gold scrolls to decorate the sides. It looked so good I couldn't wait to start beating it. The first tentative tap with a wooden spoon I had found in the kitchen yielded a dull thud. I hit it harder – still nothing of the loud, resonating noise I had hoped for. Then I realised that he had stuffed it with the innards of an old cushion so that, although his gift looked good, he would never have to be disturbed by his young son's enthusiastic beating.

Dad's ability to remain supremely detached from reality didn't stand in the way of his abiding jealousy of his brother and fellow artist, James Cook. Rivals from their boyhood, the two continued their feud through adolescence and into adult life. Matters weren't helped by the fact that they both chose the same calling. My father's artistic style was driven by a determination to depict every sheep, cow or tree in minute detail. Such was his striving for perfection that he would sometimes destroy his canvasses if he wasn't satisfied.

Given his habit of accepting commissions without asking for an advance payment, the Cook family finances were often sorely stretched. Mum even had to pack up and leave him in Dundas from time to time to find work wherever it was available. On one occasion Jane and I were moved to a sheep station four hundred miles away where Mum had found a job keeping house, cleaning and cooking for a bunch of smelly drovers.

Uncle James, on the other hand, had an interpretative approach to painting which was then much more in vogue, and he prospered while Dad struggled. But what really peeved Dad was that his brother had a far better war. Dad was seconded from his teaching job to draw minutely-detailed exploded diagrams of the De Havilland Mosquito fighter-bomber for the benefit of assembly engineers. James, meanwhile, became an official war artist, travelling with frontline Australian troops. At home I have one of his water-colour paintings of a ravaged and rubble-strewn Italian town. Next to it hang examples of my father's precise, draughtsman-like landscapes.

In death, both my father's and uncle's work have gained tremendously in popularity and appreciation. I reserve judgement on who was the better artist, but when I stand back and look at Dad's work I remember the man for what he was and I recognise something of myself in that striven-for but rarely-achieved perfection.

It was my father's love of the quiet life that helped me form my early ambition to become a vet. Jane and I were desperate to have a pet dog – but the prospect of feeding, walking and listening to a puppy was too much for him. When we actually prevailed upon him to let us keep the rather boisterous beagle puppy we had fallen in love with after seeing him in the local pet shop, he surprised us some weeks later by volunteering to take him out for a walk. To our horror, he returned dogless, announcing that he had given him away because he was too badly behaved.

My mother eventually forced a change of heart over the dog issue and brought us home a friendly short-haired Dachshund which we smothered with love and we almost forgave Dad for what he'd done with the other dog. Sadly, the new arrival must have sensed the head of the household's disapproval and tried to escape. She snared herself on the wooden palings of our dilapidated and unmended back fence, her wound became infected and soon afterwards she had to be put down. I resolved then and there never to be helpless in such a situation again.

After that, I had to settle for a box of silkworms. They didn't make any noise and cost nothing to feed as there was an abundant supply of mulberry leaves from the trees in the churchyard behind our house.

In thirty years of investigative reporting, I've been knocked unconscious a dozen times, needed hospital treatment on almost thirty occasions and I've had a score of bones broken because people object to my persistence – or to the fact that I exist at all. Growing up in Australia in the 1950s was great preparation for what was to come. It was a young country, scarred by the war – a melting-pot of different nationalities, with an unsophisticated and sometimes brutal education system.

I hadn't really taken much notice of Georgie Kadar until I noticed him cheating in class. We were both about eight years old and under the firm control of Miss Kay, our form mistress at Hunter's Hill Primary School. A tall, stiff spinster in her mid-fifties, she was one of those teachers who seem instinctively to know when a child is doing something they ought not to be. And even if you weren't misbehaving, she made you feel as though you were.

Georgie was quite a small boy with dark, curly hair and a disconcertingly intense stare that made most of the other kids avoid him at break time. His Latvian parents, according to my mother and father, had had a terrible time from both the Germans and the Russians who had fought over their homeland during the war. They escaped to the Allies in the immediate aftermath of the fall of Berlin and were given free passage to start a new life in Australia.

Not that any of this would have made any difference to my perception of Georgie as we sat in the peeling-paint austerity of Miss Kay's classroom doing our fortnightly maths test. Mathematics has never been my strong suit and, when the effort of making numbers do what I wanted them to got too much, I looked up from my book and gazed blankly across the room.

He sat two places away with his forehead buried in the palm of his right hand, elbow resting on his paper. On his knees, below the oak and wrought-iron desk, I saw the cover of our arithmetic course book peeping out. I was staring at Georgie's little deception when Miss Kay's uncanny intuition made her look up.

'It's no use looking at Kadar, Cook, he won't help you.' She got to her feet and walked towards Georgie, antennae twitching. She stopped at his side and looked down.

'Get up, Kadar. Let's see what you're hiding down there,' she said in her brittle little voice. Georgie's game was up and he was led firmly away for six strokes of the thin malacca cane the headmaster kept behind his study door.

I suppose I should have guessed who Georgie would blame from the hate-filled glare he gave me as Miss Kay led him away. At the time, though, I thought little of it. I hadn't told the teacher what I had seen.

Early the following week I walked the half-mile from our house to school as usual. It was a beautiful late-Spring day. I emerged from the shade of the eucalyptus trees that lined the cul-de-sac where the school gates stood open for the steady stream of kids heading for their classrooms.

As I walked past the main hall someone jumped out beside me. It was Georgie Kadar. He'd been hiding behind a water butt and now he was less than two feet away from me, staring intensely into my eyes. Wordlessly, he brought a metal hammer down on my head three times in rapid succession.

When I woke up I was on a hospital bed, wearing a green gown. It was stained with blood and a doctor was telling me to hold still as he tried to stitch the cuts on my head.

Miraculously, Georgie Kadar wasn't expelled for what he did. Perhaps there was nowhere else for him to go. Maybe his parents persuaded the school that their son would never do it again. When I went back to school after several days under observation in hospital, Georgie was still in my class, staring at me malevolently.

And he hadn't finished with me yet.

A few weeks later Miss Kay asked the class if we had any pets at home. I put up my hand and told her about my box of silkworms. As this seemed out of the usual run of dogs, cats and rabbits, and sounded a lot less trouble, she invited me to bring them to school to show my classmates. I heard Georgie laugh when I agreed.

Next day I walked into school – skirting carefully round the water butt by the hall – bearing my box of silkworms which lay replete and dozing after a heavy feed of mulberry leaves.

My demonstration of the process of feeding the silkworms in order to extract the highly-valuable silk threads from them, accompanied by the occasional prodding of their torpid bodies, went down well with the other children. Even Georgie Kadar seemed grudgingly impressed.

I came back into the classroom after playing footie with my friends at break time to find the box crushed under my desk. Whilst I had been out, heavy boots had squashed the cardboard flat and silkworm body parts writhed and oozed on the floor. Georgie sat at his desk with his arms wrapped around his thin shoulders. He looked me directly in the eye and smiled cruelly. I gathered up the remains of the box and the worms and walked past him, out of the school gates and back home. I dumped the crushed cardboard and the worms in the dustbin and vowed not to take on any more pets until I could trust the rest of the world not to take them from me.

*

cations of giving birth. Among those to shower me with grateful praise would undoubtedly be the beautiful daughter of the wealthiest landowner in the district. Adolescence had truly arrived.

I applied, without visiting, for a place at Yanco College, two hundred miles south-west of Sydney. It was far enough away for me to board during the week but close enough to go home to the family at weekends. It was only after I had been accepted and turned up there for my first day that doubts about the place crossed my mind.

A hot breeze fanned plumes of dust from the margins of the long drive as we approached. The hotch-potch of buildings in brick, timber and corrugated iron looked anything but welcoming. The place felt remote, vaguely threatening, and – for a busy school campus – strangely silent. The austere classrooms and dormitories stood out through the heat haze against a distant background of grain silos, stockyards and an assortment of khaki-coloured outbuildings. But it wasn't just the aspect of the place that was depressing.

Although only twelve years old, I was six feet tall and weighed twelve stone but my size and fitness granted me no exemption from the initiation rites at Yanco. The fact that my father wasn't a rugged farmer, but 'a pansy artist' didn't help much either. Like many before me, I was marched round to the back of the college kitchens by a group of senior boys who emptied an industrial refuse bin onto the asphalt quadrangle.

'Pick it up,' said one of them to me, gesturing to the rubbish. I hesitated. A fist hit me below the left kidney. I got the message.

I picked up every lump of congealed fat, eggshell, rotting vegetable and God knows what else and scraped it off my hands into the huge galvanised metal bin. When I had finished, they emptied the bin again. The result of an attempt to resist a repetition of events was a monstrous black eye that needed surgical attention – no questions asked – by the college nurse.

I did manage, however, to avoid another dangerous humiliation.

After lessons, the Sixth Year bullies at Yanco liked to take trembling new arrivals to the college dairy complex where the cow manure, pending use as fertiliser, was stored in concrete clamps, each about the size of a small swimming pool. The sadists would make the younger boys strip to their underpants and stand on one of the concrete walls overlooking the clamps.

'Dive in. It's time for a little swim, turdface,' one of the prefects would hiss, and the victim would have to pitch headfirst into five feet of stinking mire. Then it was back to the college shower rooms to wash off the mess, avoiding the masters on pain of death.

In one particularly nasty incident, an unfortunate noviciate lost a foot. We boys were never told exactly what happened. But the gory story that passed into school lore – to be whispered after lights out – involved school bullies, some pieces of rope and a severed foot, still clad in a brown suede desert boot, being retrieved from a local railway line.

There were several attempted suicides while I was at Yanco. No one much seemed to care. The prevailing atmosphere was tense and, from my lowly viewpoint, the administration appeared to have little interest in the happiness or well-being of its charges.

Whether the college staff felt that life would be easier if they let the bullies be, or whether the bullies' routine threats of reprisals against anyone reporting their attacks meant much that went on went undisclosed, I don't know. In any case, the few incidents that *were* formally reported invariably drew a response of the 'stop-whingeing-and-pull-yourself-together-boy-it'll-make-a-man-of-you' sort.

One sorry image still haunts me from that godforsaken place: the face of a poor, withdrawn Jewish boy of twelve or thirteen who had the misfortune to have been born with facial features that gave him the appearance of a cat. He had huge, mournful eyes and a wide, flat face that tapered grotesquely to an almost imperceptible mouth and tiny chin.

Universally reviled by the older boys and staff, this poor creature slunk from lesson to lesson, never saying a word – always creeping in at the last moment to sit at the back of the class. Such was his desire for unmolested anonymity that, to this day, I cannot recall his proper name. To us all, to our eternal shame, he was Pussy Rosewarn.

dumped into the swimming pool three hundredweight of orange flavour jelly crystals that I had liberated from the kitchen stores. It never set quite like my mother's desserts used to, but it certainly stopped the college caretaker in his tracks when he unlocked the pool house at six o'clock the following morning to check the chlorine levels.

My elementary but competent understanding of the physical sciences led to the small-scale manufacture of a minor explosive called, to the best of my recollection, nitrogen tri-iodide.

With the aid of a tatty old chemistry manual, I experimented at the back of the chemistry lab until I was producing glass phials full of a purple liquid. While my concoction was wet it posed no threat at all, but once it had dried to a thin film of crystals it was full of surprises. My speciality was to paint the class blackboards with the liquid. A minute or two after the mixture had dried, the merest pressure of chalk or blackboard rubber on the surface was enough to cause a minor explosion accompanied by a puff of purple smoke. Luckily for everyone else, an informant gave me away before I was able to instigate a campaign on the toilet seats.

Isolated moments of fun weren't enough to dispel the unhappiness I was feeling at Yanco and, although it took me many months to get through to him, my father eventually accepted that his son was desperately keen to get away from the place. I ended my secondary education much closer to home at a sports-mad agricultural college at Hurlstone on the outskirts of Sydney.

Despite my new school's lack of academic emphasis – the headmaster's first question to me was to enquire which rugby position I played – I kept my resolve to be a true country veterinarian. I passed my matriculation exams with flying colours and was accepted by Sydney University to study veterinary medicine.

The snag was that I couldn't afford to embark on this protracted and difficult course without financial help. Members of the so-called 'squatocracy' – families grown rich from land their ancestors had simply occupied in the nineteenth century – had the money to go it alone, but chaps like me needed a scholarship.

The alternative was to take any job during the day that you could find to pay for your tuition, which, in those days, you could elect to receive principally at night.

The scholarships were mainly commercial arrangements funded by veterinary pharmaceutical companies which seemed intent on obliging those they sponsored to devote their careers to treating dogs, cats and other small domestic creatures – usually with the kind of products they manufactured themselves. My passion for my chosen profession began to wane and it wasn't long before my career ambitions began to move in an entirely different direction.

I had discovered the attractions of journalism.

While finishing my exams at Hurlstone, I had found myself a job as a copy boy on the *Sydney Daily Telegraph*. The atmosphere inside the news building captivated me. Every evening, along with a half dozen or so full-time copy boys, I would sit in a little office waiting for the reporters in the adjoining newsroom to tear the paper from their typewriters and wave it in the air. That was the signal for one of us to rush in and bear a few more paragraphs of the next day's story via the sub-editors to the typesetters.

I liked the whole system and I liked the reporters for their lively, sometimes half-drunken sociability and the power that they wielded in our everyday lives. I gave up studying veterinary science, and switched to an English course – I was going to be a journalist.

My academic career didn't last much longer. Two things happened. The practical joker in me lived on. I had already received warnings from the university authorities for my drink-fuelled antics during a series of Rag Weeks. These involved attacking townsfolk with water pistols filled with green dye and the re-appearance of the annoying effects of home-made nitrogen tri-iodide. But my downfall came when I rode ubnsteadily into the university's main lecture theatre on my Rabbit Rolamatic Motor Scooter and, having stalled it a few feet from the podium, spent several minutes noisily, but fruitlessly, trying to kick-start it, entirely drowning out an appeal being delivered by the vice-chancellor.

I don't recall the subject of this appeal, though I'm told it was a saw a blossoming of independent broadcasting enterprise, fuelled by a boom in advertising as Australia's economy moved out of the post-war doldrums.

On the strength of my letter, 2GB had called me in to the studio and asked me to read a few news stories. To my surprise, they offered me a part-time job.

The prospect of a media career appealed to me far more than the idea of treating some blue-rinsed dowager's yapping toy poodle. So, long before the motor-scooter incident, I had begun spending less time than I should at my studies and far more time than I should hanging around the studios. The inevitable eventually happened. To my mother's intense disappointment, I abandoned university and started full-time work at 2GB.

It took about two weeks for the scales to fall from my eyes about the glamour commercial radio liked to sell its listeners and of which I now thought I was a part. 2GB, which was owned by a large commercial broadcaster called the MacQuarie Network, ran a well-known quiz programme called 'The Ampol Show' – sponsored by a well-known Aussie petrol brand. As a young boy I had tuned in to 'The Ampol Show' and marvelled at the huge wealth of prizes the successful contestants could pull in.

A simple question and answer session narrowed the competition down to two finalists. Then listeners would hear the lucky winner being handed a golden telephone in the studio and, upon hearing the words 'Ampol Treasure House, number please?' would recite a prize number he or she had selected. They could choose any number they wanted from one to a thousand.

These prize numbers, therefore, could run into four digits as if the range of goodies on offer was substantial. It was only after joining the station that I realised the warehouse-size Ampol Treasure House didn't exist. There was just a middle-aged woman in our office who answered the winner on a Bakelite phone and, whatever combination of numbers was quoted, there were only ever about ten prizes on offer.

A few months later, the station held more auditions – this time for a permanent on-air announcer. With the arrogance of youth I applied for and got the job. Suddenly, I was earning the princely sum of five hundred Australian dollars a year.

Sadly, the euphoria didn't last.

The reality of the job I was so thrilled to have landed was working atrociously long night-time hours in a cramped studio, operating every piece of equipment myself and broadcasting to a tiny audience of insomniac Sydney residents. At first it was a tremendous thrill to see the studio console light up when I threw the switches and, at times, when I slipped on the headphones and spoke into the microphone, I could barely keep the excitement from my voice. I listened to the radio professionals on both the broadcast and technical side and sucked up their advice like a sponge.

Control and delivery are not easy skills to learn, however good the 'raw material' of your voice. The next time you listen to one of the best radio broadcasters – be it Terry Wogan, Alistair Cooke or one of the Radio 4 newsreaders – don't be fooled. It takes an awful lot of hard work to sound so laid back.

But once the novelty of radio broadcasting and the mastering of the sheer mechanics of it were over, boredom and disillusionment began to set in. The hunger for content to go with the presentation set in. I felt I wasn't getting anywhere; it wasn't the kind of journalism that I wanted to be involved with. Also, I was finding it impossible to meet girls with my permanently nocturnal working schedule.

It was the Oxberry Aerial Image Animation Camera that finally lured me away from 2GB. It belonged to a marvellous man called Eric Porter and he used it to make cartoons. Until I saw his advert for a film assistant I hadn't really considered getting involved in movies – however tenuous the link he was offering was to proper film-making. But Eric persuaded me. He was a small, pipe-smoking bespectacled figure in his late fifties who put me at my ease during the interview by spending most of it talking with schoolboy-like enthusiasm about the sophisticated animation camera he had just bought in America.

He was everything my father wasn't. Where my father withdrew

Eric had come on the animation scene at the same time as Walt Disney and used to claim that he had the first fully-animated cartoon film on screen some months ahead of Disney.

Sadly for Eric, Australia lacked the studio network and financial structure to back his inventions and he got left behind by his American rivals. Typically, he shrugged off his disappointment and got on with his work – and kept on inventing new ways of improving cartoon-making, paying his way by making commercials.

His latest baby was the OAIAC – we all got sick of calling it by its proper name and its acronym, and eventually just referred to it as 'the camera'. What distinguished it from other cameras used to film drawings for animation was its ability to give great depth to the pictures. In the right hands, it could give a cartoon real 3-D depth that the animations of the 1960s usually lacked.

I learnt how to use 'the camera' and the associated film gear, and Eric also encouraged me to develop my script-writing skills. He had just started making short documentaries to be shown before the main feature films in Australian cinemas and enrolled me in their production. From long hours spent in a dark, cramped animation studio, I started going out on location with a film crew. Sadly, this was not Hollywood and among the subjects we made shorts on were the migratory habits of the pied wagtail and the history of the watercourses of New South Wales. It was valuable experience and it gave me a good working knowledge of the technical side of film-making that has made my career on the other side of the camera a good deal easier since.

I got a buzz, too, out of going to the cinema with friends and reciting the script of whatever support film I had written just as the actor voicing the commentary was saying the lines. Needless to add, the novelty soon wore off for my friends – and for other cinema-goers around me.

I spent two very happy years working for Eric. Of all the different skills he taught me, script-writing was the one I valued and enjoyed the most and when I heard of a job doing just that for the radio talks department of the Australian Broadcasting Commission, Eric actively encouraged me to apply for it.

From ABC to BBC

Landing the job at the ABC felt like the culmination of everything I had been working for. The ABC is Australia's version of the BBC – there really was no better platform for someone like me, or so I thought. I was twenty-one, ambitious and keen to show Australia's biggest broadcasting organisation what a journalistic trailblazer they had hired.

During my time with Eric Porter Productions I had been my own boss in many respects. I researched my subject, I wrote an outline of what I proposed to film, got approval from Eric, then went out and filmed, and also wrote the accompanying script. I had developed my own ideas on how to keep an audience's attention. Sadly, they differed mightily from those of my bosses at the ABC.

Like the BBC, the ABC then regarded itself as the standard-bearer of the nation's broadcasting values. In my view, however, it some-times talked down to its audience, not crediting it with the common-sense to make up its own mind about the merits of an issue. This nanny-state attitude was backed by a vast, unwieldy bureaucracy which had long since learned to stifle the new or unorthodox by doing what all self-serving organisations do best – as little as possible as slowly as possible.

At times, I felt like I was back at Yanco. The overwhelming sense that you had no one to turn to if you needed help or wanted a fair hearing was exactly the same.

In the 1960s, the ABC documentary style was to use a narrator to explain the issues, seldom allowing the listener to hear the story from the people involved simply through interviewing them. I found this boring; it gave the impression that the ABC was, in some way, filtering the facts and deciding how it should present them.

I started writing scripts for a magazine programme called 'Scope' and occasionally reporting for a weekly show called 'News Review'. In both these cases, I tried to include more interviews with the individuals concerned in the story and cut down on the waffling commentary from the reporter – who was, in some cases, myself.

I ran into trouble straight away. As a new recruit unversed in ABC culture, my scripts were monitored closely. When my section head saw what I was doing, he immediately passed the script to the news editor, who smartly passed it on to the head of the talks department. There was re-write upon re-write. My scripts would be handed back to me having passed through three or four different hands – each individual imposing house-style more and more strictly until what was finally broadcast bore absolutely no resemblance to my original, nor, in some cases, to the facts.

I got some support from middle-management colleagues, but it was more in the nature of restraint. Some of my wilder ideas – though not without merit, they said – were tantamount to instant professional suicide. Better to work from within, they said. Outside meant no outlet. Why didn't I take the odd regional posting to reflect and perhaps to cool down?

I took their advice and accepted a couple of jobs in the country, but they only served to increase my sense of professional isolation. On the up-side, however, it certainly gave me a broad grounding in broadcast skills. One outpost was so small I had to do everything, including turning off the transmitter at night and on again in the morning.

To have a new radio station was a big thing for a small Australian town in the 1960s. The mayor of this particular place had made it plain how pleased he was to have me there and that he would go to any lengths to show it. Unfortunately, these lengths included installing his daughter in my hotel bed just before I got back from work one night. I made my excuses, as they used to say in the Sunday tabloids, and left.

Back in mainstream broadcasting, nothing had changed.

I tried appealing to my section head, to the news editor, the deputy and head of the talks department – to no avail. This was how things

in a meeting, I stormed in to find him closeted with a member of
the ABC board of governors. I said my piece, mindful that with every
word I was talking myself closer to unemployment. I left them sitting
in stunned silence and went back to my desk to await the inevitable
summons and retribution.

One redeeming feature of a huge, civil service-like body like the
ABC was that it was almost impossible to be sacked. It would have
been an admission of failure on their part, so it was considered far
better to make disapproval plain and invite resignation rather than
cause a stink. Two days later, therefore, I was called in to see the
head of talks.

'Cook, we have a short-term vacancy in Western Australia which
we should like you to fill – just a few months until we can find
someone permanent over there.'

In other words, 'Take the hint and resign now, or go to Perth and
annoy someone else for a while. Meanwhile we'll quietly forget all
about you here in Sydney.'

I have a stubborn side and I decided these bastards weren't going
to force me to resign. Rightly or wrongly, I believed the listener was
entitled to hear the truth of a story from the people most closely
involved in it – be it victim or perpetrator – and I determined to
carry on until they were forced to recognise I was right, or until they
sacked me.

Perth, though a very attractive place to live, was the end of the
professional world as far as I was concerned. This was years before
the huge commercial expansion of the city and the glitzy image it
now enjoys as an international yachting centre and playground of
the rich and beautiful. Carried along by youthful pomposity, I said
goodbye to Mum and a distinterested Dad, who were still living in
semi-dereliction in Dundas, and caught the plane westwards with a
light heart. I had nothing to lose.

Perth's ABC boss was Arthur Povah, who was fiftyish and an

ABC man through and through, who had been forewarned about me.

'This is Perth, not Sydney, and we won't be wanting any of your big city tricks here,' was his message.

It was advice I didn't heed.

Barely weeks after I arrived, I landed myself in trouble with the local ABC management. In a weekly news magazine programme I decided to substitute one item I considered boring with another, totally unauthorised piece about the local housing authority's scheme to ship the local aborigines out of East Perth to a reserve several hundred miles away.

It was obvious that the council had become exasperated by the constant complaints from shopkeepers and some residents that the aborigines were causing a nuisance. Their main 'crime' was occasional drunkenness and sitting about the streets, which they did mainly because no one would give them jobs.

I felt it was ridiculous to take these people out to some shacks in the desert. They were overwhelmingly fifth and sixth-generation city dwellers to whom the ancient ways of life meant very little. Far better, I argued, to address the problem where it lay, in the city, and to try to do something about it.

My opinion was not popular with Arthur Povah and the city council.

Days after the broadcast, which included interviews with aborigines and white townspeople alike, a campaign against the proposed move began and the plan was eventually quietly dropped.

I still get a charge out of a result like that.

But it was another of my sidelines that caused the most trouble with ABC Perth.

My response to the new libertarianism of the Age of Aquarius had been to co-found a satirical magazine which gloried in the title *Grot*. My 'partners in crime' were a commercial radio producer and an advertising executive. It was first published about the time that Richard Neville and his friends started *Oz* in Sydney. Unlike *Oz*, an 'underground' magazine that was eventually published and prosecuted for alleged obscenity in the UK, we never offended anyone enough to end up in court. But at a local level, we became notorious for reprinting the first magazine article in Australia to use the word the ABC was not amused.

I had also managed to persuade the local commercial television station to run a short weekly insert entitled 'The Grot Spot' on one of its shows. With hindsight, it was an unwise move since I derived my main income from Australia's public broadcasting body. That's how Arthur Povah saw it, too, as something of a conflict of interests.

Official disapproval reached its height after 'The Grot Spot' – which was often delivered in song form – revealed that Western Australia possessed a naval vessel whose duties included the defence of a huge ammunition store. We had discovered that the one thing this ammo dump didn't have was any shells of the right calibre for the ship that was supposed to defend it. In other words, anyone could have attacked the dump and the Royal Australian Navy would have been virtually powerless to prevent it.

Eventually, we ran out of printers who were prepared to work with us and *Grot* bit the dust, but not before I received a terse memo from Mr Povah which read: 'From next week you will be moved to newsreading duties until further notice. You will never read one of your own scripts again.'

Reading the news wasn't my idea of cutting-edge journalism but I wasn't in any position to object. Besides, there was some fun to be had in my new department due to the activities of one of the ABC's most senior announcers.

Peter Harrison looked every inch the consummate professional. Tall and serious, casually but impeccably dressed, everything about him said he was a company man. Our bosses at the ABC rarely saw his other side – his immense capacity for disruption and mischief-making.

Peter's favourite targets were young newsreaders fresh out of training school. Waiting until they had just gone on the air, he would ignore the red 'On Air' light outside the soundproofed studio and wander in, putting a reassuring finger to his lips to imply he was there purely in a monitoring capacity. The nervous reader would plough on, glancing up at Peter from time to time.

The next thing the victim would see was the station's most senior newscaster dropping his twills and underpants and lowering his buttocks onto the grey metal wastepaper basket. He would stare fixedly at the now panic-stricken newsreader who would stutter, lose his place and generally wish for his mother to come and take him away.

Peter would then up the ante, and start to strain and grimace, producing barely-audible grunts. Nothing that the listener would ever hear, but loud enough for those in the studio to pick up.

The end result was usually near-hysteria and a newsreading performance that left the listener confused and often concerned for the health of the young broadcaster. The broadcaster, having gratefully handed over to the continuity announcer, would watch, slack-jawed, as Harrison pulled up his pants, did himself up and strode out of the room as if nothing had happened. Sometimes his victims would try to persuade themselves that nothing *had* happened, particularly when Peter greeted them later and nonchalantly gave them some small piece of advice about their performance.

I was lucky enough to avoid this treatment because Peter considered me a comparatively old hand at newsreading after my experiences at 2GB and the ABC in Sydney. He had another prank in mind for me.

My new duties included evening stints as a continuity announcer, informing the listener what was coming up next. On this occasion I was about to read out details of a live concert when I sensed someone standing behind the sound console a few feet in front of me. Seconds before I was due to read the script to introduce the concert, I glanced up to see Peter holding two leads – one in each hand. If what I was about to say was going to be broadcast, those wires should have been plugged together, and fast.

'You stupid bastard, what the hell do you think you're doing,' I hissed.

I turned at the sound of an urgent tapping from the engineer in the glass-fronted control booth behind me.

He stabbed his finger repeatedly at Peter, and I turned back to waited until Peter was well into his stride with the main evening news bulletin and then slipped into his studio. I carried a fire bucket, emptied of sand and filled with ice.

Peter scarcely looked up as he realised we were close to him. Two of us held his arms whilst his trousers were swiftly undone and the contents of the bucket shovelled down the front. We stood back to await results. Nothing. Peter just kept reading the bulletin as if glacial interference with his nether regions was part of his daily routine.

Another spectacular revenge attempt was staged by Big George, a local sports reporter, who had arguably been Harro's most regular victim.

Big George was, by all accounts, monumentally endowed. One afternoon, when Harrison was live on air, Big George treated him to his party trick. He backed slowly into the studio, obviously carrying something. As he approached the announcer's desk, he turned to reveal, laid out on a tray and garnished with salad, his enormous appendage.

Without blinking an eye, or fluffing a word, Harrison flicked off his microphone, and smote big George's mighty organ with a steel ruler. He then turned his microphone back on and continued to read as if nothing had happened, leaving Big George hopping round the studio in the background, trying to stifle howls of agony. Harro was absolutely bombproof, and everyone thereafter more or less gave up trying to prove him otherwise.

Those few moments of fun aside, life working for the ABC was a fairly depressing experience. My documentary output in Perth had been halted and there was absolutely no sign that the station would ever move into the second half of the twentieth century and start treating its audience as if it had a mind of its own.

I kept being reminded of what a self-censoring, toe-the-party-line organisation the ABC had become. I often found myself thinking of the brave departure of two journalists I much admired, Michael Charlton and Bob Raymond – the presenter and editor, respectively, of 'Four Corners' – the local equivalent of 'Panorama'.

They had resigned over the ABC's craven capitulation to the right-wing government of Sir Robert Menzies after the broadcast of a programme on his administration's failing housing policy. It was a well-researched exposé revealing serious flaws, and, naturally, required an official response. None was forthcoming and the government's presumption seemed to be that if the Housing Minister, one Senator Spooner, did not wish to appear, then the programme could not be transmitted.

When the programme was broadcast, it caused quite a stir. Then came the political backlash. Menzies himself got involved, the ABC was reminded where its funding came from and the back-pedalling began.

The government demanded, and got, total access to the next edition of 'Four Corners' and the minister took almost the entire programme to air his views unchallenged. Bob Raymond thought it made Spooner look the pompous prat he was, but such direct political interference and organisational toadying could not be tolerated. Having failed to get any assurance that the same thing would never be allowed to happen again, the editor and presenter resigned. Michael Charlton came to Britain to report, without undue influence, for 'Panorama'. Should I follow his lead?

What had happened to those very senior journalists was, on a much smaller scale, happening to me too. This was not the way honest journalistic enquiry should be treated and, if I stayed – or remained silent – I was acquiescing in the whole sordid process. I'd had enough of Perth and was professionally disillusioned.

Besides, I had fallen in love and a larger plan had formed in my mind which was going to take some time to bring to fruition.

I had met Madeline while working on a story on overseas students for the ABC. The research took me to the library of the University of Western Australia where I saw a beautiful, slim Oriental girl with long, black hair reading at a desk. We fell into conversation and, having discovered that she was the president of the Students' Union, I ended up making her a major part of the programme.

Her family were well-to-do Singaporean Chinese who had sent

ticket – which I still have – from Tilbury on the *SS Orient* – price £17:17/-.

The family had connections in Whitby and a belief – unproven – that the family tree links us to the famous explorer Captain James Cook. So, many of the male members of the family, myself included, have James among our forenames. My mother's family, although from Wellington, were also only relatively recent immigrants from England. After Dad died, Mum moved back to the UK until her own death in 1994.

Madeline and I started to make plans together. My options in Australia were restricted. I was partly responsible for that myself, of course, having fallen out with the biggest and most powerful broadcaster in the country. Youthful arrogance prompted me to believe that I had something significant to contribute to broadcasting; I knew about film-making, documentaries, investigations and radio. Britain – 'home' – felt like the place where I could put my talents to best use.

Madeline wasn't free to go to England for two years and I was going to need substantial financial backing if I was to survive the early times before I got established there.

My decision to start afresh lifted a weight from my shoulders. With a light heart, I wrote my resignation letter to Arthur Povah.

I landed on my feet almost immediately. Bill Warnock ran one of the most successful advertising agencies in the country from its Perth headquarters. We met, we got on and he offered me a job running the radio and television arm of the business. I stayed there for two years, saving hard for the move to England. I bought myself camera equipment for my freelance work and set aside as much cash as possible for accommodation and living expenses.

Madeline graduated with one of the best firsts Perth had awarded in years. We spent a blissful year in our own flat. We went to parties, we soaked up the increasingly liberal atmosphere of the Flower Power era and kept saving. It was an exciting and enjoyable period in my life.

I got severely bitten by the motor racing bug and nearly blew everything on a Fiat Abarth sports car until a friend pointed out the true cost of competing week in and week out – buying spares, new engines, finding race fees and paying for fuel. Common sense prevailed, but I remain permanently bitten to this day. I love watching motor racing and I have an interest in a small car manufacturing company which produces sporting, bespoke three-wheelers. I have also become a bit of an anorak on the history of Jaguar and delight in driving one of their faster models.

Madeline and I decided to get married before we left for England. It was a simple ceremony conducted in a neighbour's home by John Hudson, the ABC's local head of religious broadcasting. John had become a friend and was notoriously un-vicarlike. He arrived for the ceremony wearing a long, black cape and announcing himself as 'Batman'.

Few family members were there. The whole thing was so low-key that it hardly seemed worth asking Madeline's family to come all that way. I saw little of Mum and Dad since I'd moved out again, and I honestly felt that to involve Dad in the upheaval of a wedding – however small-scale – would be more than any of us could bear.

The day I walked through the doors of Broadcasting House in London – 14 May 1968 – I had no idea what would happen. I had arrived in England knowing nobody apart from Madeline. I had no appointment arranged, but I did have a name – Andrew Boyle, the editor of 'The World At One', the lunchtime news programme. Although I didn't know it at the time, I was in good company as I approached the cluttered, cream-painted 'World At One' office to see Andrew: Nick Ross, Jonathan Dimbleby and David Jessel all started work there at about the same time and we remain on good terms even now.

Andrew Boyle agreed to see me straightaway and I decided to take the bull by the horns. I began: 'I like what you do here and I know I can do it too, but with a rather different approach which I think you'll approve of.' It was a bit over the top, but I meant it.

I told him what I had been doing in Australia and that I could around, doing what nearly all students did in 1968 – occupying and protesting.

I found the ringleaders, did my interviews, brought the tape back and edited it. It led that day's programme and, two days later, Andrew Boyle offered me a contract.

I loved the brisk, challenging style of 'The World at One', or 'The World at Sixes and Sevens', as some wags dubbed it. You never knew what you would be doing until you arrived in the office and Andrew Boyle approved your story for the day. I thrived on the adrenaline, knowing that once you left that office, armed with your tape recorder, you had to bring a story home. Then there was the editing to make it as immediate as you could and, finally, the satisfaction of hearing it go out to several million listeners.

For three years I was totally immersed in day-to-day news. It gave me the chance to do all the things I had yearned to achieve in Australia. Instead of some sober-suited announcer filtering the facts to the audience, we gave it to people right from the shoulder. It was liberating.

Eventually, my work pattern and preference metamorphosed. I began to present 'The World At One' and the PM programme when Bill Hardcastle was on his day off, and more and more of my reporting was done for TWAO's sister programme, 'The World This Weekend', which had room for more in-depth reports which were prepared over a few days. In 1971, one of these stories set me on the path I am still following today.

For a few weeks, we had been receiving letters about the activities of a loan-sharking company calling itself the Turret Mortgage Company in Bristol. The letters seemed genuine and came from individuals unconnected with each other but all making the same complaint, that Turret was charging extortionately high interest rates and that when its customers had difficulty repaying the loan threats soon followed.

More than one correspondent wrote harrowingly of home visits from Turret employees accompanied by a pair of fierce Alsatian dogs.

I did my homework on the company and decided to find its boss to discover why he was so aggressive towards his clients. I found him at his office a couple of days later and, armed only with my trusty Uher tape recorder and microphone, asked him what his qualifications were for running a finance company, apart from being a former heavyweight professional wrestler.

By way of reply he grabbed me in a bear hug and threw me down the stairs. The entire encounter was safely recorded on the now crushed Uher and I made it back to the studio and put together the story. But not before retrieving the tape spool, which had bounced off down the road, unreeling the tape as it went.

I sat on the kerb with a pencil pushed through the middle of the spool and carefully wound all the tape back. Happily, the Turret Mortgage Company went out of business shortly after the programme, but – sadly – long before the authorities got round to regulating the activities of those offering financial services.

The public response to what we broadcast was amazing.

Letters started arriving addressed to me personally, starting with phrases like: 'It takes a brave man to do what you do, you should have a look at this company . . .' We had unwittingly tapped into a huge wellspring of public feeling. The complaints about finance companies, crooked businesses and even large institutions and government departments flooded in, giving Andrew Boyle and me an idea.

On the basis of what the public was telling us, there looked to be scope for a series of radio programmes founded on investigations. The remit should be to examine injustice, criminality and bureaucratic bungling.

To anyone reading this now, it sounds strangely naive and obvious. But in the early 1970s, there was no such thing as investigative broadcast journalism. Sure, there was 'The Braden Beat' on television but it treated matters humorously, ending with a virtual nudge in the ribs, a sly wink and a 'We didn't really mean it, Mr ICI . . .' There was also 'You and Yours' on Radio Four – but that was all about consumer affairs and could hardly be described as hard-hitting.

Although Andrew Boyle was a firm believer in the idea of an

He nicknamed me The Colonial Pirate and blocked any attempt we made to get him to listen to a pilot programme we had put together outside office hours. I heard on the grapevine that he thought I was too brash and determined for my own good and he was not about to let me loose with my own series.

For the next eighteen months I plugged away at 'The World This Weekend' and 'The World At One'. The letters kept on coming in from the public, and were filed away for future reference in case the series ever came to pass. Some actually made it to air on 'TWAO'. They ranged hugely in subject matter from door-to-door salesman rip-offs to the treatment suffered by the late Jess Yates, who presented a Yorkshire Television religious programme, 'Stars On Sunday'. The tabloid press had pilloried him for his private love-life and effectively hounded him off the screen, dubbing him The Bishop. They accused him of having an affair with a much younger woman, but neglected to mention that he had been legally separated from his wife for ten years. Who knows what he would have made of the 1990s coverage of the paternity of his daughter Paula.

We took this issue of privacy up, and gave the newspapers some of their own medicine.

Two senior reporters found themselves the focus of the same kind of impromptu interview to which they had subjected the hapless Mr Yates. One paper issued a writ without realising that one of its own executives had given us an interview confirming everything we said in our report. The writ was withdrawn.

I might have pursued press injustice even harder if I had known then what I do now, having had my own private life examined closely – and inaccurately – in recent years.

The intransigence of the BBC was making me impatient. The sense of injustice I used to feel back in Australia against the college authorities who condoned the bullying at Yanco and the management at the ABC with its head-in-the-sand attitude was fast bringing me to a new confrontation at Broadcasting House.

I decided to storm the bastion of power. I grabbed Andrew Boyle from his office one evening and dragged him down the corridor to Tony Whitby's department. I told his secretary that Andrew and I would wait outside his door until he agreed to listen to our pilot show. Poor Andrew just nodded helplessly in agreement.

The tape was duly passed through to Whitby by his secretary and, after sitting for an hour wondering whether I'd done the right thing, she came out and told us we could have an audience in the inner sanctum.

Whitby sat hunched over a large sheet of paper covered in small, inked squares each filled with cramped, indecipherable lettering. He was hard at work on a corner of his sheet with a huge eraser.

He ignored us for a full minute and then looked up: 'In case you're wondering what I'm doing, I'm putting your series into the programme schedules. It's going to work, gentlemen,' he said, as if he'd known it all along.

Sadly, a few weeks later Bill Hardcastle died. He and Andrew Boyle had been incredibly close and Bill's death seemed to knock the dynamism out of Andrew. I needed him to help fight my corner as we geared up to make the new series but he just didn't have the heart to commit himself to it and he channelled his remaining energy into 'The World At One'.

I then made the mistake of going away on holiday. When I came back I found that I had been transferred to another department. Instead of working for the news department, I was now under CAMP, Current Affairs Magazine Programmes, the same people who ran 'You and Yours'. They seemed to have no real idea of what my new series was all about. What was more, they had chosen the name of the new show in my absence – it was to be called 'Checkpoint' and it was to be a consumer programme. I wasn't even given an office, just the corner of someone else's desk. There was no researcher or secretary and we were expected to function on an almost non-existent budget.

All the same, if the new series was to go ahead at all, I had to keep quiet and bide my time and I had to keep working a full rota at 'TWAO'.

the results.

The previous form had been to go, more or less cap in hand, to the subject of your investigation to ask for co-operation. If that wasn't forthcoming, that was probably the end of the programme.

Our very first programme proved, in the words of the series producer, Walter Wallich, to be a 'baptism of fire'. We decided to investigate the monopoly that opticians then enjoyed in the supply of spectacles, the resultant over-pricing and over-prescribing. In what was then an original approach, we sent the same 'patients' to eye hospitals and to opticians and discovered that the profit-motivated opticians were many times more likely to recommend glasses than were the eye hospitals.

The opticians' professional body complained direct to the BBC's Director General, disputing our figures and saying its spokesman had been interviewed too aggressively and that opticians hadn't been given enough time in the programme.

The fuss over the programme and others that followed unnerved senior management. They apparently decided that a way had to be found to rein the programme in. That avenue opened when the target of a subsequent edition wrote to complain about my allegedly unfair treatment of him. He was sent a letter from the BBC manage-ment inviting him to complain again, more forcefully, in a form suggested in the letter. They also suggested other complaints he might like to make against me.

There were plenty of people around who wanted me to fail and they rubbed their hands with glee when I was temporarily suspended without pay.

However, the complainant, who despite his commercial failings was obviously a fair-minded man, eventually responded in a way my masters did not expect. He wrote back to say he did not wish to be manipulated into becoming a rod to beat me with. He didn't wish to complain further and, on reflection, Mr Cook had only been doing his job.

The 'internal investigation' dragged on for a few weeks more. One of the department's senior producers, who felt she too had been manipulated into voting for my suspension, resigned in protest. I was back on air, but without back pay.

Despite the faltering start, it's only fair to record that those executives who took the trouble to find out firsthand how the programme operated were very supportive – and that something as radical as 'Checkpoint' then was, would probaby not have got going at all outside the BBC.

In that first series we tackled a huge variety of subjects, ninety per cent of which were prompted by listeners who got in touch with us. We looked at cowboy estate agents, exploited au pair girls, the movement of toxic waste, fairground safety, pyramid selling and computer crime. It's amazing how some of these subjects are still being investigated today, more than a quarter of a century later.

During the course of our work, we upset the National Housebuilders Registration Council over their guarantee system and undue influence in the granting of mortgages. They protested to the Director General, then to the Chairman of the BBC Board of Governors. In 1974, therefore, the BBC felt it had to introduce a new code of practice to guide us. We were then given a series of guidelines that were, by and large, sensible, covering subjects like secret tape recording of interviews and the balance of arguments of both sides in a disputatious programme.

I still find it rather amusing that much contained in these guidelines was a virtual carbon copy of the code of practice that I had penned nearly two years previously. Later expanded and refined in collaboration with senior researcher David Perrin, I abide by that code today. I won't go into detail, but here's a flavour of the controls we imposed upon ourselves:

Except where we knew we were dealing with a hardened criminal, or someone we had good reason to believe would 'do a runner' rather than answer the questions, we would give the subject at least a week's notice of any proposed interview and a clear outline of the areas we wished to discuss.

given more staff – ending up with a producer, a co-producer/senior researcher and three researchers. We even got a suite of three small offices on the seventh floor of Broadcasting House, overlooking Parliament Hill.

At the height of 'Checkpoint's twelve year run, around 1985, we had two million listeners, second only to the 'Today' programme in popularity. We started to win awards, we got laws changed and criminals jailed – and, rightly or wrongly, I earned the sobriquet of The Most Beaten Up Journalist in Britain. It was pretty much inevitable that violence occurred. So often we pursued criminals and demanded explanations from them that could easily – and often did – result in prosecution and imprisonment.

In all, I was assaulted sixteen times at 'Checkpoint'. I suffered broken ribs, concussion, fractures, lacerations and bruises. But there is one incident that people still remind me about to this day – astonishing when you consider it happened twenty years ago.

We were investigating two families – the Sumners and the Randals – who had been ripping off individuals on a grand scale through adverts offering useless or non-existent goods or services in exchange for money sent by post; money which was not returned when the goods or services failed to materialise.

When we caught up with them they tried to pretend they had emigrated to Australia, but we found them living just outside Penrith in Cumbria. I don't like confrontations but the purpose of 'Checkpoint' was to report first hand where possible, and so I waded in.

The Sumners and the Randals swore so much in the interview that we had to get permission from the Managing Director of Radio to broadcast it, with bleeps inserted where necessary.

For the record, this is how the BBC preserves the text of that encounter:

(Sound of Cook knocking on the Sumners' door.)

COOK: Mr Randal?

RANDAL: Yeah?

COOK: Could I speak to you and Mr Sumner, please, about your business activities and about firms like Interlink and Randal Travel Publications?

RANDAL: No.

COOK: My name is Roger Cook from the BBC 'Checkpoint' programme and I've come to interview you now. There are many things you ought to talk to us about. Would you like to call Mr Sumner, please? We know he's in. There are many, many dissatisfied customers of the business ventures you tried to mount all over the world. Have you nothing to say? (A woman appears.) Ah, you are Mrs Sumner?

MRS SUMNER: Who are you?

COOK: My name is Cook, from the BBC 'Checkpoint' programme.

MRS SUMNER: Fuck off, or you'll get swilled.

COOK: I beg your pardon? . . . An explanation is due . . .

(A chamber pot is emptied over Cook from an upstairs window.)

MRS SUMNER: Fuck off!

Messrs Randal and Sumner then charged after me, tore the microphone from its lead and ripped open the tape recorder in an attempt to get at the tape. They failed, and the subsequent police investigation led to the arrest of both families. Randal's wife got eighteen months and Mr and Mrs Sumner were jailed for five and three years respectively.

What I remember most vividly was what happened next. The stakeout had taken a couple of hours. It was eleven o'clock at night and I was a long way from my hotel. I was so keen to clean myself up that I stuck some money in a car wash and walked through it fully clothed. I didn't mind the soaking, just so long as it was only water next to my skin!

I have sustained accidental damage to myself at work, even when villains weren't involved. On one occasion 'The World At One' sent me to interview the then Lord Chancellor, Quintin Hogg, at his home on Putney Common. He had warned me to beware of 'strange men' on the Common but hadn't thought it necessary to warn me

During the early 'World At One' days there was never any firm guarantee my employment would last. I was on a perpetual short-term contract that meant the BBC could kiss me goodbye at any time, so I decided to keep my private freelance work going. When the chance came to make a short promotional film for Reliant Cars, I grasped it with both hands. I also bought one of their cars.

I set off from London on an early spring morning in my Reliant Scimitar. I patted the bonnet as I left home and told the car it was going home to its factory for the day. I zoomed up the A5 towards Reliant HQ in Tamworth with my expensive camera equipment stowed carefully behind the back seat.

Princess Anne had just been caught by the police for speeding in her Scimitar and, as a long stretch of road opened up ahead of me, I thought, 'Well, what are the chances of two Scimitars being stopped in the same week?' I put my foot to the floor.

Then I smelt burning and saw the flames licking from under the bonnet.

A wiring fault had developed and because there was then no fire-retardant in the Scimitar's fibre-glass body, the flames soon threatened to engulf the whole car. I pulled into the first lay-by I saw and jumped out, racing across the A5 to avoid incineration. A police patrol car, alerted by the thick smoke hanging over the road, screeched to a halt beside me. The driver cordoned off the lay-by with red cones and radioed for a fire engine.

That was when I remembered that the insurance on my camera equipment had expired just before the weekend. I had been too busy to renew it.

The fire engine arrived and soon put out what was left of the fire. The police and I stood pondering the melted and blackened remains of the car.

A thirty-two-tonne articulated lorry approached the scene. The driver, whom I later discovered had gone well over his regulation hours, chose that moment to fall asleep at the wheel. His truck ploughed through the middle of us. Blue uniforms and yellow fire helmets scattered everywhere. A lorry tyre scrunched over a policeman's foot and the truck hit me full on, sending me flying forty feet through the air. I landed on a grit bin at the far end of the lay-by and rolled into a ditch full of stinging nettles. I think that's what they call adding insult to injury.

I was rushed to St Cross Hospital in Rugby where, after emergency treatment, the only available bed was in the geriatric ward. I had several fractured vertebrae and was trussed up like a chicken. The smell from the longer-term occupants of the ward with the relentless diet of over-cooked cabbage and root vegetables was unspeakable. I tried to have sympathy but I was in too much pain. Then the ward sister discovered that I worked for the BBC and brought me a sheaf of scripts she had written and pressed me to get them passed to the Comedy Department. Add to this that Madeline and I had been having a rough time recently. She had found it very hard to come and visit me as we no longer owned a car, and I hadn't seen her for over a week. I was anxious to get home and sort things out. I decided to discharge myself.

Plaster and strong bandages made it impossible for me to catch a train or sit in a taxi so I called Chris Drake, a friend in the BBC newsroom in London, and begged him to come and take me away. As soon as he had agreed and put the phone down I realised my mistake. Chris and I shared a passion for exotic sports cars and he was bound to turn up in something barely big enough to house a pair of double-jointed midgets.

I was right. Two hours later Chris pulled into the Ambulances Only parking space at the front of Casualty in a bright-red E-Type Jaguar.

The hospital insisted that I be strapped to something to keep my fractured back rigid. A bright junior houseman had an idea and spoke to workmen repairing a wall outside. Minutes later the doctor had laid a length of scaffolding plank from the passenger seat of the Jaguar to its rear window and I was carefully lowered onto it by three

British broadcasting career would never get off the ground.

I put these morbid thoughts to one side as we arrived at the flat Madeline and I shared in Highgate. The journey had been painful. I had felt every bump and pothole on the way as my spine jarred against the unyielding plank. I thanked Chris profusely as he undid the bandages and stood me upright on the pavement.

'Come up for a drink, mate, you deserve it,' I told him.

'I'd like to see you make it up the stairs without me,' he grinned.

With a lot of grunting and grimacing I shuffled and limped my way up three flights of stairs to the door of the flat, Chris solicitously holding my elbow and pushing when required. I fumbled for the keys and let us in. Madeline wasn't in; she was probably at work at Crawley de Reya, forerunners of Mishcon de Reya, the Queen's solicitors where she was blazing a trail as a media law specialist.

I hobbled slowly across to the drinks cabinet in the corner of the kitchen. I noticed a small, white envelope on the table but left it until Chris and I had downed a stiff Macallan and he had gone on his way.

I returned to the kitchen, sat down gingerly at the table and picked up the envelope. It was addressed to me in Madeline's neat handwriting. I opened it and read the short note. She had left me. She was sorry, but felt that we had tried everything and our relationship was over. She was going to stay with some friends for the time being and would come and collect her things in the next few days.

While success was beginning to come for me, I still had no security in my job. I had been lurching from one short-term contract to another at the BBC but Madeline had already put her foot firmly on the bottom rung of the legal ladder and started to climb. Her rise was inexorable. Although a newcomer, she impressed the partners with her grasp of her chosen branch of the law. She was spoken of as a future partner and, while my meagre income dribbled inadequately into the household, her regular and increasingly-fat pay packet kept us going and even paid for a few luxuries – like the now defunct Scimitar.

In my unreconstructed chauvinist state in the early 1970s I resented Madeline being the main breadwinner. To some extent it was a surprising attitude for someone whose own father had stood idly by while his wife gathered the children up and decamped to the outback to skivvy for sheep shearers in order to keep a roof over our heads and enough food in our mouths. But perhaps I had subconsciously decided to reject everything my father was and take exactly the opposite position.

The thought of being alone and, to cap that, physically restricted turned out to be worse than the reality. Andrew Boyle was happy for me to be fetched and propped up in the corner of the studio conducting interviews and editing my material, and I launched myself back into my work. Between us we kept the preparation of 'Checkpoint' going and eventually, with the help of the physiotherapists of the Whittington and North Middlesex Hospitals, I got mobile again.

As a present to myself and as a respite before 'Checkpoint' was officially unveiled, I took a week's holiday in Ibiza. I have never been a beach bum so I chose to stay in a small hotel in Ibiza town, close to the old bullring.

I spent the first two days asleep in my room, grateful not to have to get up and get on the Tube to the Beeb. Then I started to explore and discover the delights of the harbour and its wonderful restaurants. I tried the *zarzuela* – the Iberian equivalent of bouillabaisse – over the next couple of days, and decided to hire a small car and head off to the beaches on the south coast. I left the harbour in search of a car hire office. Halfway down the street, my world suddenly imploded. I felt a terrific blow to my neck and shoulders and collapsed on the pavement. Something heavy was pinning me to the ground. There was a lot of shouting and I heard footsteps running towards me. The wind had been completely knocked out of me and I couldn't breathe or shout for help. Then I lost consciousness.

When I came round I was lying in a hospital bed in the firm grip of a surgical collar. My first thought was that I had been mysteriously transported back to the geriatric ward in Rugby. I looked around –

drugs. The two elements had unhappily combined just before I chose to stroll underneath his third-floor balcony. I had innocently interceded between suicidal hippy and pavement, leaving me with severe bruising and two broken collar bones and him with the mistaken impression that he had died and been re-incarnated instantly on the streets outside his hotel. He wandered away from the scene, apparently unhurt, and survives to this day for all I know.

I was determined to take a relaxing break at some stage in the immediate future. After the first, successful run of forty-four 'Checkpoints' and once we had been assured by our masters at the BBC that we would have another series, I telephoned an old chum from Sydney who had recently been appointed the manager of one of the best hotels on the Caribbean island of St Lucia. His euphoria over his promotion prompted an offer of a heavily-discounted stay at the hotel. All I had to do was pay for my flights. Just what I needed.

The holiday season hadn't quite started when I arrived but there was to be a lavish welcoming party in the newly-refurbished ballroom for the few dozen guests who were already in residence, myself included. I had even brought my tuxedo with me – not bad for someone who only wears a tie about twice a decade.

I was just easing myself into a second Martini and was about to saunter, Bond-like, over to a small group of attractive young ladies when I heard a loud twanging noise above my head. Then came the blackness to which I had by now become accustomed.

The main chandelier, which had been taken down and put into storage during refurbishment, hadn't been anchored properly when it was replaced. All its weight had been trusted to one inadequate cable. When the inevitable happened, guess who was standing directly underneath.

Miraculously, considering the weight of the chandelier, no bones were broken, but I did have to spend the remaining ten days of my dream holiday lying concussed in my darkened room listening enviously to the squeals and shouts of my fellow guests enjoying themselves by the swimming pool outside my window.

In the late 1970s, 'Checkpoint' regularly worked on co-productions with the BBC1 early evening magazine show 'Nationwide'. One of these concerned a supposed cure for blindness in which sufferers were stung by bees and stung financially by a strange Middle European lady.

I took one of her victims for a walk along the shores of Lake Windermere, which he loved to visit. Sadly, he wouldn't be able to see it for much longer and we were filming what was a very poignant interview when he stumbled on some rocks. I managed to dive forward and grab him before he fell into the lake – he stayed dry and I flew straight past him into the water, dislocating my shoulder en route.

My uncanny ability to attract personal injury from positions of complete safety became legendary in BBC Radio. At my leaving party from 'The World At One', they presented me with a T-shirt that carried the simple logo: 'Stand clear. I'm an accident waiting to happen.'

Nemesis in a Leisure Shirt

After my marriage to Madeline broke up, I sold our little flat in Highgate and traded up to a small Georgian house round the corner. For the next decade I concentrated on my career. I had a series of fairly short-term relationships – once or twice women actually moved in with me – but nothing had any real permanence. I was afraid of getting hurt again and I wasn't really much of a proposition as a hands-on partner. I would head off to Broadcasting House on Monday morning and show up back at Highgate when the 'Checkpoint' investigation of that week was over. Nevertheless, there came a time when some friends thought it was high time I settled down again.

In 1982 I had introduced my sister Jane to her future husband, then one of the legal team at 'Checkpoint'. Jane, a speech therapist, had followed me to England from Sydney in the seventies. She and I had never been very close, but she clearly felt the need for a bit of sibling *quid pro quo* and I spent much of the following year being invited round to her Fulham flat to be introduced to women whom she thought were my type.

I was just gearing myself up to tell Jane that I really didn't see the point in carrying on with these fruitless gatherings when she persuaded me to go round once again 'just to meet a good friend'. And that's when I met Frances.

Physically, we couldn't have been more different. Frances was petite, pretty, bright, Irish and blonde. I was an overweight workaholic who was just about to turn forty and was becoming reconciled to permanent bachelorhood. She was working as the senior PA at a large architectural practice and was the life and soul of the evening.

She lifted my mood instantly – I was charmed by her personality and, for some reason, she seemed to get on with me.

Within six months we were married and she moved out of her tiny house in Notting Hill. It was a flying freehold – rooms built over an archway – only eight feet wide, that I found impossible to fit into.

So, I had someone to share my Highgate pad with again – but this time for keeps. And, before long, there would be three of us, with the birth of Belinda at the end of April, 1985.

'Checkpoint' had now been on the air for twelve years. The programme had become an institution and, although not exactly sharing Groucho Marx's sentiments about not wanting to live in one, I was ready for a change.

For about a year I had been wooed by television companies wanting to put a version of 'Checkpoint' on the screen – Mike Townson, editor of Thames Television's weekly current affairs programme 'TV Eye', had suggested a regular investigative edition of the show; David Elstein at Brook Productions proposed a series of half-hour programmes; as did an old friend Bob Southgate at TVS. Bob had interviewed me for a job as a newsreader at ITN soon after I arrived in London from Australia in 1968. Although he confessed to me over a post-audition drink that there weren't actually any vacancies at the time, we kept in touch with each other as he climbed the television executive ladder from one independent station to another.

Bob and I had talked about my joining him at TVS in Southampton in 1982 but he warned me that he was involved in serious political in-fighting and he didn't know how long he would be around in order to get any new series off the ground. His instincts were proved right and he soon moved on to Central Television in Birmingham where he became Controller of Factual Programmes.

'Checkpoint', or at least the Checkpoint style of journalism, did make it onto BBC TV in the early seventies. For nearly five years, almost every run of the 'Nationwide' series featured a fortnightly investigation researched largely by the radio team and presented by me. Sometimes they were even television versions of the latest 'Checkpoint'.

They were popular to the point that some talented 'Nationwide' staffers began to mumble that they were being consigned to the

ings. It was considered good enough to warrant a separate airing in
its own right. I had always wanted a solo spot on television and now,
with a recent television example fresh in management's minds, I was
presented with the opportunity to lobby for one.

I found myself at Heathrow, bound for the Edinburgh Radio and
Television Festival. I joined the queue at the check-in desk and did
what most people do when they are in a slow-moving line at an
airport – stare at the person at the head of the queue and marvel at
how long it takes to process one individual's ticket. I focused on the
overcoated figure a few places ahead of me. He looked familiar. With
a start, I realised who it was – Alasdair Milne, the Director General
of the BBC.

My brain went into overdrive – perhaps I could repeat the success
of my 'Checkpoint' lobbying of more than a decade before. It was
worth a try.

After what seemed an eternity, but was probably only ten minutes
or so, I reached the British Airways desk. Using my softest, and, I
hoped, most persuasive interview technique, I explained quietly who
I was and that it was *very* important that I had a seat next to Mr
Milne, who had checked in a few minutes earlier. The clerk consulted
her screen. I held my breath. She started to hammer the keys, looked
up and told me that she'd been able to move another passenger yet
to check in and that would be fine – have a good flight. I scooped
up the ticket, thanked her sincerely and walked through to depar-
tures. Now it was down to me.

I avoided Milne in the lounge and waited until he had boarded
the plane and found his seat before I stepped into the cabin. His
head was down, reading some papers, and I recognised his thick,
black head of hair a few rows in. The seat next to him was empty.

I feigned surprise at being in the seat next to Mr Milne and was
relieved that he seemed to know who I was. We slipped quite easily

into conversation about Edinburgh and the festival. I waited until
the air stewardesses had done their safety stuff and the captain had
assured us of his and the rest of the staff's devoted attention before
taking the plunge.

I had steered the chat towards television and radio cross-overs –
then, as now, quite a rarity.

'I really think "Checkpoint" should be given a chance on television,' I said, watching the director-general's face for a reaction.

He sipped his coffee and gave a barely-perceptible nod, appearing
to mull over the notion. He turned his head slightly towards me and
I took this as the cue to proceed with my argument for translating
'Checkpoint' from the airwaves to the small screen. I gave it my best
shot for a full five minutes, glancing at him anxiously whenever I
felt I could.

'It may work,' he conceded after a silence that had me wondering
if he had dropped off to sleep. Then he added, with a smile, 'You've
certainly made the most of your luck in getting a seat next to me.'

I smiled back at him. 'It was more than luck, you know. If I see
an opportunity, I generally try to grab it with both hands.'

He told me to speak to Brian Wenham, Director of Programmes
for BBC Television, when we got back to London. He assured me
that he would 'have a word' with Mr Wenham first. I could do no
more. I couldn't help wondering whether he meant what he had said
or whether he was trying to fob off this burly, insistent fellow whom
he had heard was always barging up to people, demanding interviews.
Our conversation turned to other, more general, matters and we
parted with a handshake at Edinburgh Airport – he to climb into his
chauffeur-driven car and I to seek a taxi. When we bumped into one
another at the festival, we simply exchanged a cordial nod.

A few anxious days later I made the call to Brian Wenham's office
half-expecting to be greeted with incomprehension. But my call had
been anticipated. 'Checkpoint' for TV was being examined – I just
had to wait for a while and I'd be contacted.

'Checkpoint' was given a six-week trial run on BBC1, albeit on
radio budgets and, apart from the camera crews, with radio staff. In
presentational terms, it showed. But the quality of the journalism
appealed to the audience. The average viewership was something
over eight million. The management pronounced the exercise a

a solo programme. As today, 'Watchdog' already had an investigative, although consumerist, bent and the perception may have been that a TV 'Checkpoint' was surplus to requirements.

Alternatively, perhaps we had been pigeonholed as a radio show. The Corporation had accepted our investigative style but seemed happier keeping it where it was, literally, out of sight. A move to television was just going to cause more high-profile ructions because of the targets we would tackle and the powers-that-be weren't prepared to fight any unnecessary battles.

The 'Checkpoint' staff were moved out of its new offices and we were offered our old jobs back at Broadcasting House.

I wear disappointment badly sometimes and it became openly known that although Auntie was always high in my affections, the time had probably come to undo the apron strings.

The telephone rang in our house in Highgate one evening. It was Bob Southgate with a proposition. Now securely ensconced at Central, he was convinced that he could persuade the company to take my kind of investigative programme to television on a permanent basis at last.

Independent television worked very differently from the BBC in the 1970s and 1980s. Where the latter retained complete control of its programme output, each department providing the requisite number of dramas, comedies, news and current affairs shows to fill the schedules, ITV was much more competitive. Every independent station – in those days the likes of Central, TVS, Thames, LWT, Granada, Tyne Tees, Yorkshire – fought its rivals for programme slots.

There was a beauty contest of contenders to fill, for example, the eight o'clock slot on Friday evenings – or to be the sole providers of a particular kind of factual programme. In those days, the larger companies had a right to a certain amount of airtime into which they could pitch programmes they particularly wanted to make. Central prepared to wheel and deal what we decided to call 'The Cook Report' onto the air. These days, the judge and jury in these regularly-held beauty contests are the senior officers of the ITV Network Control. These are among the most powerful and widely courted figures in television.

Bob confessed that Central had missed the boat to get me on air for the 1986 season but with his political skills, learned over years of intriguing in the corridors of ITN and TVS, he was confident he could land me a series for 1987.

First, he needed to recruit me to Central so we could start to plan the new series and find the right personnel. For a year, I would work on a major new regional programme – 'Central Weekend' – which then tackled one issue a week, often showing a pre-recorded investigation, on, say, medical negligence and opening the debate up to a live studio audience afterwards. I would work on the investigations and co-host the debates with two consummate professionals, Sue Jay and Andy Craig.

One of the producers, who doubled as a cameraman for the pre-recorded parts, was Peter Salkeld, who was to become a good friend and international travelling companion in the 'Cook Report' years.

'Salk' was one of the most unusual people I had ever met. Wiry and incredibly energetic, he had a large, bushy grey beard, several missing front teeth and a high-pitched, cackling laugh that was soon mimicked throughout the office. A lapsed former Baptist lay preacher, he retained an absolutely rigid sense of right and wrong which, though often endearing, could also make him incredibly awkward. Indeed, his unbending attitude almost cost him his job on several occasions. At our first few meetings I could tell we would get on well, and this heartened me for the future.

I handed in my resignation at the BBC, and it was greeted with an almost unanimous deafening silence. General relief at my going was tempered only by Michael Grade, then the Controller of BBC1, subsequently telling the press that the corporation should not have let me go.

After seventeen years with the BBC, I cleared my desk and went home. I felt a mixture of sadness, anger, mystification – and a sense of anticipation for the future.

*

us know what the weather was like outside so that we could dress appropriately before the long walk through corridors and gangways that led, eventually, to the security desk and the real world.

Belinda had not long been born, and the three of us took a flat not far from the studios so that we could be together as much as possible. Sometimes, I think that if I had known what pressure this change in my career was going to put all three of us under in the years to come, I wouldn't have done it. But, at first, the workload was gladly borne.

Two of the senior researchers, Paul Calverley and Tim Tate, had come with me from 'Checkpoint'. Although they had little experience of television, both were highly-talented investigators to whom the smallest snippet of news, however much buried in the columns of a heavy newspaper or trade magazine, could represent a programme idea. They were used to sifting through up to 400 letters a week from the public. They had contacts in most of the police forces and Customs offices in Britain.

Several times a week, sometimes two or three times a day, we would all troop into the smoke-filled office of the programme editor, Mike Townson, and engage in head-banging sessions to thrash out programme ideas. Townson had been hired on his reputation as a hard-working and inspired editor at Thames Television where, for a decade, he had run the successful current affairs series 'TV Eye'. I had first met Townson in the early eighties when he tried to recruit me to the programme.

Then, quite by chance, soon after I joined Central, I spotted him in Regent's Park. I was looking for my car, abandoned the night before in anticipation of a boozy party in nearby Primrose Hill. Mike was sitting on a bench looking as if he was searching for somewhere to commit suicide. He told me he was waiting to get fired. It was a familiar story in independent television. The guy he'd sacked several years previously had just been appointed his new boss. Revenge was imminent.

I was carrying a Vodaphone mobile with me, the size of a car battery in those early days. I dialled Bob Southgate and told him I was with someone he should talk to. I handed the phone to Mike. Bob had worked for Townson as a reporter on 'TV Eye' and there was mutual respect between the two men, although Bob knew that Townson could be tough on his staff. He recalled that, on occasion, Townson would put two teams of reporters and researchers to work on the same story without letting either side know. Whoever, in his judgement, had made the most progress in a week got to make the film. The same pattern of role reversal that was ousting Townson from Thames Television was about to ease him into a new career with Central.

Ten minutes later he had been offered the job of editor of Central Weekend with the tacit understanding that the new series of investigations would also be his. I went on to search for my car and Mike went back to Thames Television to enjoy the luxury of resigning before he could be fired.

The 'Cook Report' office was a puzzling place. Where, passing visitors to this largely empty but untidy open office space, would ask, was the staff? Where was the frenzied activity that must surely accompany the pursuit of the action-packed programmes that were the keynote of the series?

Pat Harris, the programme manager, would usually be at her desk in the middle of the floor. Next to her would be Gaynor Scattergood, Tracey Bagley or Kay Haden – one or other of the programme's hard-pressed secretaries. An accountant would be hard at work, poring over programme costs and occasionally querying expenses.

Over in the corner, in his smoke-filled office, would sit Mike Townson, consigning information to his desk-top computer, puffing at his Benson and Hedges. Mike Townson's dress sense made my casual style look positively *haute couture*. He would plod into the office, a Benson and Hedges cigarette on the go, despite Central's strict 'No Smoking' policy, wearing shabby trainers, sagging tracksuit bottoms and a gaudy T-shirt stretched tightly over his pot-belly.

He waggled his half-empty Tesco bag. 'This is it. No point in going to too much trouble.' He grinned, exposing a substantial set of nicotine-stained teeth and pushing his enormous black-framed glasses back up the bridge of his nose. He loved to shock, but behind the jocularity a shrewd and ruthless brain was at work.

A few feet from Townson sat his long-suffering secretary, Desna Markham, who had long ago learned not to get overfussed by Townson's abrupt demands, which she habitually greeted with a smile and a small, dismissive wave.

Next to Townson's office was mine and next to that was another shared by Clive Entwistle and Peter Salkeld. Newer recruits, producers and researchers alike, shared desks in the open-plan hinterland, behind an assortment of hessian-covered screens.

But where were they all?

More than likely, producers and researchers would be 'on the road', trying to convert raw information into television programmes. This meant long stints of 'phone-bashing' at the early planning stage of a new series, but that would probably be the last time anyone would see the office other than to drop videotapes in en route to somewhere else. My office would normally be empty and locked, its occupant engaged in long-haul travel. Roger Cook and his awkward demands to influence the course of investigations were thousands of miles away. Producers telephoned Townson every day to report on progress, during the course of which calls Townson issued new orders, or, more usually, added to and amended them constantly throughout the day and night by phone or fax.

Mike Townson loved the office's 'ghost-town' atmosphere. It meant that all his staff were out information-gathering or filming something for him. 'Townson's Train Set', we used to call ourselves. Not that Townson always got his own way. Over time we learned to use his control techniques against him and only fed in the information we wanted him to get – so sometimes stories we favoured – and he didn't – actually made it to the screen. Sometimes a programme was successful because of him. Sometimes, though rather less frequently, it did well despite him. And, because of his background in daily current affairs, few programmes ever got finished until minutes before transmission.

It was all a game at times. We would take perverse pleasure in being on assignment in some far-flung location where there was no way of telephoning the office – or of the office phoning us. Townson could appreciate that the person on the ground knows what is happening better than the one sitting, thousands of miles away, in the office. It's a situation I have manipulated in my own – and I hope the programme's – interest quite frequently.

Mind you, there have been occasions where I have desperately wanted to communicate but haven't been able to. I remember getting a message to phone home while I was in one particularly remote West African location. I made countless failed attempts, then, with the help of a pre-booked call, several helpful international operators and a military radio telephone, I finally got through.

Belinda answered. 'Hi, Dad. Sorry, but "Neighbours" has just started, can you please ring back in half an hour? Bye.' She hung up on me.

The question that visitors to the office most frequently asked was, 'Where do you get your ideas from for your programmes?'

It was a good question. If I'd been asked that while working at 'Checkpoint', I would undoubtedly have replied, 'From you, the listener. We get 400 letters a week and there are always stories in there.'

But things had changed. In the 'Checkpoint' days, one programme would often spawn another. If we broadcast an exposé of a rogue garage chain, for example, the next week we would receive dozens of letters about another, similar scam. New names and companies with other, equally nefarious, ways of conning the public, would be unearthed by the researchers and off we would go.

But twelve letters of complaint about a roofing company's high-pressure sales techniques and shoddy workmanship didn't add up to a half-hour television show. We had moved on in both subject breadth and the public's expectations. At first I used to check myself and talked through the latest developments in all of these subjects. Somewhere there was a programme to kick off 'The Cook Report' in fine style.

The first programme was due to air on 22 July 1987. It was now April and we needed to decide soon what to fill it with. One show was almost complete but Townson wasn't convinced that its subject was right to open with. Producer Clive Entwistle, researcher Tim Tate and I had just got back from Brazil where we had investigated the horrifyingly active trade in stolen babies in which ruthless gangs of thieves were snatching up to 400 carefully-selected babies a month – often from poor families – to sell them on to childless couples in the USA, Europe and Israel for anything up to £10,000.

Tate had found one young mother – Rosilda Gonçalves – who was scouring the country looking for her ten-month-old daughter Bruna. She had been stolen by her babysitter from Rosilda's house in the remote interior town of Curatiba. Luckily for her – and the 'Cook Report' team – the local police decided to help and told Tim Tate which gang they suspected was behind Bruna's disappearance. One former member of the gang was in the process of informing on his colleagues in the hope of receiving a reduced sentence, and Tate discovered from him that Bruna had been sold on, via Paraguay, to an Israeli couple who lived near the airport in Tel Aviv.

Rosilda and I flew to Israel to see if baby Bruna really was there. Acting on local research, we staked out a flat in a stark, modern block and waited. A few hours later a woman in her late thirties appeared, manoeuvring a pushchair down the steps at the front of the building.

From our vantage point across a busy road, Rosilda peered anxiously at the child. She gripped my arm and whispered urgently, 'Sim, sim . . . e ela.' It was Bruna. We told the Brazilian embassy in Tel

Aviv what had happened and their advice was to seek legal assistance. The search was on to find a lawyer willing to act to get Bruna back to her mother. Eventually, we found one motivated more by principle than by potential profit.

But first Rosilda needed to get a closer view of the child she believed was her own. Almost eighteen months had passed since Bruna had been taken and we were dealing with a toddler who looked significantly different from the baby who had been snatched from her cot.

The camera crew, hired locally to overcome the language barrier and Israeli red tape on filming permission, operated from the back of an unmarked van as Rosilda approached the woman with the pushchair. Once the approach had been filmed, we joined Rosilda with the crew and an interpreter.

The adoptive mother was initially horrified – doing her best to steer the pushchair and its tiny occupant away from us as we explained what we believed had happened. It was extremely awkward, though the Israeli woman admitted quite readily that she and her husband had bought the child and adopted her. She believed that she had done nothing wrong and invited us round to her flat later that day. The adoptive mother was plainly sympathetic to Rosilda, but the father was not, repeating over and over again 'It's mine, I paid good money for it.'

I double-checked with the interpreter. Had he really said 'it', not 'she'?

He had.

For the time being, at least, Bruna – or Carolina as she had been renamed – would remain with her adoptive parents as the legal process got underway. Rosilda was in with a good chance of having her child restored to her, once blood tests had proved beyond doubt that she was Bruna's mother. It was, inevitably, going to be several months before the whole process would be over. In the meantime, we had a very strong story, to which we could return later in the series with what we hoped would be a happy ending.

Clive Entwistle had an ambition to be in Rio for Carnival. Mike Townson had got wind of Entwistle's intentions to stay on for it, and had absolutely forbidden any of us to remain in Brazil for longer dry.

Victory was within his grasp when Townson had to concede that a Brazilian police offer to provide us with an interview with an imprisoned American paedophile, and an armed guard into the bandit-infested borders of Rio in search of the suspected ringleader of one of the gangs, was an opportunity we couldn't miss.

We filmed in one of the appalling mud and corrugated iron slums, or *favelas*, where gang members shelter. As we approached, flanked by machine-gun toting officers, a brightly-coloured kite spiralled up into the air ahead of us – and then another, and another – the local signal that the law had arrived.

Eventually, and by then without our increasingly-nervous police escort, which had simply abandoned us, we found and interviewed a self-confessed baby snatcher. He told us that it was not simply a matter of snatching street urchins. They had little value. The market preference was for fair-skinned, blue-eyed babies – and these could be more easily found in the Curatiba region, where many of the early settlers had been of German descent. Indeed, so bold had the baby snatchers become, that maternity hospitals in the region had been forced to hire armed guards. Back in São Paulo, as promised, we were taken inside the grim Candiru prison to meet a recently arrested paedophile.

The authorities, without telling him what he faced, led him before our camera in an interview room. Off-guard, he confessed that he had been buying and importing little boys into the United States. What he and his friends did with them doesn't bear thinking about. Our excitement about getting this key interview soon turned to depression and, ultimately, to anger. The camera may have been rolling but the cameraman hadn't loaded the film properly – it had all been fogged. He was fired on the spot.

Getting to the carnival wasn't as easy as we'd thought either, for two reasons. The first involved an incident on the Puente de la Armistad bridge over the Parana River, where it forms the border between Brazil and Paraguay. It was through Paraguay that researcher Tim Tate had traced Bruna's route to Israel, and we wanted some local footage.

Filming in Paraguay with or without permission was impossible, so it was agreed that we would film clandestinely out of the back of a van. Space was at a premium, so Entwistle would wait for us on the bridge. It was around nine o'clock in the morning, but the outside temperature was already nudging 32 degrees Centigrade, and the interior of the van was swelteringly hot. We left the rear doors slightly ajar in order to improve the ventilation. Unfortunately, as we approached the border post, the doors swung open, revealing all.

The cameraman, the interpreter and I were dragged out at gun-point and arrested. Our lives now turned into something out of a 'B' movie. We were lined up against a wall and searched. Our camera gear was painstakingly inspected, turned every which way, as if the guards had never seen anything like it – and they probably hadn't. There were shouted conversations over a two-way radio. We were bundled into ancient Jeeps and driven to the military barracks at nearby Cuidad del Este, from which the province was governed.

The colonel in charge ran the administration of the area in the mornings and the official cocaine concession in the afternoons, we were told. We were herded into his office. He was a small podgy figure in camouflage trousers, a grey Playboy sweatshirt and Gucci shoes, the soles of which faced us across his cluttered desk.

He would have none of our explanations and apologies, and to emphasise the points he was making in rapid and incomprehensible Spanish, randomly fired his pearl-handled pistol at a row of soft-drink cans nailed to a plank in the courtyard outside the window.

When he had finished we were taken to a windowless, almost airless room and left, literally, to sweat it out. Our terrified interpreter told us she'd tried to explain that we'd been making a travelogue, and had got lost. 'Lost for good,' had been the reply.

Eventually, without further explanation and minus some of our camera gear, we were loaded into the Jeeps again. It was seven hours since we had been arrested. What now? To our immense relief, we were driven back to the bridge and dumped. As a parting gesture, one

The ever-enterprising Entwistle disappeared. Half an hour later, he returned wearing a smug grin. Using the substantial cash float that he, as producer, used to carry, he had hired a light aircraft. It had been the only one available, it had ten seats, and it had cost an arm and a leg. Entwistle then scurried up and down the ticket lines until he had sold the six surplus seats, no doubt at a healthy profit.

The carnival did not disappoint. It was the biggest, noisiest and most colourful event any of us had ever seen. Pity the winner of the most beautiful girl in Brazil competition turned out to be a bloke.

Back home, Townson's instinct was still that the Brazilian baby story, although strong, wasn't right to open the first series. We needed something more relevant to a British audience. We were told to find something else – and quick.

Paul Calverley had brought with him to a meeting a cutting from that day's *Telegraph*. It listed the names of half a dozen British criminals who had taken advantage of a loophole in extradition law to evade capture in Britain and flee to Spain. They were living the life of Riley on their ill-gotten gains.

Calverley, a balding, quietly-determined Yorkshireman in his early thirties, had cut his teeth on 'Checkpoint' and had a reputation for working long and hard on the most unpromising material if he 'felt there was a sniff' of a broadcastable story to be gleaned from it. He had already read every article in the Central cuttings library on the politics of the Anglo-Spanish extradition problem and had just returned from London where he had sounded out a senior Scotland Yard contact on the strength of feeling in the police force about these fugitives and how many we might be talking about.

A year before, a gang of east London criminals had pulled off one of the most spectacular robberies in recent history – relieving a security company of £6 million in cash in a raid on one of its vans. The police knew exactly who was behind the robbery but the principals had got clean away to the Costa del Sol, now nicknamed the Costa del Crime.

'The Security Express squad is jumping up and down because the government won't go to the Spanish and get them to kick these guys out,' said Calverley. 'My man is willing to give us six more names that haven't even hit the newspapers yet. They're all there on the Costas and he'll give us their previous and their addresses in Spain. The cops really want us to go and stir this thing up to make Thatcher do something.'

The Costa del Crime had been written about before but had never been subjected to close scrutiny by television. The criminals had certainly never before had a large man with a microphone and two camera crews confronting them.

To judge by the frenetic beating of the computer keys, Townson was interested. He listened to a few more ideas from the rest of us and then concluded the meeting. A few minutes later he bellowed to his secretary to get Clive Entwistle into his office.

Townson and Entwistle went back a long way to Thames Television days when Entwistle, a former *Sunday People* reporter, had been Townson's trusted confidant. A typical 'cheeky chappy from the north', the bespectacled Entwistle was known to his colleagues as 'The Rochdale Cowboy'. Entwistle had the flamboyant approach Townson wanted for this first programme. I wasn't so sure. Entwistle, like Townson, had a reputation as a 'deliverer'. Unfortunately, like Townson, this was often at other people's expense, and he could be extremely unpleasant if he didn't get his own way.

Entwistle had been in with Townson for half an hour when Townson's secretary was loudly instructed to call Paul Calverley and myself into the office. Townson looked up from his desk and smiled at me. 'Well, Roger, looks like you're going on your holidays in the sun. Make sure you take your swimming trunks.'

He turned to Calverley and told him to go back to his friend at Scotland Yard and get that list of names, background details and addresses on the Costas.

Top of that list was Ronnie Knight. More famous for having once been married to Barbara Windsor, Knight was also a prominent East End gangster. He had slipped away to the Costa del Sol before the police could arrest him for his part in the Security Express – then, wedding party strapped to the outside of a helicopter.

Entwistle had somehow managed to find the oldest helicopter and oldest pilot in Spain to fly us. The pilot actually held Spanish helicopter pilot licence Number One, as he proudly showed us – mercifully after the flight was over. Unfortunately, the aircraft had broken down on the day of the wedding and we had to film what we could from the ground. The next idea was to overfly Ronnie's villa which was perched on a steep hillside between the mountains and the sea just to the north of Marbella. Our onboard camera would, with luck, show an assembled group of British and foreign villains scattering as we descended, hovered and circled. Another camera on the ground would show me clinging to the helicopter, a sort of *deus ex machina* come to spoil one of Knight's regular barbecue parties, while my commentary would list the fugitive guests who had turned up.

The pilot had landed on a rocky outcrop overlooking Ronnie Knight's place and we joined him there. He pointed out, through our interpreter – local freelance journalist, Nigel Bowden, who had become our eyes and ears on the Costas – that there would be a strong up-draught around the house because it was built on an escarpment and that the helicopter would be difficult enough to control even without exterior cargo. I heard this and felt a twinge of unease. Neither the pilot nor I were keen to have my ample frame hanging outside the cockpit, but Entwistle was having none of it. I was going up and that was that.

He passed me a safety harness with which I was to be supported. I tucked it under my shirt, clicked the catches shut, and passed the ends back to Entwistle beside the helicopter. Seconds later he stepped back and gave the pilot a brisk thumbs up. I clung on to the door frame and we juddered slowly skywards.

We approached the villa from the north and dropped downwards. The effect was amazing. Guests shot off in all directions, particularly when they saw the camera lens poking out of the open side of the helicopter.

God knows what they made of me. Through my headphones I could hear the pilot's increasingly agitated commentary, translated for us by Nigel Bowden, who sat in the passenger seat.

'He says his helicopter is handling like a pregnant pig, whatever that feels like,' Bowden reported nervously.

This assignment was a little out of the ordinary for Bowden, who had been a marine biologist in a previous incarnation before marrying a Spanish woman and settling down to a life of eventful uncertainty as a freelance journalist in Marbella.

By now most of the guests had cleared off in cars back to their apartments in Marbella and Puerto Banus. We decided to call it a day. We landed back on the flat-topped rocks and everyone climbed out. I tried to open my fingers but they were locked shut round the door frame and remained that way for several minutes. Eventually, I was able to prise my frozen fingers free and leaned back on my harness to ease my aching back. The result was not far short of a somersault as I fell over backwards. I pulled at the webbing of the harness. It was slack. As I hauled it towards me, I heard the clunk-clunk-clunk of the metal clasps scraping along the cockpit floor. The safety harness had never been attached to the anchor-points inside.

The cold sweat I then felt was a classic illustration of my usual reaction to some of the bizarre and dangerous things the programme has called upon me to do. 'Fear in arrears', I call it.

We always try to plan what we do very carefully indeed, but no plan and no participant is perfect. If you analysed the risks too closely, you wouldn't do the job at all.

A few days later, we called in on one of Ronnie Knight's partners in crime, Clifford Saxe. Saxe was – and still is – also wanted for his part in the Security Express robbery. Back in London Saxe had run the pub where Ronnie and his gang had planned the job. He, too, had taken advantage of the extradition loophole and fled to the Costas.

We spent some time following him from his home to the variety of bars he frequented and decided to confront him as he drank in his favourite – Wyn's Bar – an expat watering hole in the hills above Marbella.

At 'The Cook Report' we call such an engineered confrontation the doorstep, retribution is high when I turn up with a series of awkward questions and a microphone and/or camera crew. If it really was a doorstep interview, the end result would more than likely be a frustrated interviewer with a bruised foot mouthing feebly at the woodwork.

Far better to choose a location where the inquisitor can control what happens. Until British villains had watched enough 'Cook Report's to realise that cameras and recording equipment can be hidden very easily in cupboards, bathrooms and behind curtains, the hotel room was a favourite.

I have lost count of the times when the villain of the programme has got his comeuppance after I have posed as the room-service waiter. It is difficult to escape through a narrow door frame blocked by someone of my size and there is generally ample time to fire all the questions I and the audience want to hear the answers to.

If we can't get the target to the location by prior arrangement, then we choose somewhere public. There's generally plenty of space to manoeuvre two television crews and there is generally such surprise at our arrival that I can fire off sufficient questions before the subject recovers his composure and heads for the nearest exit.

Nigel Bowden had warned us that Clifford Saxe might react unpredictably when approached. In the few months Saxe had been resident in Marbella he had been involved in several drink-fuelled fights, turning on friends and strangers alike when the mood took him.

We decided to risk it. Clive Entwistle was being bombarded with calls from Mike Townson demanding to know when I would be free to join Paul Calverley in Amsterdam where he had found and secretly filmed a gang supplying child pornography – complete with instructions on how to smuggle it past Customs. My presence was also required in Northern Ireland where our undercover team was attempting to expose Protestant paramilitaries who were demanding protection money from construction companies large and small.

minutes later Bowden rang us to say that Saxe was out of his house and installed safely at Wyn's. We set off for the 'doorstep'.

We try not to provoke our targets unduly, but Saxe's first reaction when he saw the camera and me was to pick up a heavy glass ashtray and hurl it at my head. Luckily, I ducked and it bounced off my shoulder. I persisted with my questions about returning to Britain to face trial for the Security Express job. Pandemonium broke out in the bar. Saxe's drinking pals crowded round him, pulling him back as he tried to follow me outside. Suddenly, he broke free and lunged forward at me, raining blows down on my head and back.

There's no point in retaliating; it makes you look as bad as the person you are trying to interview. I retreated a few paces and asked Saxe once again for the chance to conduct an orderly interview. He swore and spat at me before being led back inside the bar, successfully this time, by his friends. It was useless to carry on. We'd tried our best and had got unique footage of one of the 180 most wanted Brits successfully evading justice in the sun.

For my pains, I had an absolutely glorious black eye and a bruised back.

Loud shouts and scuffles from inside Wyn's Bar indicated that an attempt to snatch our film was imminent. Time to climb into the getaway car. But it wasn't where we had left it. At the first hint of trouble, the driver, who had clearly never seen anything like this before, had taken fright and driven off down the road, leaving us stranded. The cameraman, Gerry Pinches, spotted the car parked at a junction a few hundred yards away and we quickly headed away from Mr Saxe and his friends.

In a subsequent programme, we asked how several prominent Costa del Crime residents survived after their original ill-gotten gains had been spent. The answer, in many cases, was by drug dealing. We decided to show the British public what they were up to now.

This led us to a memorable trip across the narrow stretch of

Mediterranean between Spain and Morocco. The trip was arranged by a former drug dealer now turned police informant. With the protection and backing – we were assured – of the Moroccan police and Customs officers, we trekked into the remote Rif mountains where the rule of law hadn't been in force for years. We were to meet the men who grew the hashish. Our claim was that we wanted to export it in considerable quantities.

Some miles short of our destination, our escorts got nervous and turned back, but we pushed on. When we got to the meeting point – a rundown mountain town – we were put up in an abandoned holiday hotel, built but never occupied because the area had become too dangerous for tourists. It was staffed by a one-eyed bandit whose culinary skills ran only as far as a seemingly-endless supply of boiled eggs. There was no bedding or electricity and the only water available – apart from the bottled variety – lay in a mixture of green sludge at the bottom of the swimming pool.

Eventually we met and filmed the grower and negotiated our theoretical deal under the watchful eye of his armed escort.

'How will we take delivery of our shipment?' I asked the dealer.

'You may pick it up at sea, beyond the twelve-mile limit,' he replied.

'And what about the police and Customs?' I wanted to know.

'No problem,' he concluded with just a flicker of a smile. 'They will deliver it to you.'

Never has an answer given me such a frisson. There we were, deep in enemy territory, with our promised protection clearly working for the other side. Luckily, we were able to talk our way to safety, saying that we needed to talk to our 'principals' before going ahead with the deal. The Rif mountain filming became part of a very successful programme.

There was just time for one more 'doorstep' in Spain before catching the plane for Amsterdam. John Corsecadden looked a lot more respectable than Clifford Saxe but, then, he was a much more accomplished crook. Dozens of creditors knew to their cost what a skilled fraudster he was. Over the past few years he had embezzled £3 million from a series of companies he had supposedly been trying to rescue from bankruptcy. He, too, had availed himself of the Spanish extradition loophole and had fled with his wife to a substantial, detached their umbrellas. Steve Phillips was so incensed he grabbed John Corsecadden's umbrella from his grasp. For one awful moment I thought he was going to belabour the couple with it, and I told him to stop. He handed it back. Corsecadden, umbrella reclaimed, rained down another dozen blows on my head, ably assisted by his wife.

Once again, I wondered why I was doing this, especially as I wasn't getting any relevant answers to my questions. And yet I already knew the answer to that: we were showing up the man for what he was, cowardly, greedy, unprincipled and selfish. His victims would appreciate it.

John Corsecadden eventually returned to Britain to receive a three-year prison sentence for fraud. He was released early due to ill-health and died shortly afterwards.

I was glad to board my flight at Malaga and relax for a few hours before landing at Schiphol.

Four hours and a visit to Amsterdam's Red Light district later, I had concussion and burns to add to my black eye and bruised shoulder.

Paul Calverley had met us at the airport and taken us into the middle of town to confront a loathsome creature called Justin who had been selling him child pornography from under the counter of his sex shop for the past few weeks.

Justin had been secretly filmed by Calverley as he showed how paedophiles smuggled the material through British Customs controls by re-packaging the videotape on typewriter-ribbon spools. Black and white footage of Justin's demonstration was already safely back at Central studios.

Calverley, accepted as a regular customer, went into the sex shop first to establish Justin was at the counter. He wore a radio mike so that we could hear that Justin was on duty. As soon as our sound recordist picked up Paul's conversation with our target on his head-

phones, I walked in with the camera crew at my shoulder and confronted him. Justin had delivered a few shocked denials before I felt
a sharp pain over my head. The lights were suddenly switched off.

Back in Birmingham, only when I looked carefully at the footage
did I see what had happened in the gloom of the shop. The burly
proprietor had returned – and he wasn't happy. He could see the
camera crew and me and obviously decided to make filming as hard
as he could by plunging us all into darkness. Then he picked up a
billiard cue and ran towards me. He started hitting me while we
were still inside the shop – that was when I felt the pain in my head
– and he was still hitting me as the crew and I beat a retreat outside.

Then he turned his attention to the microphone I was holding.
Everything he and I were saying was actually being recorded by a
tiny radio microphone out of sight under my jacket. The hand-held
mike was a legacy from my 'Checkpoint' days when we wanted it
made plain to the interviewee that he or she was being recorded. It
wasn't really needed.

My assailant tried to pull the hand mike away from me. The
struggle took us away from the shop and we lurched dangerously
close to the edge of the canal. Suddenly, he reached for the short,
fat cigar he'd had clenched between his teeth and stubbed it hard
into the back of my hand. The pain was amazing. I let go and, with
some satisfaction, he hurled the microphone into the water.

Then, quite without warning, the cigar-wielding shop owner was
set on by a group of young men and pushed roughly back inside his
own premises. Surprisingly, our rescuers turned out to be performers
from the live sex show theatre next door. They had heard the scuffle
and, when they found out that their neighbour was peddling child
pornography, angrily rounded on him. Pornography, they said,
should only be the preserve of consenting adults.

The shop – and others in the same chain – were shut down by
the Amsterdam police a month later.

Back in England, I was able to snatch a couple of days at the Birmingham flat with Frances and Belinda who, thank goodness, was rapidly
taking after her mother in looks. But, after my forty-eight hours
respite, Mike Townson was on the telephone once again.

'The UDA's taken our bait. They're expecting Mr Rogers over

Northern Ireland is one of the toughest in which to carry out an undercover investigation. In twelve years of programme-making we have embarked on seven deep-cover projects there. Six have gone to air. The seventh may one day, but only when it is safe enough for the brave people who dared to help us to come out of hiding.

Our contacts with the Royal Ulster Constabulary had always been close, going back to 'World At One' days. Paul Calverley, in particular, had good contacts within C13, the specialist anti-terrorist squad which had its headquarters in a rundown manor house on the Bangor Road a few miles east of Belfast city centre.

C13 officers are convivial to a man. When you work under the pressure they do, the odd glass of whiskey is always welcome – and it was in such an atmosphere in the bar of the Culloden Hotel, on the outskirts of the Protestant suburb of Holywood, that one of the squad's senior officers offered Paul the way into a story which might do the RUC and 'The Cook Report' some good.

In 1987, the British government was pumping £475 million a year into an intensive building programme in Ulster, replacing the appalling tenements that had blighted the province's inner cities for decades. Yet the project was going nowhere. Contracts weren't being fulfilled, the overspend was massive and, for no obvious reason, builders were going out of business every week.

The reason for the shambles, the RUC man explained, was the massive protection racket being run by paramilitaries on both sides of the religious divide. A contractor would be approached in his site hut by a small group of men offering their services as security men. It would be explained that for a down payment of a few thousand pounds and a weekly payment of a few hundred pounds, the security men would ensure that no harm befell the builder and his men and that no materials would disappear off-site in the middle of the night.

Those who expressed reluctance were taken to one of Belfast's many drinking clubs and shown the barrel of a gun. Few refused to pay up. Those who didn't pay ended up in a ditch in Omagh or Fermanagh with a bullet in the back of the head.

The political issue – and this was something Westminster was not keen to have pointed out in public – was that vast sums of money were being poured into Ulster only to be stolen by the terrorists. British troops were being murdered with bombs and bullets paid for unwittingly by the British taxpayer.

The man from C13 knew who was behind most of the building-site rackets. They were fast becoming wealthy men, and so were the organisations that they represented. For all their good inside information, the RUC was having only limited success with its network of informers. Now, if somebody from the mainland with a credible background was to come along and ask these bogus security men for protection for their new Ulster building project . . .

Journalistic experience, tempered with streetwise police advice, built a cover story for Paul Calverley. He flew to Belfast as Mr Daley, the representative of a London-based property company planning to tender for the contract to extend the shopping centre in the town of Craigavon.

He needed to find the biggest fish in the building-site protection business and arrange for him to meet Mr Rogers, the chief executive of the London company.

The story would be that Mr Rogers wanted the multi-million pound contract very badly – but he also knew that to get the building done, he was going to have to pay serious protection money.

C13 had their suspicions that one of the main gangsters involved was a man called Eddie Sayers, who ran the quaintly-named Borderline Security from a farmhouse on the North/South Irish Border in Armagh. Sayers was also an active member of the Ulster Defence Association – legal in the late 1980s but subsequently proscribed for being a front for Protestant paramilitaries.

Calverley contacted Borderline Security by telephone and explained the position. He suggested the firm call his office in London and ask for Mr Rogers. A 'Cook Report' researcher manning a telephone with an untraceable number sat in a small office in Central's headquarters in Portman Square and waited for the call.

leaked out. The paramilitaries on both sides had pretty good intelligence systems. It was a harrowing time for Calverley, our man on the ground. Not for the first – or last – time in Northern Ireland, he found himself having to change hire cars and hotels several times a week.

The day after Davies' call I flew into Belfast Aldergrove Airport, picked up a rented Ford Granada and drove it to the much-bombed Europa Hotel in the middle of the city where two 'Cook Report' technicians were waiting for me in the car park. Making it look as though they were mechanics repairing an electrical fault on my car, they carefully fitted hidden microphones in the front and back interiors.

As soon as we'd tested the Granada's mikes and found they were working, a camera crew, producer and researcher set off for the rendezvous in a 'Cook Report' surveillance van. The team arrived at the huge car park in Craigavon two hours before my meeting. The driver got out and went off for a cup of tea. Just an empty van, parked up for the day.

I set off alone for the same destination, hoping against hope that we hadn't been 'sussed'. I was excited, but concentrated on the brief that Paul Calverley had given me. I needed the men who came to meet me to make the running. They were the ones who had to make the demand for money – it wasn't incriminating enough if I just offered cash for my building workers to be left alone.

I also needed to establish, if I could, who I was dealing with. Would it be the notorious Mr Sayers? Was the outwardly respectable Ulster Defence Association really behind the protection racket? I tried not to think about what would happen if they were suspicious and wanted to search the car.

In no time, it seemed, I was at the rendezvous. I saw the surveillance van and parked so the cameraman could get a clear, unobstructed view of whatever happened. I also noticed that they were too far away to help if needed. I sat and waited.

Half an hour went by. Two figures made their way towards the Granada. Both wore ill-fitting, dark suits that flapped in the wind. A gust blew the taller man's jacket open as he reached for the front passenger door handle. I saw the black, etched diamond-design butt of a pistol sticking out of his trouser belt. The big man opened the door and sat down heavily next to me. His partner, a small, sandy-haired man, slipped into the back of the car. I felt his breath on the back of my neck.

Why do I do it?

There's the challenge of beating the odds – of bringing back the impossible story. There's the chance that what you do may change things, may do some good – and, then, when things get really danger-ous, something rather peculiar happens: it isn't me at all. I am just an onlooker.

It's difficult to explain. The best illustration of the phenomenon is the shocking footage from a cameraman at work during a South American revolution, as he calmly frames up and focuses on the man who shoots and kills him. The presence of a camera, the idea in the back of your mind that this is for television, removes you from real life. You wouldn't behave like this in real life.

I applied the lion-taming principle – show no fear and no harm will come to you.

'So, gentlemen, you know I'm pitching for this business in Craig-avon. Mr Daley says I need to speak to you first – what can you do for me?'

The smaller guy in the back answered first. 'We'll make sure you get no hassle. That's very important round here. Things can get very heavy if that sort of thing starts.'

'And how much is that likely to cost me?' I asked.

The big man next to me lifted his back from the seat and reached towards his trouser pocket. Here we go, I thought.

He pulled out a pocket calculator and looked at me. 'Tell me how much this contract is worth to you if you get it,' he growled.

I looked at his cold, lined face. 'And would you mind telling me your name?'

In circumstances like these, it really is a case of 'in for a penny, in for a pound'. You can't take your bat and go home – that could get you killed. The alternative is to play the game for all it's worth.

I knew from Calverley's briefing that I was to expect a demand for at least £10,000 per million. 'So, you're giving me a discount, are you?' I said.

He nodded and said gruffly: 'Because you came to me direct that's exactly right. Ten per cent off.'

The pair of them went on to tell me that they were backed by an armed organisation that would 'settle' any problems I might have on the site. I chanced my luck again and asked which particular group that was. I got the answer I had been hoping for: 'The fuckin' UDA,' said Sayers with a self-satisfied grin.

I had one more question. 'And if I don't agree to pay you?'

Sayers turned in his seat to face me, his watery, grey eyes six inches from mine, and said quietly, 'When you and my colleague here were talking on the telephone today, there was a man being buried in Belfast by his family. He was in the same business as you. Read the newspapers.'

The man in the back chipped in. 'We wouldn't like to say what would happen exactly, but use your imagination, you'd never work again.'

I told them I would get back to them after talking to my partners. With that, they got out and walked back to their car, passing our blue Ford Transit surveillance van without giving it a second glance, and drove away.

I leant back into the car seat, exhaled slowly and relaxed my shoulders. A minute later I switched on the ignition and drove ten miles to the arranged rendezvous to meet the rest of the team. I prayed that the microphones had relayed our conversation back to the surveillance van.

I needn't have worried, everything had been filmed and recorded perfectly. A jubilant Paul Calverley called his contact in C13. There was an impromptu premiere of our material for him in Paul's room in the Europa and something of a celebration downstairs in the bar afterwards.

I was back in the Birmingham office when I heard Sayers and two others had been arrested by the RUC for racketeering offences. Our filmed evidence in the Craigavon car park was to be the main plank of the prosecution's evidence.

A couple of hours later, Mike Townson's secretary stuck her head into my office to say there was a telephone call for me from a man in Belfast who wouldn't give his name. I asked what he wanted.

'To kill you,' she said simply.

The telephone rang. I picked it up. It was a fairly agitated man who told me that the consequences of what I had done would indeed be dire. He must have been calling from a public telephone box because, in mid-threat, the pips went and we were cut off.

Five minutes later, Townson's secretary popped back 'It's that man again.'

I picked up the call. It was indeed the same fellow. He started by apologising profusely, he had run out of money. He'd had to go to the corner shop to get some change in order to finish the death threat, which he duly did before hanging up.

The RUC recommended that, although the Protestant paramilitaries didn't have a network of active members established on mainland Britain – unlike the IRA – I should change my routine and hotel frequently.

'And when you come to give evidence at Belfast Crown Court, we'll be there to look after you,' our C13 man assured me confidently. I sincerely hoped so.

Meanwhile, I had other things on my mind. 'The Cook Report' was about to go to air and we had to choose which story to show first. Mike Townson had already decided to hold on to the Brazilian baby story and go with something he felt was more directly relevant without any pictorial illustration, of course, was likely to be a switch off for the average viewer, particularly with younger family members in the sitting room

There were a couple of other options too, including the sad victims of Britain's hopeless 'Care in the Community' policy for the recovering mentally ill, and the strange tale of several West Country families whose homes were inexplicably catching fire all the time. Secret radar-system testing by the Ministry of Defence was thought to be to blame.

In the end, Townson decided to go with the Costa del Crime programme. It had confrontation and was a subject that would raise important questions about extradition law. That said, I have made three programmes on the subject since and the situation is still as cock-eyed as ever it was.

I can vividly remember the atmosphere in the Birmingham office as we waited for the transmission of that first programme in July 1987. There was a real sense of excitement. We knew that we had a good story to tell. One or two television critics had expressed doubts as to whether the Roger Cook style could make the transition from radio to television. One newspaper critic even said that he would eat his hat if we were able to deliver a good programme and a decent-sized audience. He believed that what I did was much more effective when the action was left to the imagination on radio than when shown on TV. We secretly hoped for five or six million viewers.

Frances brought Belinda down into the bunker. Everyone tried to remain calm and have a few glasses of champagne. After the transmission, the party carried on in a bar around the corner from the office.

The next morning there were a few aching heads as we gathered to read the papers and – most importantly of all – wait for the audience researchers to telephone with the viewing figures.

The reviews were amazing. One critic described me as 'Nemesis in a leisure shirt'. Another as 'Meatloaf meets the Equalizer'. 'Powerful, purposeful and gripping television' seemed to be the consensus. However, 'We are all eating our hats' was, for me, the most satisfying comment of all. I had a gut instinct that we would surprise people with the size of the audience. We were new, different and, if you have a good story to tell, people will usually sit back and listen.

At eleven o'clock, the production manager, Pat Harris decided she could wait no longer for word on the figures and dialled the audience research department. I watched her as she wrote something down and replaced the receiver.

'We've got ten million viewers,' she shouted across the office. The news was beyond anything we could possibly have hoped for. The place erupted. Even the normally taciturn Townson allowed himself a smile of satisfaction before drawing deeply on his cigarette and continuing to pummel the keys of his computer, working on an outline script for show number two. Frighteningly late when you knew it was going to be on air in less than a week's time.

Herograms from senior management at Central flew in all directions. Bob Southgate was ecstatic. He'd risked his credibility by bringing me to Central from the BBC and, albeit at this early stage, it looked as if he had been justified. Frances rang from the flat to say that an enormous bouquet had just arrived for her from Central management.

The rest of that series failed to reach the heights of that first show in terms of audience levels, but we weren't disheartened. We were broadcasting to a nation on holiday. The sun shone, people sat in pub gardens and drank, or lit a barbecue and stayed outdoors. No other current affairs programme was reaching anything like our figures. We were down a million or so occasionally but our overall share of the viewing audience remained high, almost touching fifty per cent at times.

In other words, of those people still bothering to watch television in August, almost half of them were watching us. And that's what independent television companies – and their advertisers – like to see.

Our last programme was an update of everything that had gone before, a practice we have kept to ever since. We were able to report that the police had arrested the group of paedophiles we had discovered trading in child pornography. The head of Scotland Yard's

Freddie Foreman, a man once regarded as 'The Godfather' of the Costa criminals – and therefore another legitimate 'Cook Report' target – was expelled from Spain. The Spanish extradition procedures were improved and Ronnie Knight decided to come back to Britain of his own accord. Both went to prison – at last – for their part in the Security Express robbery. Knight got seven years and Foreman got nine.

The best result from that first series was not to come for two years. But when it finally did, it proved worth the wait.

The trial of Edward John Sayers and his UDA associates opened at Belfast Crown Court in October 1989, two years after the programme was first broadcast. I was called to give evidence for the prosecution against Sayers. Court ushers placed television monitors in front of the judge, Lord Justice Turlough O'Donnell, and counsel for both sides. Our tapes were played to a hushed courtroom. Then I was called to the stand. Sayers glared at me from the dock.

His counsel, a flamboyant figure much given to dramatic posturing, began in a vein I have heard in almost all the court cases in which 'The Cook Report' has been involved.

'Mr Cook, you set my client up, didn't you?' he asked, drawing himself up to his full height.

'Yes,' I replied. There was an awkward silence. A ready admission had not been expected and the defence was not going as planned.

Counsel cleared his throat. 'Such tactics are surely unethical,' he ventured.

I disagreed. 'They would be if we had encouraged an innocent person to do something illegal and out of character, but we never do that. What we did in Mr Sayers' case was give him the opportunity to demonstrate on film what he routinely does – extort money from people. And that film proves he needed little or no encouragement.'

The defence changed tack. Throwing back his gown and taking a step forward with his thumbs planted behind his lapels, Counsel intoned: 'Mr Cook, I suggest that you were solely motivated by a desire to impress your audience and that you were involved in nothing more than an exercise in blatant theatricality.'

I couldn't resist. Back-chat is frowned upon in court, but hoping I'd read the judge correctly, I ventured: 'You should know.'

Lord Justice O'Donnell raised an eyebrow and intervened. 'Quite so, Mr Cook, quite so,' he murmured and gave a faint but knowing smile.

My evidence took two days to complete. At the end of Day One, I was escorted to the police yard at the back of the heavily-fortified court and driven to a 'safe house' – a small hotel in Donaghadee on the pretty coastline of County Down, thirty miles to the east of Belfast.

My two RUC minders took great care of me. They had been issued with automatic weapons and powerful walkie-talkies and we drove fast through the countryside in our unmarked car.

We had dinner at the hotel and then adjourned to the bar to partake of the landlord's selection of whiskies. My minders tried to involve me but, although I love good malt whisky – and there was plenty on offer – I knew I had to keep a clear head for giving evidence the following morning. My minders nodded in agreement. 'Sure and we'll get you to bed early and you get your head down,' they told me.

By one o'clock they were a little the worse for wear but reluctantly eased themselves from their barstools, picked up their weapons and ambled back upstairs with me.

'Get a good night's sleep, Roger. We'll be here if you need us,' said one as they headed back to their rooms.

We were to sleep in three bedrooms at the back of the hotel. They put a walkie-talkie in each, leaving them switched on so that we could alert each other in an emergency. Within five minutes of climbing into bed, the pair of them were fast asleep and I was forced to listen to their prodigious snorings until I finally dozed off at 4 a.m.

Three weeks later, Eddie Sayers was sentenced to ten years in jail. His accomplices got ten, seven and four years each. In court, Lord Justice O'Donnell praised the courage of those who appeared in the programme, which itself he described as brave, skilfully made and

One of the contractors told me that it was the courage of the victims of terrorism we had shown in the programme that prompted him to speak out.

Even today, when I go to Northern Ireland, I have to be careful. Since the first programme on Mr Sayers and the UDA, 'The Cook Report' has twice exposed the terrorist past of Sinn Fein's Martin McGuinness – once showing how, despite his reassurances to an elderly Londonderry woman that her son would be safe to return to the North after a fall out with the IRA, he was shot dead within hours of being persuaded by McGuinness to come out of hiding. Three years ago, McGuinness was blamed for the savage punishment beating of a former IRA sympathiser.

I remain very much unforgiven by the bad boys on both sides in Ulster. I was invited to take part in a discussion programme on Ulster Television a year after the Sayers trial with the singer Midge Ure and my old friend Trevor McDonald. The show's host had hardly had time to introduce me to the studio audience when the phone rang in reception.

'Tell Mr Cook he's not welcome here,' said a man's voice. 'In fact, he'll be leaving in a box.'

The RUC were waiting at the end of the show. I had to forget the drink I had planned with Trevor and spend another night in a safe house miles from Belfast.

After the successful first series, there was nothing to stop 'The Cook Report'. There was so much criminality to uncover, it was going to be a long time before we would work ourselves out of a job. We were told that our initial commission to make six programmes was extended to twenty-six half-hours. It was a totally unrealistic target, and I said so. Nevertheless, Frances and I felt financially reassured by the network's commitment to us, and decided it was time to find somewhere permanent to settle down with little Belinda.

One thing had become clear in my short experience of Mike Townson – my life was going to be lived constantly out of a suitcase. Two things caused this. One was the nature of the job. Six programmes were being worked on at any one time. As each one developed, it required my presence and I found myself boarding planes from one African country to another, over to Europe, across the USA and then back to inner-city Glasgow or London in the order in which producers and researchers needed me. But I believe the second reason was that Townson just didn't want to have me hanging around. He was a control freak whose game plan seemed to be to keep all of us on the move while he conjured up the bones of each programme in his head, free of interference, and rattled them onto his keyboard. This sometimes meant that one of us would return to base to find that Townson's computerised creation bore only a passing resemblance to the story we were supposed to be pursuing. Fortunately, the facts always won out in the end.

Life with Mike Townson could never be described as dull. I veered from revering him as a near-genius for his populist touch in serious programme making to regarding him as a near-despot for whom almost any means would justify the programme end he had in mind. There were times when the possible personal cost to others simply didn't enter the equation.

The end result was that it didn't matter where the Cook family decided to settle because I would be away travelling so often. So, when Frances and I paid a chance visit to friends in the West Country and I remarked to her as we drove back to Birmingham that where we had been 'felt like home', we quickly agreed we'd go back there and find ourselves somewhere to live.

Over the next few weeks we house-hunted like crazy, mindful that the next series was looming and that soon Townson would be barking down the telephone ordering me to far-off places.

In those early days, security wasn't such a priority with us or I don't think we would have chosen somewhere so close to a main road. At least we chose a house surrounded on three sides by impenetrable woodland and a steep escarpment and that has been a comfort, particularly to Frances, when the death threats have been made. I won't disclose the location. It's not a matter of being melo-dramatic or precious. Over the past few years our personal security off in our absence. They came in with a sniffer dog which ran up to her bedroom and so terrified her hamster that it immediately keeled over in its cage and died of fright. Try telling a six-year-old that it's a small price to pay for peace of mind! To this day that incident is known in our household as 'the night the police murdered our hamster'.

Takes Two, Three and Four

It was to be eight months before 'The Cook Report' went back on air. During that time, Peter Salkeld and I were keen to develop new ideas, but the good luck that had helped us in the first series seemed suddenly to have vanished into thin air.

We were particularly keen to develop new ways to catch out the bad guys on screen. We'd started experimenting when trapping the child pornography dealers in Amsterdam and, despite the unwieldy nature of the hidden camera, had succeeded. There were pratfalls, of course, as I like to call them. Nowadays, everybody's into secret filming – in programmes ranging from current affairs to light entertainment. Our earliest 'box of tricks' was a briefcase containing two bulky and rather primitive cameras, aiming out of each end. One recorded in colour for shooting outside and the other in black and white, which picked up images far better in low-light, indoor conditions.

The trick was to remember which end of the briefcase had which camera pointing out of it and to switch on the right one in the right conditions. Paul Calverley and Tim Tate mostly pulled this off except on one occasion when Tate managed to film an hour of his own legs as he sat pointing the 'dead' end of the case at a pornographer.

For Series Two, we had developed a new means of filming secretly based on the very first Pulnix high-resolution mini-camera. We installed this very expensive device in several housings, including a briefcase, a portable television and a rather fetching flower arrangement. It was in this last guise that the camera was first used.

In 1988, the British tabloid papers were involved in their usual circulation war with one another and the *Sun* had gained the competition. We got wind of a fiddle being worked by a small group of printers who helped produce the cards for *Sun* Bingo. They were supplying winning cards in advance of publication to their friends, who were duly raking in many thousands of pounds to be distributed amongst the gang.

Our informant, posing as another printer, persuaded one of the gang to come to a meeting to explain how the scam was working and to see if he was interested in getting involved.

The gang member stipulated that the meeting take place in a quiet corner of the foyer of the Hilton National Hotel at Manchester Airport. We arrived early and placed our own, impressive flower display on a convenient table, the Pulnix safely hidden inside, its lens pointing at the seat opposite where we planned that the target would sit.

He arrived and duly sat exactly where we manoeuvred him.

Then, as he started to tell us how to make a lot of money out of *Sun* Bingo, an elderly Hilton maintenance man ambled slowly towards the table, carrying a small watering-can. He reached us just as the informer began to name names. There was a faint fizz and a brief crackle as the water hit the flowers. Hilton man moved slowly on, oblivious to what he had just done.

The rest of the conversation was pointless. You can never ask a criminal to go back over what he has told you, 'I've forgotten the detail, I'm afraid', unless you want to arouse his suspicions.

As soon as our villain had gone, we bore the sodden display and its £7,000-worth of short-circuited electronics back to Birmingham to view the film in Townson's office. Everything had worked perfectly at first – you could even make out the maintenance man hoving into sight behind our target. Then the sound spluttered out and the TV screen turned to a flickering snowstorm.

The following week, before we could arrange another meeting, the gang disintegrated, each member betraying his colleagues to the police, leaving us without a programme.

The lead-in to the second series was also a time in which my worst fears about Mike Townson's controlling tendencies were confirmed. The team would spend weeks on complete wild goose chases as he chopped and changed his plans. In theory, the selection of

In the end, we started the second series with the Brazilian baby trade programme that we had almost finished the previous year, and followed it with shows on the dangers of prescribed medicines, loan sharking in Scotland and, more spectacularly, badger-baiting. For weeks, Peter Salkeld and I had hunted the badger-baiters together in all weathers, ending up by leaping from a helicopter to confront half a dozen of these brutal men in the rugged hinterlands of West Wales. We interrupted their preparations to stage a fight to the death between their dogs and a badger they were digging from his sett. They stood their ground rather than flee without the dogs, which were still underground. One badger saved, six men shamed. Don't ask how much the helicopter cost.

The jaded 'Cook Report' team convened for the transmission of the first show in Townson's office. Memories of Rosilda, Bruna and the atmosphere of Rio at Carnival came flooding back as I sat crammed onto a sofa in the corner of the room. I looked around and thought how tired everyone looked. No surprise really when you consider that hundred-hour working weeks were not uncommon – *and* that there was still a long way to go before we completed every programme in the series.

The second programme we made about Bruna and Rosilda gave us enormous satisfaction. I'll never forget the emotions we felt when the Israeli judge found in Rosilda's favour, nor when, at the end of our return journey from the successful mission in Tel Aviv, the aircraft door opened at Curitiba Airport to reveal a welcoming party of more than a hundred thousand people.

Bruna's story had become a *cause célèbre* in Brazil. It had also become one in Israel, but for very different reasons. The Israeli media attacked us for interfering in their country's internal affairs, quite forgetting that it was not Roger Cook who had authorised Bruna's return to Brazil with her natural mother, but an Israeli judge following a conclusive DNA test.

both mother and daughter decided that Rosilda was an exceptional mother – not an unfit one, as the press had implied – and that despite their protracted separation, Bruna's best interests would be served by sending her home.

Ignoring all this, the Israeli media line that we had interfered was taken up in the UK by the *Mail on Sunday*, who despatched a reporter to Brazil to interview Rosilda. Rosilda didn't believe that the reporter wanted to do the kind of sympathetic story she claimed she would write and sent her away with a flea in her ear. Despite this, the *Mail* persevered with the story.

To it were added the claims of an Israeli cameraman that we had falsified the footage of Rosilda's first sighting of Bruna in Tel Aviv. The facts are that, despite instructions to the contrary, he had filmed the event in such a way that it couldn't be edited and from such a distance that Rosilda's reactions on seeing her child couldn't be clearly discerned. At the cameraman's suggestion, close-up shots were taken the next day – with Rosilda's co-operation and understanding – to try to reproduce what had happened twenty-four hours earlier. One of those brief supplementary shots – mistakenly – involved the use of eye drops to replace the previous day's genuine tears of emotion.

Mistaken, yes. Deliberately dishonest, no – but the end result was a disproportionate amount of fuss over two seconds of air time. Mind you, there was no fuss at all when the programme was broadcast.

The cameraman only complained months after the initial filming, when he realised that he wasn't going to be re-engaged to shoot the second Bruna programme. We had been given the services of a top-notch Brazilian crew free of charge. After pressure from 'The Cook Report', the *Mail on Sunday* published a full apology.

The day after transmission the viewing figures confirmed the way I felt: just over six million, compared to ten for our first ever outing. The undeserved bad publicity had done us no favours. The figures did not recover for the rest of the series. Even the badger programme, which had involved six weekends of highly-exciting, and expensive, helicopter pursuit of the Welsh badger-baiters, failed to dig us out of the doldrums. Fortunately, in audience terms, we've never had another series like it, although our figures were still streets ahead of

Alfred Cook.

Lin Cook.

Aged nine months.

In Perth, at the Australian Broadcasting Commission.

Broadcasting on ABC Radio, 1966.

In London, about
to 'do battle' on
Carnaby Street.

Editing a 'Checkpoint' tape
at Radio 4, 1980.

Baby Bruna – stolen and sold to Israel – on her way home to Brazil.

On location with the editor, Mike Townson.

A unique vantage point for the filming of Ronnie Knight and friends.

On the Costa del Crime: Mr and Mrs John Corsecadden put their umbrellas to a novel use.

Clifford Saxe takes aim …

… and fires.

A Dutch child pornographer attempts to avoid the famous doorstep …

… and resorts, inevitably, to violence.

A memorable moment
in Zambia with white
hunter and trumpeting
elephant.

The elephant killing
ground.

In a warehouse for illegal
ivory in Tanzania.

In Hong Kong, ivory trader Mr Poon throws a rock at the camera.

Salk gets to grips with the wildlife.

any of our rivals. A third series was commissioned without hesitation.

Everyone took a much-needed break after the second series ended.
I went to the West Country to try to get to know my little family
again, especially five-year-old Belinda. I had been alarmed by reports
from her primary school about how much she was being affected by
my prolonged absences.

She and her classmates had been asked by their teacher to take
part in a public-speaking exercise – 'My father's job'.

'My father,' said one youngster, 'is a doctor and he makes sick
people better.'

'My father,' said another, 'is a farmer and he grows food for us
all.'

'Mine's a train driver,' chimed in another.

And so on, until it was Belinda's turn.

'My father,' said Belinda firmly, 'is a telephone.'

'He's a telephone. My Dad's a telephone,' explained Belinda under
interrogation. The teacher gave Frances a call.

For the previous four months, while the second series was being
made, nearly all the contact I had with my daughter was brief, tender
moments on the line from whichever hotel I was staying in. No
wonder the poor child was confused. We took a long holiday together
– this time there were no telephones.

My prolonged absences were accepted – but never welcomed.
Frances had learned that a telephone call from me in Birmingham
often heralded a trip away of anything up to three or four weeks.
Very sensibly, she took up a mature degree course – studying day
and night, in between looking after Belinda.

When Belinda was very small, I would sneak away at the end of
shoots wherever we were in the world and head for the nearest and
most expensive-looking children's clothes shop. I would emerge with
several beautifully-made but over-priced and over-fussy outfits which
I would proudly produce out of my suitcase back at home under the
quizzical gaze of Frances. Some outfits she allowed Belinda to be
dressed in. Others I never saw again.

Nobody really tells you how to be a father. I certainly hadn't had
much of a role model in my own Dad. We were never close and I

always had the feeling that yes, of course, my sister Jane and I were his children but we were rather a lot of trouble. He was an artist first and foremost and he was driven to be as much of a perfectionist as he could be. There isn't much room for impromptu fun and frolics when all your energy is going into paint and canvas. So, without much of a memory of how it should be done, and a whole lot of guilt that my job made me such an absentee parent, I often got it wrong.

Where Dad and I were alike, however, was the striving for that seldom-achieved perfection. Perhaps I wanted to dress Belinda like a little doll because that was how the ideal little girl would look. Or perhaps I was just over-compensating for my absenteeism. The real solution, of course, would have been to control my rampant workaholism and to spend more time at home. But it wasn't that easy.

Belinda soon realised what a soft touch I could be. As she grew a little older, she realised the true strength of her bargaining position when she wanted something. One day I'd be confronting one of the world's biggest drug barons or a multiple murderer to demand an explanation for their hideous crimes. The next, I would be promising almost anything to a little girl who would finally win her argument by looking up at me and asking, 'Okay, Dad, how cute do I have to be?'

Home was a million miles from the punishing schedule of 'The Cook Report' and was heaven to return to. But there is a balance to be struck. Anyone who has ever seen me during an enforced lay-off from work – often caused by injury – can tell you that I can't wait to get involved with the job again.

That's when I can become a little Townsonesque myself. Colleagues can expect a telephone call at work or home as I demand to know the latest development on some story – and the gossip. The 'Cook Report' office was full of highly-talented journalists and programme-makers with contacts absolutely everywhere. To tap into it was to learn the most extraordinary things.

At any one time, the inside-track knowledge in the office would include details of secret police investigations, imminent arrests of high-profile public figures, ongoing international criminal activity as well as scandals brewing in the political world.

More than once, we've all sat down to weigh up whether it really is in the public interest to investigate the private sexual activity of a member of the government. On occasion, we've been actively encouraged by one section of law enforcement to look at someone's behaviour – only to be taken aside by another department which asks, or demands, that we lay off.

In the early nineties, we were getting monthly reports of a squad of police officers moving to arrest one leading Conservative politician – who then received a heavy rebuke from a more 'secret' police team with orders to hush things up and prevent any investigation.

Personally, I believe sexual activity between consenting adults is, and should remain, their own business. With some of these untold stories I think that everything has its own time-scale. It will come out eventually, even if it isn't 'The Cook Report' that finally breaks the news.

Salk was keen to produce more programmes on the plight of wildlife. He firmly believed that the British public's love of animals would win us back our flagging audience. He loved filming them and the two of us agreed that we would support each other at 'Cook Report' meetings if Townson resisted research into the general subject.

In early September, the telephone rang in the Cook household. Frances passed the receiver to me. It was an excited Salk. He had found that elusive animal story and he also thought he had found a way to convince Townson to let us make the programme.

Intensive scouring of animal welfare magazines had yielded a cutting from a correspondent in Hong Kong who had implicated a company there in large-scale illegal ivory dealing. Salk had also amassed a wealth of material on the impending disaster facing the African elephant. In 1988, the world was only just waking up to the fact that the trade in tusks was threatening one of the best-loved creatures on earth with extinction.

'What's more,' cackled Salk, 'you'll have to go to the Far East and at least three African countries. Townson will love it – he won't have to talk to you in the office for months.'

He was right. Townson saw the attractions of the story straight away. If 'The Cook Report' could be the first to present the desperate truth about the threat to the African elephant with filmed proof, the programme could win back the viewers it had lost in the second series *and* it meant I would be out on the road while he was left to his own devices . . .

For a week, Salk hit the telephones in the Birmingham office to find a starting point in Africa. A call to one of the wildlife charities put him on to a white hunter turned conservationist operating in Zambia. For months, Alistair Gellatly had been sending in reports of the wholesale slaughter of the elephants in Luangwa, in the east of Zambia, where he now ran his photo safaris. Salk eventually tracked down a number for Gellatly and, on a crackling line, discovered that the killings were happening almost every week. Gellatly told him he was welcome to join him – while there were still some elephants left to film.

Salk and his sound recordist, Bill Dodkin, arrived in Zambia two days later to find heavy flooding all over the bush. They made it by safari truck to Gellatly's camp but were warned that it would be impossible to venture out until the crocodile-infested waters receded.

The following day, they woke to the sound of voices outside Gellatly's house. A black African game warden was talking excitedly to the ex-hunter. Gellatly shouted across to Salk and Dodkin and pointed down a mud track behind the encampment.

Six African rangers were walking slowly into the camp in single-file. Each had an ancient rifle strapped across his back and a stick resting on his shoulder. From each stick dangled a grey, tufted tail three or four feet long. Despite the storms and floods, proof of the continuing massacre of the elephants was on its way.

The rangers told Gellatly that they had found the bodies of five elephants lying in a small group a few miles away in dense bushland. They had been machine-gunned down. The sixth, a tuskless female, had managed to run off. But the loss of blood from her wounds had brought her crashing down in a clearing half a mile from the other herd members. All the magnificent ivory tusks had been cut off and transported away by the poachers within an hour, leaving their prey to the bush scavengers and the flies.

Salk started the lengthy process of dialling Townson on Gellatly's decrepit old telephone. Eventually, Salk heard his editor's brusque voice bellowing down the receiver to him to speak up. Salk explained the situation in equally stentorian manner.

'Right,' yelled Townson. 'Roger's on his way. Aren't you, Roger?'

I guessed I was. I had rushed into Townson's office to catch the last part of the conversation. It had been impossible to miss it. Everyone was staring at Townson's office wondering what the hell was going on.

I called Frances to tell her I was flying to Zambia that evening. In anticipation of this, I'd already had the necessary jabs a week before and was well underway with the malaria tablets.

'Take good care of yourself and don't get shot by poachers,' she said.

Or deafened by mad editors on the telephone, I thought.

I had been booked to fly to Lusaka on a now, happily, defunct African airline which consisted at the time of one ageing DC10. This one plane, however, had been taken out of service when I arrived at Heathrow and we were to use a hired-in replacement.

I knew it was going to be one of those flights when a fight broke out during boarding. Cabin staff were trying to seat us according to a DC10 seating plan, which simply did not work because the replacement was a rather smaller DC9.

No one got the seats they paid for. You took what you got, or you got off. I ended up right at the back, crammed between a very large, chocoholic German lady and a very tall African gentleman who constantly hummed an out-of-tune dirge and rattled through his worry beads.

The plane pressed into service had come from the aeronautical equivalent of rent-a-wreck. It didn't have the range of the DC 10 and our direct flight now included a stopover in Cyprus. Unfortunately the air crew seemed to have great difficulty in finding Cyprus, and then in finding the airport. They also had trouble raising the wherewithal to pay for the fuel, landing fees and on-board catering. After a delay of several hours, the pilot reluctantly agreed to pay for the fuel and landing fees on his personal credit card. Food, we had to forgo.

It was a rough onward flight to Zambia. The ancient plane creaked and groaned. A lady up front, soaked by a regular trickle of condensation, hysterically proclaimed that there was a petrol leak. You can imagine the reaction of her fellow passengers.

During a particularly unpleasant spell of turbulence, the overhead clamshell lockers all opened as if choreographed, disgorging their contents over passengers and into the aisles. My immediate travelling companions took this latest hiatus badly. The worry beads clicked like high-speed maracas and the large lady, who had been scoffing chocolates as if they were the last supper, announced that she was going to be sick – which she duly was, all over me and the worry beads.

In the interests of personal hygiene, I headed for the lavatories. Of the two nearest to my seat, one had been – literally – boarded up, and in the other the bowl was clogged up with what appeared to be a straw hat. The hand basin produced no water.

On my way to the alternative facilities, I was bowled over by one of the rent-a-wreck hostesses as she charged past me carrying a mask and an oxygen cylinder. My confidence in my chances of surviving the flight from hell, already pretty near rock bottom, plunged to uncharted depths when I realised that her destination was the cockpit.

Somehow, we limped into Zambian airspace and made the descent, landing at Lusaka without further mishap. The fact that the first airport taxi I engaged caught fire with me in it didn't faze me at all.

I seem to have been on some of the world's worst flights. Later, during the same shoot, flying with Salk up to Dar es Salaam in Tanzania, our post-lunch reverie was rudely interrupted by a loud bang and a violent juddering. Salk pointed out of the window towards what appeared, to me, to be a large chunk of engine spiralling earthwards.

The captain's eventual attempt at reassurance didn't really wash in the face of the visual evidence. 'Not to worry, ladies and gentlemen,' he said. 'We were going too fast and may have overshot our destination, so I have just had to apply some reverse thrust.'

At thirty-two thousand feet?

Fortunately, the other three engines stayed put and we made it to Dar, where they put screens around the affected wing before they would let us off the aircraft. They told the passengers travelling onward to stay aboard. Sensible people didn't stay long, but the plane was still there when we left the country two weeks later.

I firmly believe that bad things happen in threes. Later on the elephant shoot, Salk and I had to leave the game reserve by light aircraft. Although the aviation fuel, hand-pumped from a stack of drums beside the bush airstrip, had been filtered through a pair of tights, the pilot wasn't sure it was entirely clean. He also thought it might have contained some water, but there was nothing we could do about it. In any case, the engines eventually cranked into life, so we thought the fuel couldn't be too contaminated.

It was. At fourteen thousand feet over the Luangwa Valley, the engines cut. We fell nearly eight thousand feet before the pilot managed – with commendable coolness – to re-start first one, then the other.

Stories about your life flashing before your eyes at moments like this *are* true. But nothing flashed before Salk's eyes. He'd managed to sleep through the lot.

After that first rent-a-wreck adventure, I finally found a taxi that wasn't about to self-combust and got to a hotel for a much-needed sleep. Several hours later, suitably refreshed, I was joined by 'Cook Report' researcher Kevin Dowling for the onward flight from Lusaka to Luangwa. A serious, schoolmasterly man of about forty-five who had covered the world as a newspaperman, Kevin had joined 'The Cook Report' a few months earlier and this was the first time he had been abroad for months. He was clearly relishing the chance to travel. I wondered whether he'd feel the same after a week or two in the bush.

Salk and Bill Dodkin came to meet us at the Luangwa airstrip. The sound man was wearing khaki shorts and a green safari shirt. His legs were covered in mosquito bites and he was clearly suffering, to judge from his inflamed legs and the time he was devoting to scratching himself. Salk was wearing what he always wore wherever he travelled in the world – a two-piece grey suit, a white shirt and a tie. He'd even gone skiing on an assignment in Colorado wearing the same outfit.

But Salk's eccentric dress sense was paying dividends in the Zambian bush. 'Bill's even got mosquito bites on his mosquito bites,' cackled Salk in his high-pitched voice. 'The mozzies can't find anywhere to get me.'

I too was glad that I had my usual khaki colonial 'uniform' of long-sleeved shirt and long cotton trousers on. I prayed quietly that my malaria tablets would work.

Before my arrival, Salk had been hoping to get some preliminary filming done by boat but Alistair Gellatly had said no. Hippos had followed the crocodiles into the floodlands and he was fearful that the boat would be overturned. The hippopotamus may look like a smiling, benign cartoon character but, in reality, they kill more people than lions and crocodiles put together. It's apparently not uncommon for a human to be bitten in half by an enraged hippo, despite the fact that they're vegetarians. Salk had taken Gellatly's warning on board and agreed to wait for me to arrive and for the waters to go down.

By the time we all got back to Alistair Gellatly at his camp, the waters had receded enough for us to make an attempt to reach the scene of the elephant massacre.

We set off in Gellatly's truck at daybreak. Our team comprised Gellatly himself, three Bantu African rangers, Salk, Dodkin, Dowling and me. There was talk that the poachers were still in the area, scouring around for more prey, armed with Kalashnikov automatic rifles. Our rangers carried World War Two Lee Enfield rifles but, we were dismayed to learn, only two bullets each.

All the dirt roads had been washed away by the rains. The flood waters might have receded, but there were still vast, deep lakes where the scrub would usually have been. Gellatly had anticipated this and, whenever the waters started to lap over the hubcaps of the truck, he would hand one of the rangers the looped end of a long roll of cable. The other end was secured firmly to a winch on the bonnet of the truck. The ranger would then wade ahead until he found a tree some fifty yards ahead. The cable would be tied round the trunk and, after a wave of approval from the ranger, Gellatly would switch the winch mechanism on and, foot by foot, we would move forward, the cable stretched taut in front of us. It was a slow, tortuous process.

We had only gone about a mile and a half before we realised that our task was impossible. The water was getting deeper and suitable trees to which we could attach the winchrope were becoming fewer and farther between. Gellatly turned round to me from the front passenger seat. 'The rangers say we're still a couple of miles away. We can go back and try again another day but the longer we leave it, the less there will be left to see, if you catch my meaning. Or we can get out, carry your gear and wade.'

I looked across to Salk. We weighed it up. There were crocodiles and hippos out there – not to mention the possibility of trigger-happy poachers toting Kalashnikovs. The pictures, though, would be the most eloquent, though disturbing, evidence of the wholesale slaughter we were trying to show the world. In two days' time the ravages of heat and scavengers might render that evidence unrecognizable.

'Sod it, let's get out and walk,' said Salk. He hefted his tripod onto his shoulder and climbed gingerly over the side of the truck. His long, suit-clad leg sank knee-deep into the mud-coloured water.

Everyone but the third ranger would press on to find the scene of the massacre. He would drive the truck back to the camp and we would make the entire journey to and from the scene on foot.

The going was difficult. The ground under the water was deceptively uneven and strewn with rock and fallen branches. Sometimes we left the water behind altogether, thankfully squishing through deep mud or even finding stretches of dry land. We walked in single file, the ranger who had first discovered the elephants was in front.

Everyone helped carry the camera and sound equipment, while keeping a constant vigil for crocodiles and hippos. Several times one of us would stumble and almost plunge headfirst into the water, inches away from ducking the camera, batteries or tapes and making the hazardous trip a complete waste of time.

Four hours later, the leading ranger turned to Gellatly and pointed. 'Not far now. A few hundred yards more of this and we'll see what you've come all this way for,' Gellatly told our sodden, mud-streaked and panting group.

There was the sound of faint, ragged cheering from the middle-aged and unfit 'Cook Report' personnel.

We could smell it before we saw it. Kevin Dowling pulled a handkerchief from his pocket and clapped it round his nose and mouth. The stench was overpowering. The flies swarmed about us in clouds. Dowling turned away and vomited violently. It was all I could do to avoid doing the same.

Ahead of us, on a raised, dry mound of bleached earth, lay the bodies of the elephants. Each face had been, literally, hacked off to make the removal of the precious tusks easier.

Salk and Dodkin set up the camera and sound rig, while Dowling and I joined Gellatly and his men to try to find the female which had managed to run off, before crashing down to die alone.

She was there, half a mile off across the marshy bush-bog, lying on her side, riddled with bullets, smelling hideously of decay. Slaughtered even though she didn't have the tusks the poachers' paymasters in the Far East coveted so much.

Today, the world knows all about the illegal ivory trade and how it nearly wiped out the African elephant. There has been a ban on the culling of elephants – about to be lifted in some countries – for years. But as I stood observing the grisly scene in the African bush in 1988, it was virtually a secret. The anger welled up in me. But at least I had it within my power to do something about it.

For the next few hours, we filmed everything. I memorised and delivered a number of pieces to camera for Salk until we realised that it had become too dark to film anymore.

'Shit,' said Dodkin, 'we've got to walk back in the dark. Who do you think will get us, the crocs, the hippos, the poachers or the lions?'

He had a point. Four or five miles of bush-trekking and flood-wading in blazing sunshine was one thing but how the hell were we going to find our way home safely on a moonless Zambian night?

Gellatly didn't seem at all fazed. 'It's not a problem. My guys will find the way for us. They know every part of this reserve, day or night. It'll be like an evening stroll.'

Some stroll. The rangers walked slowly in front, their World War Two rifles – complete with two bullets – slung over their shoulders. They sometimes stopped to confer but, as Gellatly assured us, this was only to best pick a route that avoided the worst of the flood water.

Bill Dodkin was the first to hear a noise off to our left.

'It's a lion,' he whispered hoarsely to Salk, who was just in front of him. Salk passed on Dodkin's fears to Gellatly who murmured quietly to the two rangers at the head of our group.

'No, it's not,' said Gellatly after he'd heard the Africans' reply.

'Well, what is it then?' returned Dodkin, who was growing more uneasy by the minute.

'It's not a lion, that's all they'll say,' replied Gellatly.

'How the hell do they know?' Dodkin was getting beside himself.

'Because if it was a lion, you wouldn't hear anything until it was too late,' said Gellatly with a finality that made further comment useless.

The noises continued. Totally unreassured, we trudged on.

Suddenly, I felt my legs sliding away from me. I hit the ground. I tried to get up but found I couldn't. Something was gripping my legs. Strangely, there was no pain, just downward pressure. I called for help.

Gellatly swung his torch around and shone it down on me.

'You've fallen in something. Let's have a look at you. Oh my God, Roger. You really are in the shit,' he said.

And I was. I had fallen into a pit full of elephant droppings and sinking mud left by the receding floodwater. The suction gripped my lower legs. I didn't know whether to laugh or cry. I consoled myself that at least nothing had bitten my legs off.

I was pulled out by the armpits until, with a satisfying slurp, my legs came free. My boots and socks had remained behind, however, in the stinking gloop of the pit. I finished the homeward trek in bare feet. We joked warily that it was the smell of elephant dung that kept the stealthy lions away from our exhausted band that night.

The next day we all slept in. After a leisurely breakfast of fruit, rice-cakes and mugs of tea Salk and I decided we had better call Townson and let him know what we had got.

'It's been great not having him on the phone every half hour,' Salk muttered as we walked over to Gellatly's office. 'There are compensations for falling up to your armpits in elephant shit,' I replied.

One thing we weren't going to tell Townson was the state of Bill Dodkin's health. He had woken up with such back pain that he was actually crying. There was no way he could keep on working but he'd begged us to keep quiet about it. Rumours were rife that Central Television was about to make substantial staff cuts. He feared that if the company got to hear of it, he'd be the first to lose his job. The 'Cook Report' team decided to let him rest.

Townson was delighted with what we'd filmed in the bush but, as usual, wanted us to pull a stunt that would look spectacular for the viewer but put his staff in mortal danger.

'Go out into the bush with this Gellatly character and get me a shot of the biggest male elephant you can find. I want it rearing up at the camera as if it is about to charge,' he demanded – and hung up.

'He doesn't want much, does he?' Salk mused as we went to find Gellatly.

Luckily, Gellatly knew exactly how to achieve what our demon editor wanted. The next day Salk and I left an agonised Bill Dodkin lying in bed. Kevin Dowling was preparing to fly out of Zambia to arrange interviews in Burundi, the country given as the source of hundreds of tons of illegal ivory on the forged paperwork which usually went with it.

We knew the ivory couldn't be coming from Burundi, as we had established that they only had one elephant left – and that was in Bujumbura Zoo. We also suspected that if so much dubious documentation originated in Burundi, the likelihood was that those behind the trade could be found there too. We were right, as it turned out.

We dropped Dowling off at the airport and joined Gellatly in his truck and headed out in search of the biggest male elephant in the whole reserve. By now, the floods had all but dried in the intense heat of the sun and travelling was relatively easy. A couple of hours into the bush, Gellatly picked up his binoculars and searched the tree clumps in front of us.

'What do you make of that?' he asked me as he passed the binoculars over.

About three hundred yards ahead of us, moving slowly through the trees, was a truly enormous elephant. We were down wind of him and he hadn't yet noticed us. There was a hillock behind us and we retreated there to plan our approach. We decided to leave Salk to set up his camera and tripod on the hill. Gellatly and I would walk through the waist-high grass towards the elephant and, as he sensed our presence, hope to get him to issue a warning, which Salk would film.

Gellatly and I moved to the bottom of the raised ground and waited for Salk to give us the signal that he was ready to roll the camera. We walked slowly forward. Gellatly, who was holding his rifle over one shoulder, suddenly touched my arm with his free hand.

'He's seen us. Just stick close to me,' he whispered.

Sure enough, fifty or so yards ahead, the male was staring at us suspiciously, a large, leafy tree branch hanging from his mouth. We'd got his attention all right, but how, I asked Gellatly, do we get him to give us Townson's 'angry' shot?

Gellatly produced two stones the size of small paperweights from his pocket. 'I'm going to crack these two together. Elephants have piss-poor eyesight, but fantastic hearing. When he hears an unfamiliar noise, he'll think he's under attack. It's my bet this big fellow will stand his ground. He might even decide to charge us.'

I looked back at the truck and Salk, both several hundred yards behind us. It seemed a long way away.

'What do we do if he does charge us?' I enquired as nonchalantly as I could.

'Run like fuck,' said Gellatly – and he struck the stones together.

The effect was instantaneous, and terrifying. The huge creature swung round and faced us. His enormous ears rose up around his head and his trunk shot up vertically into the sky. He let out a deafening and outraged trumpet and started to shift his front legs from side to side as if preparing to charge.

'Hold still,' said my companion. 'Do you think Salk got his shot?'

'If he didn't, I'm not bloody going to do this again for him,' I replied.

We stood, statue-like, in the grass as the elephant continued his menacing posturing. Then, after a minute or so, he must have felt he'd been imagining things, because he slowly turned his back on us and returned to stripping the nearest tree of its leaves with his trunk.

We moved nervously back to the hillock. Salk was happy with what he'd got. It was an image that Townson was to use at the beginning of the programme to such effect that viewers remembered it for years to come.

Two days later Salk, the still-crippled Dodkin and I left Gellatly and headed for Dar es Salaam to interview government officials on the threat to the elephants. After a couple of weeks roughing it in the Zambian bush, we decided we wanted the home comforts of a good hotel. Our travel department back in Birmingham had chosen the Kilimanjaro Hotel which was registered in the travel books as five-star standard.

The building was in darkness as the airport taxi dropped us and our luggage by the entrance. We staggered in with the countless bags, suitcases and metal boxes that all television crews are destined to travel the world with. A candle flickered at the back of the foyer and, through the gloom, we made out the check-in desk and two or three members of the hotel staff standing behind it.

With much fumbling and holding up of registration cards to the candlelight, we became guests of the Hotel from Hell.

The entire establishment had been without electricity for weeks. Not only was there a huge fault in the city's main power station but the back-up generators had also failed. We had been allocated rooms on the eighth floor. We grumbled but were told they were the only rooms they had left. We were halfway to the lifts before we remembered what was needed to power them.

If Bill Dodkin had been in pain before, it reached new heights as we helped him lug his baggage up eight floors. At the top of each landing stood a guttering candle stuffed into the neck of a beer bottle. After an eternity, our bags were safely stowed. Despite his back, Dodkin decided to join me for a meal. Salk, who wasn't a big eater at the best of times, declined and stayed in his room.

Dodkin and I can't remember to this day what they served us in that 'five star' restaurant, it was too dark to see. I just recall the aftereffects – the worst vomiting and diarrhoea I'd ever had. It didn't help that during the night, the water supply failed.

Two days later, I felt well enough to want a bath. I turned the tap – still no water. I managed to summon room service and asked for water to be sent up so I could, at least, have a body wash. Ten minutes later a bucket was handed to me. It was full of mud.

Dodkin was now in a very sorry state, so we decided to send him home. The plan was that he would leave some basic sound recording gear with us and we would say nothing to the office that he had left us. The rest of us embarked on an intensive schedule of filming in Tanzania, Kenya and back in Zambia. We weren't too bothered that we now had no sound recordist – Salk had been one in a previous incarnation and I had mostly been my own technician in radio days. No problem.

In Dar es Salaam we had been given permission by the government to film in a large warehouse full of illegal ivory. It contained thousands upon thousands of tusks – herd upon herd of dead elephants. Under the corrugated iron roof, the temperature soared to nearly fifty degrees Centigrade. We had worked out a complicated piece to camera which involved us weaving our way through the rows of musky tusks – from the baby ones on shelves at the back to the monster-sizes formed into arches at the front of the building.

Sweat dripped from my every pore. Salk had to take his own shirt off to mop me down with it between takes. There were fourteen of them before we were satisfied that we had what we wanted. Then Salk clamped the headphones over his ears to play back the tape and check it was okay. He looked up at me, puzzlement and then profound embarrassment spreading over his face.

'We've got an air gap here,' he said. 'Two so-called pros forgot to plug in the sound lead between the camera and the mixer. We've just made a silent movie!'

These mishaps occur in television from time to time and it's no big deal. But it was bloody hot, the equipment was in danger of overheating and neither of us felt like doing much except having a beer and going to lie down in our hotel rooms. Fortunately, the hours of wordless rehearsals produced a perfect fifteenth take.

There was one key witness we wanted to interview in Burundi – a secretive middleman we believed to be the link between the African elephant poachers and the ivory traders in Hong Kong. It was a circle we badly needed to square. We joined up with Kevin Dowling in Nairobi and tried to get into Burundi. However, there was a civil war going on and we had to think again.

To add to our problems, other programmes being shot in Britain and America were in an advanced stage of readiness and I was required. Also, Salk had found out that ITN were planning to broadcast a programme on elephant poaching on 16 May 1989. Our first show was scheduled for 15 May. We desperately wanted to go out before our rivals.

Townson told us to fly the ivory middleman Dowling had unearthed down from Burundi into Kenya and do the interview there. Our man refused, politely but firmly, saying that he had a religious festival to attend with his family. I asked him what his religion was. Ismaili, he replied. I tried a long shot.

The head of the Ismaili religion is the Aga Khan. Years before, I had met his cousin, Sadruddin Aga Khan, who was a keen conservationist and founder of an influential environmental organisation called the Bellerive Foundation. I telephoned him at his home on the shores of Lake Geneva and explained the problem. Could he, perhaps, apply a little pressure?

'Leave it to me,' he said and took down my contact details.

Within hours a note was pushed underneath my door. It was from Sadruddin Aga Khan and it read simply: 'Pressure on.'

Within three days, our unwilling interviewee had arrived in Kenya and confessed all on camera. When a blood relative of the man regarded as your supreme religious leader tells you to do something, you just get on and do it.

Next stop was Mr Poon in Hong Kong, owner of the company implicated in trading ivory which had set Salk on the trail in the first place. It turned out he was the biggest trader by far.

Frances had long since given up feeling surprised about my movements around the world. At least, she said, the long-haul trips of the series were almost over. I reassured her and Belinda that I would be home in a few days' time. I didn't mention the trip that would follow almost immediately – to the USA to confront a British taxi driver suspected of multiple murder.

Salk and I flew into Hong Kong and headed straight for Poon Brothers' shop in the downtown area. These greedy people played a major part in keeping a despicable and cruel trade going. We tried to get into the shop but they saw us coming and retreated to the back office.

Then, the glass front door opened a couple of feet. One of the Poons stood at the entrance. I fired off a couple of questions. His response was to throw a huge paperweight at Salk. It smashed into the lens of his camera and bounced off his shoulder. The lens was completely shattered. Further filming was impossible.

As we walked back to our hotel Salk turned to me and said, 'For the first time, I know what it's like to be in your position, Roger. When I saw what he had in his hand I wanted to get the hell out of there but I knew I had to stand my ground, take whatever was coming and get what we came for.'

His bravery had got us what we wanted.

We made it back to Birmingham, exhausted but with the vital link between the African poachers and the traders of the Far East. ITN brought their programme forward in order to beat us to the punch, but, in fact, their efforts served as a trailer for ours. The viewing figures were nine million. More importantly, the film gained international recognition and Sadruddin Aga Khan was kind enough to say we had 'played a pivotal role' in achieving the worldwide ban on ivory trading which followed the transmission of the programme. The reputation of 'The Cook Report' was enhanced and the team felt it was well and truly back on track.

Viewers liked the mixture of wildlife, scenery, detective story and confrontation that the ivory programme contained. Townson decided to tap into this rich vein of audience-captivation and mine it for all it was worth – so it wasn't long before he despatched us on another story that had me and the trusty Salk swallowing our malaria tablets and digging out our sunblock for the long haul to the plains of Africa. It was also a trip that ended with a regrettable but unavoidable incident that could have seriously dented the reputation of 'The Cook Report'.

Soon after the ivory programme was broadcast, I received a letter from Charles de Haes, then director general of the Worldwide Fund for Nature – formerly the World Wildlife Fund – congratulating us for our exposure of the illegal trade in tusks. A few weeks after that, we were contacted by a senior member of the WWF who wanted to convey a different message altogether.

He told us that the WWF had recently commissioned a report on its own internal workings and to evaluate its performance since it was founded in 1961. The report's findings, written by a Professor Phillipson, had shocked the organisation so badly that it had suppressed them immediately.

In a nutshell, Phillipson said that each of the WWF's major projects – to save the elephant, panda and black rhino – had failed miserably.

Money was being wasted and the WWF was getting itself involved in grand conservation schemes best left to the international aid agencies. African elephant numbers were down – 150,000 had been killed since the fund took up their cause. Black rhino numbers had dwindled from uncounted abundance to 3,000. Most embarrassing of all, the WWF had pumped £1 million into a project to protect the panda in China but, instead of using the money to set up a panda breeding project, the Chinese had devoted much of it to building a dam that had actually flooded part of the panda's natural habitat.

Our early investigations also discovered the existence of a report exposing the late Jomo Kenyatta, president of Kenya, as the chief organiser of his country's illegal ivory trade while he was in power. Senior WWF figures had read the report and quietly kept it a secret for seventeen years. Meanwhile, the Fund had awarded Kenyatta the Golden Ark – the highest possible accolade for wildlife protection.

Secret WWF documents were leaked to us – including a fax from Prince Philip, the organisation's international president, in which he voiced his great concern about the Phillipson Report. He pointed out that the WWF was damned whatever it did. If it hushed the report up, someone would find out and accuse the fund of a cover-up. To go public willingly would expose the organisation to the full blast of criticism contained in the report.

But what shocked me most was the discovery that the WWF was actually involved in a scheme in Zimbabwe to provide white hunters with prey. The charity gave out leaflets telling you which Zimbabwean game ranches to visit to join the hunt. For $500 dollars you could shoot several species of antelope. For a few thousand dollars, you could kill one of the WWF's cherished elephants, provided you were prepared to join the three-year waiting list for the pleasure.

This was part of an experiment in 'sustainable utilisation', a controversial policy which decreed, amongst other things, that the best way to preserve a species was to give it an economic value, not only to the hunters but to the local population as well. You might find it extraordinary, as we did, that an endangered species like the elephant should be available to hunt in any circumstances.

Salk and I booked ourselves into the Humani Ranch in the middle of Zimbabwe. We decided to apply for permission to the government to film officially. The Zimbabweans agreed and said that they would inform the WWF of what we planned. We caught the plane to Harare from Heathrow, into which I had flown only three hours before from another assignment in Islamabad.

We arrived to find a message from the 'Cook Report' programme manager, Pat Harris, waiting for us at our hotel. The Zimbabweans had decided that it was too sensitive for us to film the shooting of animals in their country.

'Bollocks to that,' said Salk in his usual succinct way.

I agreed with his sentiment. We'd already made the journey. There was no way we were going home empty-handed. A little subterfuge was all that was required.

We had brought with us a small Super VHS camera for those occasions on which it was advisable not to appear as a TV crew. We ditched most of our equipment and half our baggage at Meikles Hotel in Harare and telephoned the Humani Ranch. Two tourists wanted to book a few days' hunting – did they have room for us? They did? Good. We'd be on the next light aircraft.

On the flight out, we discussed the dilemma we had created for ourselves. Yes, we stood a good chance of filming the shooting of all manner of animals, which was what we had originally come for. But what would happen when we had one of them in our sights? We'd soon be rumbled if we refused to pull the trigger.

'But think of the newspaper headlines back home if it ever came out that "The Cook Report" had actually shot the animals it says it's out to protect?' insisted Salk.

It was undeniable. It would be no use trying to explain to the tabloid reporters that we had to do it to expose the practice in the first place. I'd already had experience of the treatment meted out to people like me if Fleet Street thought they detected the slightest whiff of scandal, real or imagined. We'd be crucified. The animal welfare lobby, with whom all my natural instincts lay, would be mobilised by the popular press and Central would have no alternative other than to apologise publicly and quietly pull the plug on the programme.

Our worst fears were realised as soon as we met the white hunter who was to be our guide. He could have stepped straight out of the pages of a *Boy's Own* comic: young, enthusiastic, festooned with ammunition belts and never without his hunting rifle slung across his back. He was determined that we would be bagging everything from warthogs to antelope from dawn till dusk.

'We're going to have a job avoiding killing anything with him around,' murmured Salk after the first encounter with our guide, whom we quickly nicknamed 'Blashers'.

We were out at five the following morning. We travelled in an open safari wagon. Salk filmed the other hunters when they killed anything, then I would stand near the scene and pretend to be sending a jolly message to the folks back home as Salk focused on me.

The first part of my speech would go something like, 'Hi, kids, here's Dad out on safari. Bet the weather's not as good as this back home . . .'

Then, when no one was paying us any attention, I would slip into 'Cook Report' mode and deliver a pre-prepared piece to the camera about WWF sponsored hunting. I then finished off with another set of witless observations for the family and raised no suspicions from our fellow hunters. It would be a simple job for Graham Puntis, our film editor back in Birmingham, to cut out the dross and use the central part of my message in the programme. The out-takes would probably find their way into our Christmas compilation of cock-ups to be guffawed at by the 'Cook Report' staff after a few drinks.

But the fundamental problem still remained. Blashers would direct the African driver across the bush and then order him to halt. 'Look, over there,' he would whisper to us. Through the trees we would see a warthog, or an antelope – well within shooting range. By now we had decided that under no circumstances would I actually pull the trigger to kill an animal. If anyone was going to do it, it would be Salk. So Salk was now seated next to our gung-ho companion with the rifle across his knees.

He bought time by going on the offensive. 'Listen, all I'm interested in is shooting a kudu,' he declared. 'It's no use you showing us warthogs and that type of thing. We want a kudu – I've set my heart on one.'

Salk was taking this aggressive line because no one had seen a single kudu in the two days the hunting party had been in the bush and he was banking on things staying that way. For another two days, our luck held. Then, on day four, disaster struck.

Our safari wagon was bucketing along one of the few dirt tracks near the Humani's tented, central camp when Blashers gave a shout and signalled the driver to stop. He jammed the binoculars to his eyes and stared across a grassy clearing to a clump of thorn trees about a hundred yards away. Something was moving inside the canopy of the trees. I made out a shape about the size of a cow grazing slowly through the shade. The huge antelope was russet and black – I was almost certain what we were looking at. Then the head lifted and we all saw the magnificent, curlicued horns of a fully-grown male kudu.

Our white hunter ordered the driver to move us slowly off the track and onto the edge of the clearing. He waved Salk off the side of the wagon. 'You aim below the shoulder and fire. If you miss or wound it, I'll finish it off,' he whispered as the pair of them crept towards the kudu, which was munching leaves amongst the trees, still blissfully unaware of our presence. I made a bet with myself that even if Salk shot the animal clean through the heart, Blashers wouldn't be able to resist squeezing off a shot of his own.

Salk and I hadn't had time to confer but we both knew that there was no avoiding killing the kudu. We'd painted ourselves into a corner by specifying the species. The tactic had been useful, though. The delay meant that our 'tourist video' tapes now contained copious scenes of hunting on a ranch recommended and actively encouraged by the WWF. I knew that the British public would never be able to look at the charity in the same way ever again.

I saw Salk bring the rifle up to his shoulder and rest his cheek on the butt. The young white hunter did the same a few feet behind him.

'Come on,' whispered Blashers urgently. 'You'll miss your chance.' Salk continued to squint down the barrel, following the animal's movements. I watched as he began to squeeze the trigger. Then from behind us, a shot rang out, with Salk's subsequent effort adding to the echo of the first. Blashers, who had been promised the trophy for himself, had, literally, jumped the gun. The kudu slumped to the ground. After a few reflex kicks, it went still. My God, I thought, I wish we hadn't had to do that.

Blashers was ecstatic. He virtually dragged Salk by the elbow to where the kudu lay. I followed, picking up the video camera as I left the wagon.

I filmed as Salk and the hunter examined the carcass of the kudu. For an inexperienced shot, the cameraman had done well. The professional's bullet had entered a few inches in front of Salk's. Both bullets had penetrated the animal's side and ripped through the area of the heart. At least it hadn't suffered.

A few minutes later, Salk took the camera from me and I knelt by the kudu and delivered one of my disguised pieces to camera – starting and ending with an excited message to the folks back home and sandwiching serious words for the programme in the middle. I was holding Salk's rifle for him as I crouched next to the carcass.

I looked up during our filming to see Blashers holding his own stills camera. Before I could do anything, he'd snapped at least half a dozen pictures of Roger Cook kneeling, gun in hand, by a magnificent creature which he had, apparently, just bagged as a trophy. The effect the pictures would have if they appeared in the newspapers after I'd broadcast a programme supposedly exposing the Worldwide Fund for Nature's game hunting activities couldn't be anything but devastating. The *real* story would be lost in a rush to pass judgement on us.

'Bad news,' I murmured to Salk when we'd finished filming. 'He's taken a load of pictures of me next to the kudu.'

'Mmmm,' Salk mused. 'Let's get back to the camp and think of a plan to get that film off him.'

Before we could leave, the kudu had to be lifted onto the back of a truck. The quality of such animals is measured by the length of their horns – and this one had attracted the attention of one of our fellow hunters. Bob was not only keen on game hunting himself, but he had a professional interest in the activity too.

'I'm a taxidermist back in the USA,' he drawled as he pulled a tape measure from his trouser pocket and held the extended tape against one of the kudu's dark, shiny horns. 'Yup, I wouldn't mind betting that's the best one killed in this area for a year or two,' he said. 'Congratulations.'

This news only made Salk and me feel worse about what had happened.

Back at camp, the two of us sat in our tent and discussed what we were going to do about the pictures. No obvious plan came immediately to mind but we decided to talk to the young hunter and find out how many pictures he had taken and whether he would consider giving – or even selling – them to us as souvenirs.

No dice. Blashers obviously took his photography seriously. He had taken eight and he wanted them for a new brochure he was designing for his own soon-to-open game business. He didn't mind getting copies for us, however, and asked for Salk's address back in the UK.

Thwarted, we retreated and tried to think of something else. We were getting desperate. There was the added problem that the longer we stayed on the Humani Ranch, the more animals we were likely to have to shoot in order to maintain our cover. Time was running out.

Then came our chance. The hunter came over to the tent later in the evening. He apologised, but said that we wouldn't be able to go out hunting at dawn tomorrow because he had to go into the nearest town to collect some supplies – but we could be out on safari after lunch. We made our plan for the next day over a glass of whisky before bed. As soon as the hunter had left, Salk would keep guard outside his tent while I went in to see if he'd left the camera behind.

He left by truck at nine the following morning. Salk and I crept out and headed across the compound to Blashers' one-man tent. Feeling like a pair of sneak-thieves, we glanced nervously around us for passers-by. All was quiet. Salk undid the tapes of the tent flap and I slipped inside.

As I rummaged guiltily for the camera, the sound of luggage zips and buckles being undone seemed deafening. Salk hovered anxiously outside, resisting the temptation to ask me if I'd found anything yet. After what seemed like an age, I did find the camera – not packed away at all, but hanging by its strap from the frame of the camp bed. I backed cautiously out of the tent and turned to face my co-conspirator.

'You've got it,' said Salk triumphantly. 'Now let's get back to our tent and see what we can do.'

Blashers had taken twenty-four pictures. Eight of those – the last eight – were of me and the slain kudu. Salk pulled out his coat from under his camp bed and put it over his knees. Then he pushed the camera under the heavy fabric and opened the back of it.

'I'm getting the film out without exposing it,' he explained. 'Now I'm going to rewind it to the beginning and put it back in the camera.'

A couple of minutes later, the film was back to frame one and Salk had pressed the shutter sixteen times as he held the camera under the coat. Those first photos would survive. Then he walked out of the tent and, pointing the lens directly at the fierce sun directly above his head, pressed the shutter another eight times.

'They'll be well and truly over-exposed,' he giggled. 'He'll think there's a problem with the camera but I don't think he'll ever find out he's been sabotaged and make a stink about it.'

The camera was returned to Blashers' tent and, with a lighter heart than in many days, we downed a couple of cans of lukewarm beer and began to address our remaining problems – how to avoid shooting any more defenceless animals and how to get our film back to Townson, who, as usual, had been leaving us telephone messages several times a day urging us to come back and get on with something else.

After several hours of contemplation, we came up with an idea. Salk would tell the ranch managers that he had just called home to hear that his daughter was ill. He had to get back to Britain as quickly as possible to see her in hospital. I, as his friend, would, obviously, have to go with him and comfort him on the way home.

'I don't like saying it – it's tempting fate,' said Salk. 'But it is the only thing I can think of that will get us out right away – and it'll shut Townson up for a bit, at least.'

We made a telephone call to Townson in Birmingham and told him about the kudu, the camera and our plan to escape. 'Okay, do it,' he barked down the line. 'And, so far as the rest of the world is concerned, the bloody kudu thing *never* happened, got it?'

We got it. Though by the time the programme was broadcast some weeks later, what we'd done and why we'd done it had been included – and there were no complaints.

If I'd thought there would be some respite from the globe-trotting when the WWF film was finished, I was mistaken. They were crazy times. In one three-month period, Salk and I later worked out that we had flown thirty-three times – to France and Libya on the trail of the missing National Union of Mineworkers' funds, back to Spain to check on the activities of the ever-industrious British criminal fraternity, back and forth to Africa to make the WWF film and, in the summer of 1990, a veritable frenzy of air travel that culminated in what must be the ultimate in traveller-masochism – a day trip to Australia.

The pressure was beginning to tell on the 'Cook Report' staff. Divisions were appearing in the ranks. Some, who felt worn down by Mike Townson's 'hands-on' management style, gravitated towards my office to sound off about his latest demands. Others, who believed that Townson possessed some unique magic power to convert ideas into audience-pulling television, more readily accepted the immense workload placed upon us.

Townson himself appeared to thrive on the self-imposed pressure. As long as he had a cigarette to dangle from his mouth, his secretary to bellow at for coffee, and the power to summon members of the team at his whim, he seemed happy.

I was tired. But being away from home and a routine meant something worse was creeping up on me. For weeks on end, my body clock would be continuously wound forwards and backwards as I crossed from time-zone to time-zone. My metabolism seemed to change. I ate when an air stewardess or night-duty waiter put a plate in front of me. I slept when the journey ended and the taxi dropped me at a hotel. Exercise was reduced to extended trudges through airport corridors or leg-stretching in the aisles of Jumbos on long-haul flights. Poor Frances grew used to the sound of my dopey voice mumbling down the telephone line at unusual times of the night.

I had always been heavily built, but now I was piling on the pounds because of my unhealthy lifestyle. What's the point of trying to diet when your body doesn't really know when the next meal will materialise? My body's philosophy became 'Grab it while it's there.'

Occasionally, I was able to spend a few days at home and restore my body to some semblance of normal routine under Frances and Belinda's loving care. Frances, quite rightly, does her best to keep me on the straight and narrow when I'm not away at work. Fortunately, she's a very good cook and there's no hardship in eating salads and low-fat foods when she's responsible for the meal. I enjoy cooking myself, but with less culinary artistry and technique at my disposal, I tend to go for really good ingredients and flavours: fresh seafood, Scottish beef, Welsh lamb, local ham. I also love good cheese, but I know how fattening that can be – particularly for someone with my working lifestyle.

But wine is one of my great indulgences. The New World wines – the Chardonnays of Australia and New Zealand – are close to my heart. They are the countries of my earlier life – and that's as good an excuse as any for supporting them.

Bob Southgate, who brought me from the BBC to Central Television, was a soulmate for my enjoyment of the finer things in life. In an era when television executives were encouraged to adopt the leaner, hungrier style at work and play, Bob was a beacon shining in a fairly joyless world. His office in Birmingham was an oasis in an otherwise arid environment. A fan of Loire wines and the Sauvignon blanc grape in particular, Bob could be relied upon to have something chilling in his fridge. A corkscrew and glasses were always within easy reach near the cabinet that held part of his collection of food, wine and hotel guides.

Such was his love for Sancerre – one of the Loire's finest white wines – that he would sometimes sign his memos with the words: 'Yours Sancerrely, Bob.'

I would dream of such luxuries while recuperating at home, but eventually the call from Townson would come and off I would go again, my healthy diet and exercise abandoned.

Peter Salkeld was also finding the pressure hard to bear. I numbered loyalty and industriousness amongst his many qualities, but he was – and is – a stubborn bugger. And when Salk feels his principles are being compromised or unfair conditions are being constantly imposed upon him, he has to take a stand.

After a series of arguments with Townson over policy, working practices and the ethics of programme-making – none of which Townson was ever disposed to make concessions on – Salk decided to leave. It was a hard decision for him and one which I urged him not to take lightly. After much thought, he resigned.

Anyone who knew him appreciated that he had the drive and energy of someone thirty years younger, but he was in his early fifties and doing something regarded as a young man's job in our industry. The world of television was growing tougher and new job opportunities fewer and farther between. Salk struggled and was eventually forced to sell his beautiful beamed medieval home on the Welsh borders. We kept in touch and at least he knew that, in his absence, life at 'The Cook Report' wasn't getting any easier.

Series Four – broadcast in the summer of 1990 – was getting audiences of around twice the size of the disappointing second series. And it didn't take a rocket scientist to see that the audience we had built up had a predilection for exciting, confrontational subjects. When we took on Arthur Scargill and asked him what had happened to his union's funds during and after the miners' strike of the early 1980s, we pulled in figures of twelve and a half million. Costa del Crime villains, similarly, attracted very good audiences. When we strayed over to subjects such as the National Health Service there was less interest.

However, the risk that important issues might not pull in record-breaking audiences doesn't mean that 'The Cook Report' shouldn't cover them. In fact, I've often argued that the programme ought to tackle difficult subjects precisely because of its audience-pulling abilities.

British audiences usually find Northern Ireland and 'The Troubles' an instant turnoff, but we have returned to the province whenever we felt that there was a worthwhile story that needed telling. This has yielded six programmes. One covering building-site racketeering by the paramilitaries. Two on the financing of the IRA. Another about Clenbuterol, a drug that the IRA sold to unscrupulous farmers to enhance the size, and therefore the value, of their animals – putting the health of anyone who bought and ate the meat at risk in the process. The final two were about the hypocrisy of Martin McGuinness, as told by the people who have suffered directly or indirectly as a result of his actions.

McGuinness is a man who despised being governed by the British, yet took unemployment and housing benefit from that same government; a man who now denies ever having been a member of the IRA, yet was once convicted of membership in the South – and had openly boasted about it in the North.

I have rarely come across a more hypocritical figure than McGuinness. In 1993, when the first programme on him was made, he was embarked on a campaign to be accepted as a purely political operator. Questions about his activities as the most important member of the IRA Army Council were brushed aside by him in interviews with surly counter-questions about the politicians who fronted the various Protestant paramilitary organisations. Any attempt to examine McGuinness's clandestine past and present was met with a wall of silence by those loyal to him. But away from the Sinn Fein hardliners, there were people whose lives he had torn apart and who were willing to talk.

I had no compunction about examining McGuinness's criminality. I found myself thinking of my early days at the BBC when Andrew Boyle and I realised how desperately the public wanted someone to address their problems head on. We had said then, twenty years before, that my remit would be to examine injustice, criminality and bureaucratic bungling. Two out of three of these elements would apply to a programme about Martin McGuinness.

By the late 1990s, several books had been written by repentant IRA members who firmly placed McGuinness at the heart of the killings and bombings both in Ulster and on the British mainland. In 1993, however, such exposure was unheard of.

I sat in the Birmingham office with Townson and Clive Entwistle, who was to produce the first McGuinness programme, and talked the subject through. There was no problem dismissing the allegations of partiality that came from the Sinn Fein camp. The fate of Mr Sayers of the Protestant Ulster Defence Association and his companions after we had exposed their extortion racket was more than adequate proof of our unbiased stance.

Entwistle's research had already found the victims prepared to speak out against McGuinness and his cronies. They included one man in his early thirties who was living in fear of his life in England after escaping from his IRA torturers in Londonderry. Paul McGavigan had been passing low-level information about the IRA in his native Bogside area of the town for months before he was found out by the Provos. Like McGuinness, McGavigan was a keen fly fisherman and would meet his Army intelligence handler as he flicked his line over the waters of the River Foyle, which flows through Londonderry to the sea. But he was being watched and, as he walked home to the Bogside one afternoon, he was kidnapped by a group of men who took him to an empty house on the other side of the estate.

For the next few days, McGavigan was held underwater in an overflowing bath, had gun barrels poked into his mouth and was forced to lie underneath a mattress on the floor while his captors took it in turns to jump up and down on his body. One man paid visits to the house during his ordeal to ask about the progress of McGavigan's 'confession' – occasionally taking part in the torture. That overseer was Martin McGuinness.

McGavigan eventually made a run for it when an Army patrol, probably on the lookout for him, stopped outside the house. He then contacted his handler, who arranged for him to be spirited away to the mainland.

Researchers Howard Foster and Sylvia Jones found McGavigan living in a rundown suburb of an English city. Like almost every fugitive from The Troubles, the pressure had taken its toll on him. Frazzled nerves, family break-ups, the removal of his children into care, had worn him down. He had sought release in drink and now had a reputation in the street for causing trouble. But he was willing to talk about Martin McGuinness.

Another of those willing to testify for us against McGuinness was Rose Hegarty. Her son, Frank 'Franko' Hegarty, had been a Special Branch agent as well as the IRA quartermaster in Londonderry. After leaking the whereabouts of three massive ammunition and weapon dumps in the province he was forced to leave Northern Ireland and to go into hiding. After the heat died down, he expressed an interest in coming back to Londonderry and Rose decided to test the water through McGuinness's offices.

McGuinness himself promised Frank Hegarty immunity if he came back to Londonderry. Rose Hegarty told us the story of what happened next in one of the most moving, simple and truthful interviews I have ever seen. Quietly, evenly, and only occasionally giving in to her emotions, Rose described how Martin McGuinness came to her house and, taking her hand in his, told her that her son would come to no harm if he came back to the town. He persuaded her and she sent word to her son that all would be well.

Two weeks later, the local BBC television news heard a police report that a body had been found lying by the side of a remote country road near Castle Derg in County Tyrone. It was Frank Hegarty. His hands had been tied behind his back and black insulating tape wound round his eyes before he was shot through the back of the head. He had been tortured before being murdered.

We built the programme around these moving testimonies – helped by a variety of people whose identities we keep secret to this day. God help them should their names ever emerge.

Raymond Gilmour, a local man who infiltrated the IRA for the RUC and foiled many terrorist attacks, had also experienced the soft-soap treatment from McGuinness, who tried everything to coax Gilmour back to Londonderry.

'McGuinness was a two-faced bastard and I'd never trusted him,' he wrote in his 1997 book, *Dead Ground*, about his time as a 'mole' inside the IRA. In it, he described how McGuinness tried to force him to withdraw his evidence against thirty-five IRA suspects.

Gilmour emerged from hiding to help Entwistle and Sylvia Jones expose McGuinness's past. He hadn't seen his wife and family for seven years and had lived in more houses in Britain and abroad in that period than most of us would see in a lifetime. For him, the reality of crossing the IRA was constant upheaval and the fear that someone would betray him to the Provisionals' 'Internal Affairs' hit men. So far, luckily, the death sentence he lives under has yet to be fulfilled.

Throughout the latter part of making the programme, the 'Cook Report' team had been trying to track down McGuinness so that I could confront him and give him the chance to put his side of the story. We knew it would be madness to show up at his house. Remember that Rule One of the 'doorstep' is never actually to arrive at someone's front door to demand an interview. All you are left with is the closed door and, in this case, the likelihood of an angry and potentially violent mob to deal with afterwards.

At one stage, we knew McGuinness had gone on a fly-fishing trip to the Republic of Ireland, but that had finished before we had all the allegations against him in the can. With just days to go before the programme's broadcast, we asked Sinn Fein to arrange an interview with him for us. They demanded to know what was going to be said in the programme, and who was going to say it. Naturally, we didn't want to put the brave participants at risk or have such pressure put on them that they withdrew their testimony and left us with nothing to broadcast. We could not tell Sinn Fein the exact content of the interview, so we were informed that no interview would be forthcoming. McGuinness seemed to disappear from the scene, removing the chance that we might be able to film him arriving at some public gathering where I could catch up with him.

We talked to the Central lawyers and decided that we would go ahead with the programme without McGuinness. This decision was reinforced by the government order of the time which would have compelled us to overdub McGuiness's voice with that of an actor. This was part of the Thatcher legacy that was intended to deprive terrorists of the 'oxygen of publicity'. For us it would have meant turning a potentially powerful interview into a complete parody.

I felt in my heart of hearts that we were on safe ground but I must confess to a little trepidation as we watched the programme in the Central building that night.

Predictably, there was uproar amongst the Sinn Fein-controlled parts of Londonderry. The local newspaper decried the programme, digging furiously to discredit the participants. We waited to see if McGuinness felt he could risk taking legal action. Nothing happened – and hasn't to this day, almost seven years later. The real satisfaction for me and the team that had made this difficult and, at times, dangerous, programme possible came from knowing that almost ten million people had watched 'The Cook Report' about the real Martin McGuinness.

What went without saying was that the Cook family wouldn't be going on holiday to see Frances' family in Eire for some time to come – I had now badly upset both sides. Back at home in the West Country, security was under review again.

CHAPTER 5

Heroin and Hot-dogs

After three years or so of broadcasting, 'The Cook Report' had big budgets, an investigative team that was second to none, and the whole panoply of Central's resources behind us – reference library, editing and graphics facilities, cameramen and sound recordists, a travel department, press and publicity team and an accounts department dedicated to keeping track of our increasingly diverse financial needs.

We kept on getting letters from the public and we continued reading them, grateful for the feedback. If, as was often the case, we couldn't help someone, we rang the sender back, commiserated and offered to pass on the details to a more appropriate outlet – another television or radio programme or to friends in the national or regional press. If a government agency seemed to be the most appropriate remedy to a problem, we suggested it.

More and more, however, we looked to our extensive range of contacts for new material. The team had a lot of top-level contacts in the police, customs, secret services, armed forces, political parties, interest groups, and we had made invaluable contacts abroad.

I was generally very happy with this state of affairs. The variety of subjects suggested to us was immense. When I look at the list of what we broadcast in the first few years – cult abductions, wildlife charity failures, fugitives abroad, cosmetic surgery, the IRA, drugs, credit card fraud – I am reminded of the vast amount of ground we had covered.

Mind you, it is easy to forget without any physical reminders. I used to keep, and occasionally review, copies of past programmes. But I was always disappointed for one reason or another, so now I keep nothing. No tapes, no files, no reviews. There isn't a programme I've done that couldn't have been done better.

But the viewers were obviously less critical and appeared to find the programme and its presenter memorable – as the ratings and the sizeable fan mail seemed to indicate. The fan mail was usually complimentary and always answered, but like the reviews – with one exception – never kept. The one brief letter I did keep came from a lady in Leamington Spa shortly after I had joined Central TV. It goes as follows and it still makes me smile:

> 'Dear Mr Cook,
> I have been an admirer of your bravery and your probity for many years on BBC radio, and I am pleased to see that your investigative skills have been taken up by ITV.
> Keep up the good work, it is much needed and much appreciated. However, I hope you will not mind if I make one further observation: you were much slimmer on the wireless.'

Nevertheless, whatever shape I was in, I was now recognised almost wherever I went. This, for me, was the downside of fame. The higher profile amazed and unnerved me. It was one thing to be recognised in Britain but when a Malaysian airport official asked me who I was after in his country – and much the same was happening in India, South Africa, Holland, Scandinavia, Spain, France and the USA – I was again reminded of the power of television.

I try to remain as private a person as I can. It's one thing to promote yourself as an entertainer and willingly build up a following of fans. But, for me, public recognition is a by-product that spells hassle and actually interferes with me doing my job properly.

A lot of people expect me to be a combative, confrontational type, but they couldn't be more wrong. In reality, I'm fairly shy and retiring. When, in 1997, it looked as if 'The Cook Report' was coming to an end, one of the suggestions my agent, Jon Roseman, made to keep the wolf from the door was after-dinner speaking. I was mortified by the thought. I'm happiest at home with my family, or with motor cars, or good friends and colleagues where there is no need to explain myself, where I can relax and truly be myself.

By 1992 my face had become well known – and the price of fame was potential danger. It didn't take me long to learn the ground rules. Ask for a discreet table at the back of quiet restaurants. Ask for the car to pick me up at the side door of the hotel – one I had probably checked into using an alias anyway.

My recognisability did have its lighter side too. I once turned up at a posh hotel to see a friend who was staying there. I rang up to his room from the reception desk and he asked me to wait for him in the foyer. I took a seat. As I sat down I noticed out of the corner of my eye a well-dressed man in his forties with an expensive looking attaché case on the seat next to him. As I settled into my seat, he saw me and suddenly sat bolt upright as if someone had electrocuted him. He threw a couple of nervous glances at me and peered behind me as if expecting to see a film crew. Then, with a half-choked cry of 'Jesus Christ!' he leapt up and ran for all he was worth. I wish I knew what he had had to hide. There was definitely a story there somewhere.

In the world of professional programme-making, that Cook high profile could help us get the stories. If there was a scent of danger, a whiff of adventure involved in a subject, journalists and film-makers in the freelance market often brought it to us first. And if that exciting subject happened to coincide with a breaking news story, so much the better.

In 1990, two teenage Birmingham girls, Patricia Cahill and Karen Smith, were stopped as they tried to fly back to Britain from a holiday in Thailand. The police at Bangkok Airport searched their baggage and found half a hundredweight of heroin. Protesting their innocence, the girls were thrown into the infamous 'Bangkok Hilton' women's prison to wait for their trial. The press had a feeding frenzy back in Birmingham, interviewing the outraged families of the girls as they prepared to fly out to Thailand to see them.

The 'Cook Report' team, for once, had an investigation right on its doorstep. Townson called a council-of-war in his office. Who had put these girls up to it? Researchers and producers made calls to the West Midlands police and their underworld contacts alike. Progress was quick and we soon traced the girls' 'sugar daddy', who had been paying for trips abroad for them in recent months. He lived less than a mile from the studios. We put researcher Graeme Thomson on the case to find out everything possible about him, while Clive Entwistle, cameraman Grahame Wickings and I prepared to fly out to Thailand and, if possible, get an interview with Cahill and Smith. Our plan was to speak to the girls and put to them what we had uncovered about their case back in Birmingham.

Two things were worrying me, however. First, we still had some weeks to go before our programme would be aired. Any one of the dozens of newspapermen covering the story could discover our exclusive line about the sugar daddy and print it, nullifying the lead we had on everyone else. Second, there was no guarantee that the girls would be allowed to see us – or, indeed, that they would want to. We needed something else to raise the story and make it run for thirty minutes.

As we were about to set out for Thailand, Entwistle took a phone call. It was a freelance producer called Patrick King. We knew his work – he was an ex-British Army soldier who had turned to film-making when he had left the services and he had brought adventure-based ideas to us before. He asked whether we would like to meet the man responsible for supplying the heroin Cahill and Smith were carrying.

Entwistle came into my office and explained the situation. King had recently been into the Burmese jungle to find Khun Sa, one of the most elusive drug warlords in the Far East. Khun Sa produced vast amounts of opium from his private kingdom in the heart of the rebel territories of Burma. To do so, he had raised an army resilient enough to repel everything the Burmese government troops could throw at it. King had found him, filmed him and had left him, he was pretty sure, on good terms. Now he was willing to organise our trip for us.

Naturally I liked this idea very much. But I could tell Entwistle was holding something back from me. 'Come on, Clive. What's the catch?' I asked, staring at him.

He licked his lips and looked right back at me.

We would have to make the journey by mule. It would take three or four days and we would have to cross the border illegally from Thailand to Burma and spend the time before reaching Khun Sa's territory dodging Burmese army patrols.

Entwistle could give me all the assurances in the world but the dangers from just about every quarter were obvious.

Okay, I thought, this is what I joined for. This is what I do. The potential story was great. Add to which we still had the chance that Patricia Cahill and Karen Smith might agree to talk to 'The Cook Report' and give us what we needed to get to the bottom of their story.

Let's take it in two stages, I said. The prison first. If we weren't satisfied with what happened there, Patrick King could set our border crossing up with Khun Sa and his merry men.

King joined us for the flight out to Bangkok and worked with Entwistle to try to get into Bangkok women's prison to see the prisoners. After three days of applying to prison and government officials and traipsing back and forth from our hotel to Cahill and Smith's lawyers, it looked pretty bleak. The world and his dog had asked for the all-important exclusive interview and no one was prepared to let us in.

Graeme Thomson was finding out more about the men behind the heroin smuggling operation by the day, but it eventually became clear that we weren't going to get the chance to put our questions to the women who were, after all, on trial for their lives and for whom the smallest piece of evidence about how they were set up should have been vital.

I asked Patrick King to come to my room. We agreed that we should make the arrangements to leave Thailand for Burma as soon as possible. He switched into military mode, left the room and started to make telephone calls to Khun Sa's men at the Thai/Burma border.

Twenty-four hours later, our small team found itself doing something even the hardiest members had never done before. We had flown from Bangkok to Chang Mai and were taken onwards by lorry deep into the thick jungle by a group of Khun Sa's men. They were tiny, some looked barely fifteen, but they clearly knew how to survive in this climate. They had brought mules for us, which now stood chewing grass at the side of the mud track, ignoring us completely.

The leader of the Burmese group called to his men. They walked towards us, carrying an assortment of dark green waterproof ponchos with hoods. Entwistle, Wickings, King and I distributed them amongst ourselves according to size. I was given the biggest poncho and the biggest mule – what were they trying to tell me?

We mounted the mules with the help of our guides, who, if they were amused by this clumsy sight, didn't show it.

It started to rain. All around us were moss-covered trees and broad-leaved plants. The raindrops gathered up in the branches and period-ically delivered a pint or so of warm water that hit the leaves below with a resounding 'plack!' Sometimes the payload landed on us and I thanked God we'd got our ponchos.

Every so often the riders in front would stop and turn to us, signalling everybody to keep quiet. I was concentrating so hard on just keeping in the saddle and avoiding low branches that I almost forgot we were actually making an illegal foray into a foreign and hostile country. Here, if the Burmese Army didn't shoot us as sus-pected heroin traffickers, we could, at the least, expect to be held in jail and tried for just being where we were.

The terrain gradually became steeper and more dangerous with it. A mule carrying our water bottles and other supplies slipped over on a scree and had to be cajoled back onto its feet by its handler.

'Still glad you came?' asked King, leaning over to me as I clung on to my mule.

In truth, I was rather enjoying myself. My backside was sore and my back, legs and arms were aching, but we were all together in adversity. Four white men in the hands of half a dozen members of a Far Eastern rebel army, in enemy territory and on our way to one of the biggest opium dealers on the planet. I could have been doing the garden back at home or sitting in my office listening to Mike Townson demanding a cup of coffee from his secretary. However, as long as we steered clear of the border patrols and the official Burmese Army, we would be fine.

At the end of day one, we broke open tins of food and the men lit a fire under cover of the wide leaves at the side of the track. It was warm and still raining. The team tucked into the spicy-flavoured rations. We drank copiously from our water flasks and compared notes on the soreness of our bottoms.

After we remounted, the going got even tougher. I was ordered not to climb or descend any of the huge screes on muleback. The lead guide didn't say why he'd singled me out, but I'm sure it was down to the fact that I was the heaviest member of the group and the mule couldn't be spared.

We stopped for the day at about five o'clock in the afternoon. Wickings checked his camera gear, which had been strapped, under his close supervision, to one of the pack mules which swayed from side to side under his anxious gaze just ahead of him. The Burmese put up small, green tents and showed us how to shake all the water off our clothing before slipping into our sleeping bags. We ate our rations and, surprisingly, all slept well.

I was awoken by the sound of our guides' high-pitched voices talking rapidly and excitedly just outside my tent. An intense 'Shhhhh!' went round our small camp. I lay back in my sleeping bag and held my breath. I could hear the blood pounding in my ears as I strained to pick up the sounds around me. This didn't look good. I couldn't make a run for it even if I wanted to. I began to rehearse my defence speech for the trial.

After about twenty minutes – which felt like five hours – our guides burst into chatter again. Whatever the danger was, it had passed and we clambered out of our tents. After some breakfast, we remounted, instantly reminding ourselves of how painful our backsides were. We started to cross streams and rivers followed by steep ascents and descents as we passed through a succession of lush, steaming valleys. The rain never eased and I began to wish the journey over. Grahame Wickings helped pass the time counting the natural obstacles we had overcome on our journey.

'Thirty-four streams and rivers and six mountain peaks,' he announced.

'And the same again when we go back,' I rejoined, tentatively feeling my bruised rear.

After another night under canvas and a third morning's trekking, we came across civilisation. Rows of large, tin sheds built in a clearing in the jungle. Small figures emerged to greet us. Our Burmese guides dismounted and we gratefully followed suit. We were led to one of the sheds and ushered inside.

Standing in front of a large yellow and white flag pinned to a wall below a map of the world, stood a figure dressed in smart, dark blue battle fatigues.

It was hard to guess Khun Sa's age. He had smooth, burnished skin, stood erect and tall at about five feet ten, with thick, black hair. He smiled at me and extended his hand. He had a grip of iron. He repeated the hand-mangling operation with Entwistle, Wickings and King, also giving Patrick a friendly pat on the elbow.

Through our interpreter we explained why we had come. Heroin was a massive trade in the West. Even as we spoke, two British girls were sitting in a Thai jail and stood to lose their lives for possessing the deadly drug. We wanted to know the train of events that had led them there.

To my surprise, Khun Sa readily admitted that heroin was a 'dirty trade'. He said that he hated it but that there was nothing else that would bring in the money to feed, clothe and protect his people, the Shan tribe. During the course of our long conversations, it emerged that Khun Sa had long since met 'representatives' of the US government, for whom he had offered to destroy his crop for its wholesale value. But the Americans hadn't wanted him to do that – they actually wanted to buy the produce of his poppy crop for their own use. It turned out that he had been dealing with the CIA, who, at that time, wanted to use his heroin to fund their clandestine war in Cambodia without letting a hostile Senate and House of Representatives know what was going on.

Before he was interviewed, Khun Sa showed us how he spent his heroin revenues. Over the past two years he had planned and begun to build a big hospital with the latest equipment. There was a substantial new school. His people looked healthy and well-fed and clothed. As we rode with him on the back of a battered Japanese pick-up truck, the response from passers-by was friendly and relaxed. He ran his fiefdom with the help of a small army, but no one displayed any fear.

Khun Sa himself slept on a camp bed inside one of the tin buildings. The floor was of earth. He told us that he ate the same food as his men and that they respected him. We were given identical food and facilities when we arrived, and even though it was primitive, I had the best and most welcome shower of my life – standing under a piece of perforated bamboo with water piped straight from a mountain spring.

When he was outside the perimeter of the camp, Khun Sa was surrounded by armed guards. The Burmese government had been trying to capture him and destroy his people's land for many years and attacks could come at any time. When the British had relinquished Burma after the last war, they had promised independence for the Shan people. It had never come and so they had to fight and be prepared to die in defence of their land.

Khun Sa was totally unlike my concept of a drug baron. As we drove from clearing to clearing, people came out of their huts to greet him, shaking his hand and smiling – ignoring his armed guard. The more I saw of his set up, the more I was inclined, albeit reluctantly, to admire it. The Shan had tried mining and forestry as a means of financial support but had failed. Now there was only opium. He hated it, but it was a simple choice between that or starvation.

We did the interview and filmed the Shan people going about their daily business – and captured, inevitably, the vast fields of long-stalked poppies that enabled this isolated tribe to stay independent and alive.

The next day – before we reluctantly mounted our mules and headed back – Khun Sa staged a military cadet parade for our benefit. They looked so young and proud to be wearing their uniforms, which were far too big for them. The tiniest actually stepped right out of their oversize boots as they heard the order to march forward. It was a strangely touching scene and I almost felt sorry to leave.

The return journey was painful but uneventful. Back in Thailand we tried, once more, to get our interview with Patricia Cahill and Karen Smith. Still no dice. We had to make do with some telephoto footage shot through the prison bars. But we did have Khun Sa – a fascinating insight into a very topical subject. It drew the highest audience of the series.

We sent a copy of the programme to Khun Sa. A few weeks later we received a letter from him. He thanked us for the film, which he thought was critical but fair.

He also added that the mule which I had ridden into the Shan territory and back again had, sadly, died soon afterwards.

He made no comment as to why this had happened but mentioned that that particular mule had been the pride and joy of a close friend of his. While he understood the difficulty of despatching a mule to Burma from England, his friend had rather set his heart on a 50cc Honda moped. Could I kindly forward the cost of one? The letter caused much merriment in the office. Great guffaws emanated from

Townson's office when the translation of Khun Sa's letter was read out to him.

The story of Patricia Cahill and Karen Smith ended the 1990 series on a high note for us. It ended pretty well for them, too, bearing in mind the fact that convicted heroin smugglers in Thailand normally face the death penalty. After serving just a few months of their twenty-five year sentences, the Thai Government announced that it was prepared to show them mercy, and they flew home to freedom and family celebrations.

That drugs turned up, either directly or indirectly, in many of our programmes is an indication of the all-pervasive part they have come to play in our society. Early in 1992 we were the first to warn that Ecstasy was not the harmless recreational drug its promoters proclaimed. In graphic terms, the parents of one of the very first victims, Clare Layton, told us how their sixteen-year-old daughter had died in agony after taking her first and only tablet. 'She had bloated up to three times her normal size and was bleeding from every orifice.' It was truly shocking.

I can't think of another current affairs programme that has ever staged a rave, but 'The Cook Report' did. At that carefully monitored event we told guests of the risks posed by 'E'. We told them of Clare's horrible demise. Sadly, the almost universal reaction amongst the youngsters was: 'There must have been something wrong with her – it wouldn't happen to me.'

Though it does seem to be true that some people are much more sensitive to Ecstasy than others, finding out into which category you fall is the equivalent of playing Russian roulette. On top of that – as with other illicit drugs – you can't be sure what noxious extras have been added during the manufacture of the 'E' you bought, nor whether it really was Ecstasy (abbreviated chemical name MDMA) or the similar but even riskier MDA. Russian roulette, game two.

Our film was taken up and used by a number of educational authorities and police forces also interested in sounding a warning about 'E'; but the arrogance of youth is difficult to counter and the death toll continued to climb.

We also exposed the health risks taken by those using anabolic steroids to build their physiques for purely cosmetic purposes. Steroid use had moved out of the gyms and into the wider world, with tens of thousands of new users.

We met Zoe Warwick, a former female body-building champion, who had virtually turned herself into a man through steroid use and had irreparably damaged many of her vital organs. In constant pain, and unable to cope with the consequences of this chemical self-mutilation, she was later found dead from a massive morphine overdose.

We also met the mother of Jimmy Kevill, another youngster who had used steroids to give him the muscles he thought girls admired on shirtless young men at raves. He started on steroids when he was sixteen and soon began to display the classic symptoms of so-called 'roid rage' – fits of violent and uncontrollable temper. Unable to cope with him at home, his mother finally had him committed to a psychiatric hospital. One visiting day, without reason or warning, 'roid rage' consumed him again. He circled the room, lowered his head and charged at the wall with colossal force, killing himself.

Other users made their friends and partners victims of 'roid rage'. There had been numerous serious assaults, several murders and a number of deaths from liver cancer directly attributable to steroid abuse.

Steroids are not over-the-counter drugs, so where were they coming from? Paul Calverley organised the infiltration of a gang led by John Stiff, one of the major importers and distributors. We traced his supply route to a manufacturer called P&B Laboratories in India. There, the sales director, Humandra Patel, claimed that he had no idea what was happening to his products in the UK, and that he would cease dealing with Stiff forthwith. He was lying, but we didn't know that at the time.

Back in the UK, we secretly filmed dealers in action, offering to supply us wholesale. In one sequence, which had the editorial team in stitches – so much so that we inevitably included it in the programme – one dealer jokingly said to our man on the inside: 'I hope this isn't some stunt for that bloke on the telly – what's his name again? – yeah, Roger Cook.'

He was not amused when I called on him later.

Another dealer – this time a glamorous woman – when confronted on camera insisted that she didn't want to talk to me, 'Because it would damage my reputation.'

In the months after the first steroids programme John Stiff, the man whose gang we had originally infiltrated, also found himself the focus of police attention, and so decided to hand his business over to someone else. So thorough had Calverley's infiltration been that Stiff offered his business to 'The Cook Report'!

We took him up on the offer in order to make another programme. From this advantageous position, we could now get inside the entire network, from manufacturer to supply chain, and on to local distributors. That's when we found our friend, Mr Patel, had been lying. He had continued to supply the British black market and had also provided phoney paperwork and bogus packaging in order to fool the authorities.

We confronted him again, this time after a secretly filmed meeting in a room in Bombay's Holiday Inn. He came with a business plan designed to boost his production and maximise 'our' profits. He left in a hurry, threatening all kinds of mayhem. Fortunately nothing happened to me. Unfortunately, nothing happened to Patel either. The Indian authorities weren't interested, claiming that if Patel *was* committing an offence, it wasn't on Indian soil.

I was staying at the time in another, rather grand hotel near the city centre. We were already well behind schedule and, as I lugged my luggage across the foyer in order to catch the late night flight home, the duty manager collared me. He claimed that I had vandalised a glass table in my room, and that if I didn't pay him a thousand rupees (about £100) on the spot, he would call the police. I would then miss my plane and be likely to spend a day or two longer in a rather less comfortable room than the one I'd just vacated.

The glass table top, I recalled, had been broken on my arrival. I was beginning to argue the toss when another hotel guest bound for the same plane overheard the conversation and barrelled over. 'Look here,' he said, 'this chap's just accused me of buggering up the taps in my bathroom. He wanted a hundred quid from me too. This is obviously a try on! Let *us* call the police.'

The duty manager bolted, and we just made the plane.

Back in the UK meanwhile, the team had infiltrated part of the national steroids distribution network based, surprisingly, in genteel Torquay. There, the south coast distributor boasted that he even supplied the army – unofficially and illegally, of course, and without the army's knowledge. So confident was he that at one of the meetings held in our camera-rigged house he even brought along his little daughter and sat the toddler on his knee as he talked big drug deals. He wasn't only talking steroids.

Steroids have now been re-classified as controlled drugs, but, regrettably, it doesn't stop people getting their hands on them. The same is true, of course, of those even more dangerous drugs cocaine and heroin. That's why we were able to find heroin addicts as young as nine years old, who were supplied by lower-level pushers who made their playground deliveries on push-bikes. That's also why, in another drugs programme, Keith Hellawell – then Chief Constable of West Yorkshire, but now the government's new 'Drugs Czar' – told us: 'My concern is that by the year 2005, nine out of ten of our sixteen-year-olds will be drug users or drug dealers in one form or another.'

I wish him luck in that new job: he's going to need all he can get.

The first person I saw when I strolled into the office to start work on the fifth series was Salk.

'What are you doing here?' I asked. I was delighted to see him again but, the last I'd heard, he was struggling in the chilly world of freelance camera work after finally losing patience with Townson's incessant demands.

It appeared that he'd brought in a story that Townson wanted to turn into a programme. That was one of the things about Townson – he could be an absolute tyrant and make your life a complete misery without turning a hair. You'd think you had burnt your bridges with him because you had finally cracked and gone for him, then he was perfectly capable of welcoming you back into the fold as if nothing had ever happened.

Salk had met a Turkish journalist while working for an independent production company. He had told him a story of the plunder of his country's heritage to feed the West's hunger for Greco-Roman artefacts. The journalist claimed he could take him to villages where all the ancient statuary had vanished – taken by thieves in the pay of rich dealers who passed the artefacts through the world's most famous and, supposedly, most upstanding auction houses in London and New York.

'It's got the scenery, grave-robbing, toothless bandits and smooth auctioneers in expensive suits,' chuckled Salk. 'Mike's already got a title for the programme – so I suppose he'll have to make it now.'

Townson's choice of titles for 'Cook Report' shows were usually as cringe-making as they were inappropriate. Several producers had totally failed to recognise their own programmes when Townson started referring to them by the titles he had decided to give them.

'What's he going to call it?' I asked, holding my head in mock weariness.

'"Raiders of the Lost Art",' Salk replied, breaking into his infectious cackle. 'My title, this time. What do you think?'

'I think it's good to have you back on board,' I replied as we settled down in my office to chew over the events of the past year and to laugh about some of the times we had spent together in far-flung parts of the world.

I had to hand it to Mike Townson. He did possess a knack of assembling a series with a truly diversified, yet almost eclectic appeal to the public. And he always did it with the outward appearance of having made his decisions as a result of the findings of the researchers and producers.

Of course, there had to be a selection process, however it was managed. Investigative journalism is an expensive and labour-intensive business and, with detailed research and background filming on a given story sometimes taking a year or more, we simply couldn't afford to pursue all the stories discussed before each series.

We couldn't afford false starts either. Once the filming juggernaut was rolling we had to be sure we could deliver the story. Since there was no back-up budget, the alternative was a half-hour hole in the airwaves. Fortunately we were never in that position, though we often changed tack before filming started. Sometimes the programmes would be self-selecting – stories which had already had some work done on them but hadn't been made last time around for pressure of time. Some hadn't yet been made but now their time had come – made relevant by current world events.

As we began to prepare for a new series, we would all sit together and throw ideas around. These early get-togethers could be really enjoyable. There was a freshness that a month or so away from the grindstone had allowed into the faces and demeanours of my colleagues. In a month or so, the same people would huddle anxiously over the telephone or sit, agonised, in hotels waiting for their contact to deliver the goods. But now, relaxed from their time off, they sat, stretched out on their chairs, legs extended in a carefree fashion. We also had some new blood in the team – Steve Warr, then a bright researcher who had cut his teeth on national newspapers and seemed eager to make his mark in television.

Over a couple of weeks, the 'goers' amongst the story ideas would emerge and stake their claims as future programmes. There were always about twice as many strong contenders as there were pro-grammes to be made. Then, when everyone had had their say, and you thought you were about to enter into a democratic debate about the merits of what you'd heard, Townson would look over the top of his enormous spectacles and peer down at the back of one of his countless packets of cigarettes, cough and demand silence.

'So, I've decided we'll make the following,' he would say, and he would read out six subjects – including one or two that had never come up in discussion at all – and assign producers and researchers to them. As often as not, first choice had already been allocated.

When you got to know the system, you realised what had gone on. Clive Entwistle had long been Townson's close confidant and the two of them would have been in conclave several times before the public gathering. By then, the make-up of the series was often largely cut and dried. The previously unheard-of stories would often be the ones Entwistle had got from his contacts. He played them very close to his chest.

I was always slightly at odds with myself when this happened. I felt that people in the team were being railroaded.

This time, I had to admit that on first hearing I remained to be convinced about the subject Entwistle had chosen. A half-hour programme on hamburger vans sounded distinctly unpromising – until Entwistle and his researcher, Steve Warr, explained.

Entwistle had heard an item on Central's regional news programme about the murder of Gary Thompson. He had been killed
by two unknown assailants who had stolen tens of thousands of
pounds – the proceeds from just one weekend's fast-food selling by
his vans and stalls – from Thompson's home. The news piece said
that the dead man was the biggest hot-dog trader in the Midlands.

'I didn't know there was that much money in burgers,' said
Entwistle, who had then sent Steve Warr to the funeral for a quiet
look.

Thompson's funeral had been reminiscent of an East End gangland
burial. Large numbers of heavily-built male mourners throwing hate-
filled glances – and, later, punches – at press photographers. The
whole thing reeked of criminality. Entwistle persuaded Townson to
give him the green light, not on the murder of Gary Thompson, but
to investigate the burger trade in general.

Warr interviewed a series of very frightened traders. They all
wanted to remain anonymous and would only meet late at night in
cars in country lanes. It appeared that everyone in the business was
scared because there was going to be a gang war for control of the
burger stand empire that Thompson had run until his murder. People
were going to get hurt in the process.

One reluctant interviewee even pulled a gun on Warr to reinforce
his stated desire never to be identified.

The gun-toting interviewee named a Derby man who, using force,
was the main contender to assume Gary Thompson's mantle. He
painted a reassuring picture of him. 'He is a very, very, very violent
person. Like a mad dog.' Everyone in the team sat up a little and
listened as Warr continued. The man's name was Joe Persico. I
hadn't heard it before but, in the coming months, it was to become
very familiar.

Entwistle and Warr brought the meeting to a close by announcing
that they had applied to Leicester Council for a permit to set up
their own burger stand on a pitch habitually used – illegally – by
one of the Persico-controlled vehicles.

Agreement came through the following day. Warr hired a large
burger trailer and went off to find someone who knew how to work
a hot plate without setting himself alight.

A few nights later, researcher Paul Calverley and a young gofer from the Central newsroom called Kester Demmar, towed the white-painted trailer out to the pitch in the middle of Leicester, stopping at Sainsbury's on the way to buy burgers, hot-dogs and buns.

Warr and a camera crew followed in an unmarked surveillance van and parked down the road from the burger pitch. Calverley and Demarr manoeuvred the stand into position and unhooked it from their car. Half an hour or so later, their griddle was sizzling and they were in business.

It was an indication of the profits to be made from this business that, wherever the team set up the stall, we always made good money – even though we were buying our raw materials at retail prices. If you were big enough and tough enough to control all the pitches at a major event – a pop festival or a motor race meeting – you could easily make several hundred thousand pounds at a weekend.

It was getting late when a truck pulled up about fifty yards from our stand. Three men got out and walked purposefully towards Calverley and Demarr. Warr could see that one of the men in particular was extremely angry. He was clenching and unclenching his fists and seemed to be having difficulty controlling himself.

'Mr Angry' was a short, scruffy figure with long, lank hair. He was wearing a bomber jacket and dirty jeans. He stood with the other customers and started to swear loudly at Paul, who feigned incomprehension. The cameraman focused on the agitated figure and waited for developments.

The man was demanding to know which firm Calverley and Demarr worked for and where it was based. One of his companions made a grab for Calverley. 'Mr Angry' shouted 'Leave him alone', and pushed his friend away. Suddenly, and with surprising agility, 'Mr Angry' vaulted the five-foot high counter and ripped the council licence off the wall behind Calverley's shoulder. He held it up to the flickering gas lamp at the back of the rig and pored over it.

He stabbed his finger at the type – almost poking right through it. 'This is no good,' he screamed into Calverley's face. He started pushing Calverley around the cramped cabin of the burger trailer. 'This is Gary Thompson's pitch. If I ever see you here again . . .' He left the threat unfinished, hanging in the air.

He climbed out of the stand and beckoned his friends to walk with him back to their truck.

The truck moved slowly towards the Cook wagon. It reversed towards the hitching equipment at one end of the stand. The trio climbed out of the truck and, without a word, started to rock and pull the stand off its blocks and to hitch it to their vehicle. Paul Calverley and his friend leapt out quickly and stood at a safe distance as it was dragged down the road and dumped at an alarming angle a hundred yards away. The truck roared off into the night.

We had just met Joe Persico.

A week later, two men were arrested and charged with Gary Thompson's murder. Violence erupted as two warring factions vied for control of the burger business. Persico was one of those trying to fill the vacuum and he was not afraid to use force.

Our interviewees grew more frightened. I arrived at the home of one stall owner who was obviously suffering from a bad bout of flu. The crew and I trooped upstairs to set up the interview at his sick-bed. Next to the bed was a large claw-hammer.

'Things have got so bad, I've got to have protection twenty-four hours a day,' croaked the interviewee, shivering badly – but whether from flu or fear, I couldn't tell.

We were also focusing on the problems faced by Westminster Council in central London where illegal street trading – mainly from unlicensed hot-dog and burger handcarts – was rife. Warr's inquiries showed that the threatening atmosphere of the Midlands burger scene was replicated all over the country and in London particularly.

Westminster Council was engaged in a full-scale battle with the illegal hot-dog sellers. There were threats and actual instances of violence against the enforcement officers as they tried to clear the unlicensed handcarts off the streets.

Joe Persico was trying to be the Mister Big of the burger business in the Midlands. In London, the man we were told to watch out for was Ozdamir Mahmut, a Turkish Cypriot who surrounded himself with burly enforcers. His name was spoken in awe by the Council men and burger vendors alike.

'If you try anything he doesn't like, there'll be violence and you'll come off worst,' warned a Westminster Council officer. 'It's bad enough for us when we set out to do his stands, we can always take the police in there with us. If you go it alone, you'll be attacked for sure.'

When you get information like this, and you do the sort of job I do, there's a thought process to go through. In the past I've been accused of seeking confrontation, of generating a showdown because it 'makes good telly' and the public expect it. I don't see it that way. If a programme turns out to be 'sensational' it's because the subject matter is, by its very nature, sensational – not because we choose to make it so.

The confrontations are, inevitably, a by-product of living the story. By placing myself at the sharp end of the investigations – in this case, by playing the part of a burger seller in the street – 'The Cook Report' gets involved in a way that other factual programmes rarely do. I don't enjoy the confrontation, it's just that often it is the only satisfactory way of concluding a programme and making the point.

I'm often asked why – if things do turn violent in these circumstances – we don't call the police and have the assailants arrested. This one is a real Catch 22. If we do call the police and charges are laid, then the film of the assault is part of the prosecution evidence and becomes *sub judice*, meaning that we can't broadcast it until after any subsequent trial. With a programme approaching transmission and relying on the same evidence, that would involve unacceptable delay. So we don't press charges, we just have to grin and bear it.

As usual, we had thought through the other options in this potentially dangerous story very carefully. We could enlist the help of a genuine hot-dog seller – if we could find one brave enough to go against the bully boys. But what might happen? He could be seriously injured. We could have the police standing by to come in to rescue him but, from then on, he would be a marked man if he tried to ply his trade in London.

We could always film the hot-dog and burger traders at work and describe the intimidation and violence that went on behind the scenes – but would the public really be any the wiser? Would that really bring home the reality sufficient to cause an outcry or create the sense of injustice that could stop what was happening?

Of course, there are times when it's just not possible to take on the role of active participant. The disguise doesn't always fit. But when, for example, I masqueraded as a businessman in Northern Ireland in order to catch the paramilitaries at their extortion games, it wasn't something I did lightly. In Belfast, the RUC had told us it would be impossible for an Ulsterman to pull off a sting on the UDA. We could simply have told our audience about this awful crime committed by the men with guns but it wouldn't have had the same effect and, without the filmed evidence we obtained, it's highly unlikely that Eddie Sayers would have got ten years in jail. As it is, the crime he and his friends committed remains in the mind of the viewer ten years later. The terrorists haven't forgotten either, to judge by the death threats I receive whenever they find out that I'm in the province. But our options, as with this hot-dog story, had been limited.

So it was, then, that Steve Warr paid a visit to a catering outfitters to buy me a hygienic white coat and trilby, stopping off at a theatrical costumiers to pick up an adhesive moustache and a large pair of spectacles with plain glass lenses. My disguise made me look rather like Ronnie Barker in 'Open All Hours', but at least I wasn't going to put the villains off by looking like Roger Cook working at his night job.

We were quite meticulous about hygiene and food quality. Our hamburgers were steak mince from a well-known hotel chain – far better than the congealed grey slurry usually sold from a burger van. However, I must confess that we did breach regulations – although unintentionally – on several occasions.

It turned out that the adhesive we used for my false moustache somehow lost its grip when exposed to the steam as I cooked. The result, more than once, was that customers got a little more than they bargained for with their burgers – but there were no complaints.

Westminster Council found us a hot-dog handcart and furnished us with a permit to occupy a sought-after pitch in the West End, opposite the Dominion Theatre on the corner of Oxford Street and Tottenham Court Road. The official who issued the paperwork restated his warning that we would be in for trouble – at eight o'clock every night, Ozdamir Mahmut's men would be turning up, expecting to set out their stall exactly where the Cook stand would already be open for business. They always worked without permits, instead preferring to pay a fine of £100 a day – which gives a good indication of how much money there was in the trade.

Warr dropped my handcart and me off from the back of a big Transit van a hundred yards from the pitch. With great difficulty, I manoeuvred the unwieldy cart along the road towards the wide area of pavement where I would start cooking. Those carts are not designed to mount kerbstones. Steve Warr was within an inch of coming over to help me when the blasted thing finally mounted the kerb and I was able to push on to my destination.

Warr and cameraman Grahame Wickings had negotiated late-night access to a film-cutting office three floors above street level. Under cover of darkness, Wickings felt bold enough to lean right out of the window with his camera. Getting good sound, however, was going to be a problem. As usual, I wore a radio microphone which transmitted from a little pack hidden in my pocket. Although generally an effective way of recording events, radio microphones are notoriously prone to electrical interference, particularly at long range.

We needed to get the receiver reasonably close without attracting attention to ourselves. The answer had come to us when we realised that our sound recordist was to be John Biddlecombe – a delightful chap blessed with a balding head and a bushy beard. 'Don't wash or comb your hair,' we'd told Biddlecombe on the phone the day before, 'and bring a blanket with you.'

As I grunted and heaved my way down Tottenham Court Road, Biddlecombe was watching from the darkened shop doorway across the road. He sat on the pavement, leaning back on the shop door, his slightly-dishevelled head poking out from an enormous tramp's blanket. The recording gear sat in his lap, safely hidden from view beneath it. Every so often, a passer-by would drop fifty pence or a pound in front of him. What with that and the profits from our hot-dog and burger sales, we were coming dangerously close to becoming a self-financing programme.

Clive Entwistle hovered around the scene, disappearing period-ically into Tottenham Court Road tube station and emerging to wander past me. Occasionally he would bring a message from the crew. 'Grahame says do a bit more cooking, he wants some shots of you at work,' Entwistle hissed out of the side of his mouth on one of his sorties past me. I kept my thoughts to myself but scraped industriously away at my sizzling griddle and re-arranged my soft baps and soggy onions.

I'd been at work for about half an hour when two men walked up to me. I'd seen them conferring twenty yards away and guessed I was the object of their interest. They looked like trouble – short, swarthy and thickset with mean expressions. One of them sidled up close and turned full on to me, his hands in his jacket pockets.

'Unless you move, you'll be dead – know what I mean?' he said evenly. He sounded like he was used to delivering threats.

Both men turned and disappeared into the darkness. I almost had to pinch myself. Had that really happened or had I just imagined it? Entwistle appeared for the last time – he had a habit of absenting himself when things were about to get dangerous. 'Sit tight. We're watching out for them,' he hissed through gritted teeth. It clearly hadn't been my imagination.

Steve Warr came down from the office and stood a little way down the street, a Hi–8 tourist camcorder bag over his shoulder. If I was going to get my head beaten in, it was reassuring to know that the team was going to have it captured on as many cameras as possible.

It's a strange feeling when you've been told something nasty will happen to you unless you go away – and you deliberately stay put. I knew damn well that there was no way I would move. We were there to show what happens when the bad boys move in. I had people around who would try and warn me when trouble approached. Of course, nothing would be done to stop it unless I was in real peril.

Faced with danger, that feeling that it wasn't me there at all, but someone else, had taken over. What I found slightly harder to handle was standing out there like a piece of live bait waiting for the confrontation to take place.

I tried to keep my mind on the job. Customers came up to the stand. I sold them dogs and burgers, took their money and gave them change. I cooked some more food. Sometimes I glanced up and down the road but found it impossible to tell if any premeditated attack was about to be launched against me.

Then I saw them. It was the same two, but this time they had brought muscle with them. Now there were four of them. They all looked of Turkish extraction – dark, tough and purposeful. This time there were no words. The two I hadn't seen before started crowding in on me, pushing me away from the cart, holding their arms out to invite me to retaliate – which, of course, I didn't.

While I was being hustled out of the way, the other two set about wrecking my cart. I could see them rocking it. Then it tipped right over and there was a tremendous crash as tins and metal fittings crashed onto the pavement. A crowd of onlookers gathered as my assailants finished by tipping the cart right over on its side. I was pushed and shoved. No punches, just a final 'You've no fucking right to be here', from one of them before they all made off down Tottenham Court Road as if nothing had happened.

The crowd melted away as I started to put my cart back together again. I imagined this sort of thing wasn't all that uncommon in the West End. I'd taken enough money to see that there could be rich pickings in the hot-dog game. I hadn't been hurt and I just hoped that Wickings and Warr had got it all on tape.

We rendezvoused at Warr's Transit van half an hour later. Everything had recorded perfectly. We would be able to show the Westminster Council officers the tapes to identify who had attacked us.

Steve Warr had made a tour of the other hot-dog stands around the immediate area to check if there was any more 'aggro' going on. There wasn't. But the guy who had uttered the original threat to me was still hanging about. We didn't think he was Ozdamir, to judge from the physical description of him that we had been given by the Council officials. But he seemed to be important enough to be policing the hot-dog pitches and hadn't shown any inclination to evaporate into the night after his exertions with my handcart.

We decided to doorstep him there and then.

'You'll have to put that back on,' said Warr, pointing to my left hand. I looked at it – I was holding my false moustache. It had been itching like crazy and I had been glad to rip it off once the earlier encounter was over.

I reluctantly pressed it back above my top lip. I wouldn't be wearing my white hat and coat when I went into action, but it had to be obvious to the man I was going to confront that he was being tackled by the same man whose business he had just trashed.

John Biddlecombe abandoned his shop doorway pitch, ditched the blanket and hooked his sound recording gear up to Wickings's camera. Warr went ahead of us to spot for the target. He would stand near him when he found him, giving us something to aim for.

Warr halted about a hundred yards down Oxford Street. I strode towards him, searching for my attacker. I wasn't angry enough for it to interfere with my journalistic task but I felt I would be asking him what he thought he was doing with the degree of self-righteousness that must be experienced by all other victims.

There he was, talking to a group of men next to a hot-dog stand. He looked startled when he saw me and the camera. But then he threw his head back and laughed defiantly. I asked him who he thought he was to go around intimidating and attacking people who had every right to carry on their legitimate business.

He turned to me, his face alive with malice. Did he think he ran London? I asked.

'I run the fucking planet, mate. You don't like it, it's tough shit, innit?' he guffawed, turning back to his mates and ignoring us. His arrogance was amazing. He was obviously not going to answer any more questions.

It was only when Warr and Entwistle showed the tapes to the Council men that we discovered that Ozdamir Mahmut *had* actually been present that night. He'd been watching the destruction of my cart from the other side of the street, well out of the way, but Wickings had captured him on tape.

We had an address for Mahmut in north London, so we decided to go for him. He operated from shabby premises on a small industrial estate. We couldn't do any surveillance on him because we would have been spotted by one of his gang, so we climbed into the back of our Transit van and drove into his yard at a time of morning the Council had told us he was usually arriving for work. And there he was, sitting in the passenger seat of a small van outside his office.

The crew and I slid back the door of our van on Mahmut's blind side. Just as I got to his window, his driver saw us and drove away at high speed. Mahmut himself covered his face as soon as he realised what was happening. We jumped back into our vehicle and gave chase. We lost him, but picked him up again, and I tried the frontal approach once more. Again, he turned his face away from the camera and said nothing other than that he denied any wrongdoing whatsoever. For a man so much in the front line of intimidation and public harassment, he seemed strangely shy. I wondered why.

Entwistle took our film to a friendly commander at the Metropolitan Police. He and his men identified several of my attackers as 'well known' to the law. When we showed him film of Mahmut and passed over his name, our friend took down the details and promised to get back to us.

Back in Derby, the war for control of Thompson's empire had intensified and we were finding out more about Joe Persico. He had just been released from prison after serving a five-year sentence for kidnapping and torture.

Most recently, a small trader had obviously upset someone. Although he only ran three hot-dog trailers, one of the big boys had decided he needed a warning. Three petrol bombs were hurled into one of the trailers and the fire completely gutted it – effectively cutting the man's income by a third. He agreed to give us an interview, in which he explained just how determined Persico was to take over the burger business.

But the war wasn't all going Persico's way.

Persico's cousin came out of his house one morning to find a dead piglet lying on the passenger seat of his van. It had the name 'Joe' daubed on its body in black paint. A scar had been cut into its face to match one on the real Joe Persico. A few days later, a gang attacked Persico's house, firing shotguns into the sitting room. Luckily for Persico, he wasn't at home at the time.

Then, the inevitable happened. We had been talking quite openly to the victims of this warfare – filming interviews where possible and sending crews down to the scene of the latest mayhem. Persico got to hear of our interest.

I had always assumed that Persico would be the last person to talk to me voluntarily and I had almost prepared myself for a classic doorstep with this violent criminal with convictions for torture. But he telephoned me in the office to ask for an interview.

We were invited to his favourite hotel where, as we waited for Persico to arrive, we were given an interview with his henchman, who tried to tell us that he and his boss never intended anyone any real harm but that people usually did what they were told when an axe was waved in their faces.

Persico eventually appeared and tried to schmooze me with a performance that veered between soft-spoken contrition and barely-controlled hatred. He claimed that he couldn't recall leaping into our trailer and threatening Paul Calverley and said that he was only trying to earn a living in one of the toughest trades in the country.

When I pressed him on the violence we knew he had committed, he lost his veneer of charm. 'It's all about an eye for an eye and a tooth for a tooth,' he snarled. 'If someone is good to me, I'm twice as good to them. If someone is bad to me, then I'm twice as bad back to them.'

Persico invited us to film him and his father at home displaying a fearsome array of weapons which, they claimed, they needed for their own protection. It was the last shot we needed for the programme.

Our police chum had run Mahmut through the records and – would you believe it? – he was on the run from jail. He'd walked out of Ford Open Prison in West Sussex ten years before and he'd never gone back. No wonder he was so worried about his face being shown on television!

'Hot-dog Wars', as Townson had named it, was due to be transmitted on 8 April 1991. Mahmut had been free for ten years so we didn't have to do a lot of arm-twisting to persuade the police to leave him alone until the show had been broadcast.

The Mahmut case is typical of one of the greatest obstacles to producing 'The Cook Report' in the way we like to do it. When we uncover criminal activity and show it on television, we inevitably attract the interest of the forces of law, order and officialdom – be they the police, Customs, Inland Revenue or Social Security.

If the law has been broken, then we have to allow the consequences to follow on. The reasons for this are obvious. If we let a criminal carry on, innocent people are going to be hurt. Justice – and this is my personal credo as much as the requirement of the law – must be done and be seen to be done.

So, if it's asked of us, we give our tapes and our evidence on the people we all agree should be prosecuted, to the authorities. We willingly give statements and appear as witnesses ourselves at trials. We will also put the authorities in touch with our witnesses – but only if they agree. But all this can cause us problems – and I don't just mean retribution from the criminals, or their associates. If we film criminals at work breaking the law, we often have to let the police – or other relevant parties – know. But, as has very occasionally happened, if we do that, arrests can follow before the programme is broadcast. And once someone is even arrested, let alone charged with any offence, their case becomes *sub judice* and we cannot refer to it in any way, shape or form.

What that means, of course, is that we can be left with no programme to broadcast – with no time to make another in its place and certainly no budget to spend. It's something which gives factual programme executives sleepless nights. It worries the accountants too – but I don't particularly care if they don't always get their eight hours.

What we aim for is a mutually beneficial game plan between the law enforcers and ourselves.

That's what happened with Mahmut, who was picked up on the night 'The Cook Report' went out. He went back inside and, a few nights later, we were out with our cameras on the streets of Central London with Westminster Council officials when forty of his hot-dog stands were seized. It was a satisfying moment.

Townson was cock-a-hoop about our burger and hot-dog film. It appealed to his populist nature, and I had to agree with his thinking. What people want from a factual programme like ours is the surprise element, particularly if it springs from an everyday, familiar source. The British public has grown up with the hot-dog and burger van. It is there after the pub shuts, at pop festivals, at football grounds. The content of the burgers is the butt of many jokes, but it's what you turn to when it's cold and you're hungry and away from home.

If you show the public a programme like ours and afterwards, in the office, or over a drink, people turn to each other and say, 'Did you see Roger Cook last night? I never knew all that was going on with those burger vans. There are people who've been killed . . .', then you've shown them something they didn't know and encouraged them to look a bit differently at a small part of life.

More than twelve million people tuned in to 'Hot-dog Wars' when it kicked off our fifth series in April 1991. In the Midlands, seventy-five per cent of the people watching television that night were watching 'The Cook Report'. I don't think people can look at the burger vans and hot-dog stalls in the same way again – even all these years on.

Joe Persico emerged from the programme as a violent and unpredictable man with a nasty streak mitigated with periods of charm.

He seemed to love me for portraying him in this light and, for a while after the broadcast, he phoned me quite regularly to tell me what was happening in his sordid world.

Part of the film had involved my driving a huge trailer emblazoned with the name 'Happy Burger' around sporting venues to show how stall holders got ripped off by unscrupulous show organisers or catering franchise holders by being put in remote parts of the site unless sizeable backhanders were paid. Persico called me one day and asked if he could buy the trailer.

'Let's face it, Roger,' he drawled, 'you've made us hot-dog guys famous. Everyone will remember "Happy Burgers", I just want to cash in and put "As seen on Roger Cook" on the side of it in bloody big letters. How much do you want for it?'

Needless to say, we didn't sell him the trailer, which in any case had long since gone back to the company that we had hired it from. It wasn't long before Persico was back behind bars again, so, mercifully, the telephone calls stopped.

Whenever we have made programmes with a Midlands criminal slant since 'Hot-dog Wars', the Persico family have almost always entered the equation somewhere, but our paths have never really crossed since.

CHAPTER 6

Dangerous Ground

Towards the end of the run of the fifth series – which was getting tremendous viewing figures of ten and eleven million – Townson, rather uncharacteristically, took two weeks off. It was then that the trouble really started.

You can never predict how long a half-hour investigative programme will take to make. The villains don't read the script and won't do what you'd like them to, or do it in the right time-scale. But you can reckon on between three months and, with a 'slow burner', a year or more.

When Townson went away, he had commissioned only five of the six programmes. Steve Warr and Graeme Thomson had been working on something that I thought, in terms of time, would just about scrape underneath the wire as show number six. They had discovered a network of baby-smugglers operating in Rumania. Rumania was in the death-throes of Communism and the rule of law and order had all but disappeared in some regions. The babies were 'liberated' from destitute families in remote parts of the country. Childless couples from all over Europe were flocking to Bucharest to buy a child illegally, smuggling it out on forged papers provided by the underworld and corrupt officials. The desperate purchasers included British would-be parents, so, all in all, it seemed like a good programme to make.

The team had, for some time now, been split, albeit in a rather loose and not particularly antagonistic fashion, into two camps. One camp was centred on Townson and Entwistle, the other on me; the divisions usually marked out by what we wanted to do and how we should go about doing it.

Salk, Tim Tate, Paul Calverley, Steve Warr, Graeme Thomson and John Cook, as regular researchers or producers, moved – indeed, on occasion *had* to move – between the two camps. Such political pragmatism was sometimes the only way to get anything constructive done. Nevertheless, most of the time we all worked surprisingly well together and most of us – the usual non-Townson camp – were genuinely good friends. We'd been through a hell of a lot together.

What was particularly memorable about the Rumanian proposal was that Entwistle seemed to have changed sides, leaving Townson, for once, on his own. As we were to find out later, this was an illusion.

Townson's attitude was that only he knew what was best for 'The Cook Report'. In his view, no one could manage the programme like him. He kept the details, both in management and editorial terms, very much to himself. I doubt he could even have told me what he had in mind for a particular programme until he had seen all the tapes and imposed his complex series of script ideas on the pictures. The only team member, apart from Entwistle, who understood Townson's arcane approach was Graham Puntis, the videotape editor – and his knowledge had been won through long, arduous experience often running late into the night. Puntis, a jovial, bearded character, was blessed with a good sense of humour which seemed to sustain him through the wee, small hours in his edit suite, trying his best to make the pictures fit the labyrinthine script lines Townson had fashioned on his computer.

However, Townson acknowledged that, in programme terms, I was 'the right man for the job', despite our differences about what the job description should include. So, from time to time, when he felt that he'd put my nose out of joint, I would be invited into his smoker's den to be buttered up.

'I know you didn't get the time to polish last week's script to your usual high standard,' began a favourite line in flattery, 'but not to worry, Roger, with a voice like yours you could make the telephone book sound good.' Townson's own gruff voice would brim with insincerity.

It's hard to remain angry with someone who is, at least, trying to be pleasant, however poor a job he is making of it. He was clearly under a lot of pressure. He still ran 'Central Weekend' – a regional live audience participation show that went out every Friday night –

as well as 'The Cook Report'. Unbeknown to us all, Townson was burning himself out. And when his body – and mind – finally cracked, it was devastating.

I should have known something was afoot. Towards the end of his tenure as editor, Townson began to share decisions with me and would call me in to his office to discuss the structure of the programme in hand. I thought this was perhaps because he had come to appreciate my talents more. With hindsight, it was probably only because the pressure – both external and self-generated – was beginning to tell.

He was smoking almost a hundred cigarettes a day. The office air extraction system couldn't cope any more. My office, next door to his, was a strictly no-smoking area. On the notice board behind my chair I had pinned a card that read: 'You can smoke as much as you like around me – so long as you don't exhale.' And I meant it. As a callow youth in Australia I had affected a pipe for a while – until I almost lost my voice. My voice was vital for my career, so I packed it in.

Townson stuck exclusively to his office for his almost industrial tobacco consumption. He could sometimes be found with a newly-lit cigarette and a glowing butt between his stubby fingers at the same time. And I swear that on more than one occasion his shirt would part over his paunch as he leaned back in his chair to reveal a navel full of cigarette ash.

As time went by, the pervasive odour of tobacco smoke in my office was almost overwhelming. Then, one day, I found out the cause. I was leaning back in my chair and looking up at the ceiling above my head. Thick, grey smoke was snaking through the air-conditioning vent, swirling over the ceiling tiles and sinking slowly downwards to wreath me in Townson's exhalations. Although the temporary malfunction was corrected, Townson didn't feel inclined to ease up on his habit. He just lit up another B&H and smiled defiantly as he blew the smoke from the corner of his mouth.

Townson was always having new – but not necessarily better – ideas about how to pursue a given story. For those of us out on the road this could be both frustrating and aggravating. Investigations like ours were hard enough to do without the staff being subjected to constant badgering. Any member of the Cook team could expect to arrive at a hotel anywhere in the world to find a sheaf of faxes from Townson. However jet-lagged a crew might be, Townson would override the protestations of programme manager Pat Harris and telephone them whenever he thought of a new order – even if it was three o'clock in the morning where the comatose recipients of his edicts were to be found. It wasn't uncommon, either, for slumberers to be constantly interrupted by the sound of envelopes stuffed with new Townson missives being pushed under the hotel room door.

The producers and researchers were largely excluded from the editing process, which increased their frustrations still further. For sanity's sake, it became a matter of honour amongst the rest of us to do our jobs and, despite Townson, try to have a bit of fun in the process.

This might take the form of staying on in a particularly pleasant location for an extra day or so – schedule permitting – or telling Townson that for some spurious reason his hare-brained scheme for filming would not work, and continuing on the path that everyone on location knew was right.

On one occasion, Salk and Howard Foster had had several nights of broken sleep as Townson bombarded them needlessly with telephone calls and faxes delivered to their hotel rooms in Seattle while investigating problems with some of Boeing's aircraft designs following the Kegworth air crash. Eventually, an interview with a lawyer who was suing the company came into prospect. Salk and Foster could conduct the interview in Seattle, said the lawyer's PA or, if we had to do it at the weekend, we would have to fly to Aspen, in the Rocky Mountains, where he and his wife kept a small skiing lodge.

Both keen but inexperienced skiers, Foster and Salk had no hesitation in deciding that the interview would have to wait until the Saturday morning.

On Friday night they boarded a flight to Denver from Seattle, then changed planes to a twelve-seater to the winter playground of the rich and famous. The interviewee was keen to get his interview completed by nine the following morning, so that he and his family could enjoy a full weekend's skiing. Salk and Foster wouldn't stand in his way. By ten o'clock, they, too, were on the slopes of the Buttermilk Mountain.

An odd pair they must have made as they slithered uncertainly on hired skis in thick snow – Foster in jeans and a Barbour jacket and Salk in his customary grey suit, white shirt and tie.

'This snow's getting worse,' Foster observed to Salk after an hour or two on the piste.

'It certainly is,' Salk replied. 'I don't expect we'll get out of here for a couple of days.'

'Shame,' said Foster.

They phoned the office that night to explain that flights out of Aspen were on hold until the blizzards subsided. In two days' time they would be back in Seattle and the huge pile of Townson communications would resume. For the time being, a couple of days off would do no harm – either to the story or their own sanity.

When Townson took time off in May 1991, I felt it was important that the rest of the team presented a united front over the making of the Rumanian babies story when he came back to work. There was no time to make anything else, we would tell him at the morning meeting upon his return. Warr and Thomson had already booked plane tickets. Interviews were in place and camera crews on stand-by. I had my trip to Bucharest pencilled in for a few days later. Even Entwistle seemed to agree that this was the best course to take.

On Townson's return, we all gathered in his office to have our say. Two minutes into the meeting and it was obvious that something had gone amiss with the united Cook team approach. Townson seemed to know what was going on and, far from supporting the making of the Rumanian programme, Entwistle was now arguing against it.

The penny dropped. Entwistle must have telephoned Townson the night before and they had devised their own plan for the last show. Entwistle had seen a story in a national newspaper about parts of the Mosside area of Manchester being a 'no-go' area for the police because of the growth of gangs armed with a fearsome arsenal of weapons. Townson took up the story. Forget Rumania, he said. Too expensive. We were going to make a programme on guns. He wanted 'The Cook Report' to show how easily they could be procured in Britain today. We were going to turn the shortage of time into an

My Ronnie Barker impression goes down a storm in Leicester Square.

Being turned over – literally.

In Indonesia:
canoeing in a mangrove
swamp in search of
Goffin's Cockatoos.

Confronting Arkan with
evidence of his war crimes
in Bosnia and Croatia.

Arkan's brutal
paramilitaries,
The Tigers.

A Triad gang attacks undercover agent Joe Tan.

Triad boss, Georgie Pi, makes a run for it.

In Red Square, armed with the briefcase bomb.

With plutonium seller Gennady.

Irish Naval officers approach a Spanish trawler loaded with illegal fish.

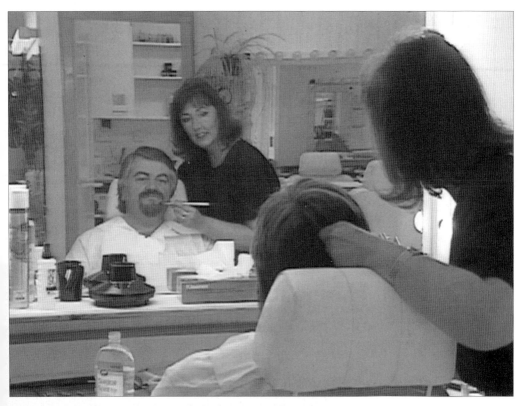

All in a day's work: a four-hour make-over.

The fake Sheikh, ready to tackle the falcon thieves.

The start of the heroin trail in Burma: Khun Sa exhibits an opium parcel.

With Khun Sa, inspecting his troops.

Caught in mid air: a lioness is violently knocked back by gunfire at close range in a so-called canned hunt.

Making a killing: white hunter Sandy McDonald is confronted in South Africa.

Proud and happy parents.

Frances and Belinda:
the two people who make
it all worthwhile.

With Frances celebrating
a win at the Baftas.

advantage. We had precisely one week in which to research, interview, film and edit a high-risk programme. We were about to break
the law by trying to obtain a wide variety of pistols, rifles and even
machine-guns. We had to find a villain who was in the supply business
and trap and expose him.

There was nothing we could do to dissuade them. Entwistle had
already set the wheels in motion – sending Warr to South Wales to
meet one of Entwistle's criminal contacts. He would return several
days later almost incapable of speech. Salk and Thomson were
despatched to Newcastle to find more weapons. The rest of the team
moved up to Manchester to attempt to infiltrate the gun gangs.
There we found a man who offered to sell one of our undercover
informants a sawn-off shotgun and to obtain almost anything else
we wanted. He became our target for the 'doorstep'.

Entwistle's 'contact' had taken Steve Warr on a long series of
nocturnal pub crawls to procure the weapons. The contact, who had
close associations with the old London criminal 'firms', the Richard-
sons and the Krays, kept himself awake for the gun-hunt on strong
lager and little bags of powder he called 'pink champagne' – a mixture
of cocaine and amphetamine – constantly snorting pinches of it and
blowing his eternally-streaming nose.

In three days, Warr had been shown and had filmed rifles, shotguns, handguns and a frightening World War Two heavy machine
gun with enough power to rip through the walls of a house. In
Newcastle, Salk had had similar fortune.

Townson rubbed his hands with glee as the tapes arrived around
the clock from his exhausted staff. He set to work with Puntis in the
edit suite behind his office. For once, researchers and producers were
allowed into the room – a rare privilege, but only because on this
occasion Townson hadn't had time to absorb all the material that
was flooding into the Central studios. He needed input from other
people so that he didn't get his facts wrong.

To this day, I don't know how we managed to make that programme. By the end of that week, everyone concerned with it had
worked themselves to the point of exhaustion – and that included
Townson and Entwistle. I hardly remember the programme being
transmitted – or if I was even in the office to watch it with the others
– I was so tired. I do remember that I wasn't very happy with it.

It was the third week of May and already that year I had worked on programmes in Turkey, Germany, Brazil, Thailand, Burma and Ghana as well as all over Britain.

There were two months before we would broadcast the 'update' programme in which we kept the audience abreast of any developments in any of the stories we had ever covered. I, and everyone else, needed a rest.

I make no secret of the fact that I enjoy the company of my fellow journalists and programme-makers when we can meet and talk over a good meal and a few bottles of good – not necessarily fine – wine. I also think that a lot of creative energy is generated when you are relaxing over a glass and a meal.

As the wine begins to flow, so do the ideas. After the second shared bottle, lateral thoughts tend to generate themselves. It is at this point in the liberating, creative process that my more convivial colleagues – such as Salk, Howard Foster or Steve Warr – made sure they had a pen and notebook to hand. It's sometimes hard to remember that brilliant idea you had when you wake up the following morning with a bit of a headache.

Although I should say I resist getting drunk. I have only been really totally incapable once. That was when I was in my early teens in Sydney, having consumed, with a schoolfriend, most of the contents of his father's cocktail cabinet. Enough to fell a small herd of oxen, apparently, so medical intervention was a necessity. I never want to be that ill again, nor that far out of control.

As time went on, the biggest challenge for 'The Cook Report' was to keep fresh ideas coming in. It was a constant challenge to avoid the tendency to feel you'd seen every investigative story before. It was sometimes tempting to concentrate on drugs. If you scratch the surface of almost any organised criminal activity you find narcotics dealing. To say that the situation is getting worse is an understatement. Money-laundering, gun dealing, smuggling, the Black Economy, car crime, the IRA – the list of stories we have investigated only to find that the money behind them all is generated from drugs is mind-boggling.

Just like compassion-fatigue and charity donations – when the public reaches the point where it just can't care enough about the plight of its fellow creatures to keep responding to endless appeals – you can't keep making programmes about the same subject all the time. It loses the impact and almost reduces the unacceptable to the commonplace by endless repetition.

Five years into 'The Cook Report', we were by far the most watched current affairs television programme in Britain. It is a ranking we retained for twelve straight years. We also consistently scored well above the factual average on the scale used to measure perceived quality and audience appreciation. Twelve million people were watching us seven or eight times a year. I'm inclined to bang on a bit about audience sizes – but size *does* matter. A bigger audience means more resources and, more importantly, the bigger the audience the more people will be made aware of the problems we seek to highlight. The greater the awareness, the more likely we are to 'get a result' – a criminal brought to book or a law changed for the better.

Good stories, well told, make enjoyable viewing and it is that that pulls the audiences. The challenge we face is to attract and involve our viewers without compromising the high standards of journalism that they – and our lawyers – have come to expect. That we seem to have risen to that challenge more often than not is the reason for the programme's success. However, it is possible to have too much of a good thing.

It was only a matter of time before commercial television realised that advertisers would pay heavily to have their adverts placed around 'The Cook Report' for as many times a year as we could produce the shows. The pressure to make more was growing – and I was against it. There comes a point when more is not necessarily better and I didn't want any dilution of the strength of what we did.

It was an argument I resisted successfully until 1993. By then, the demand for more had become universal within ITV. Central Televison asked whether I would allow them to offer twice as many 'Cook Report's as part of their bid to renew their franchise. Loyally, I agreed. Sadly, there was no going back. Even the blandishments of my somewhat cynically-minded agent Jon Roseman, who pointed out that as TV companies purchased programmes by the yard, I now also finally had the chance to earn a decent salary, didn't help. I relished the challenge but dreaded the prospect of a doubled workload and feared that we might not be able to find enough good yarns to supply the yardage required.

The equivalent of three extra half-hours were squeezed into the run – and my schedule got even more hectic.

As a result my already high profile was about to become even higher. Members of the public were recognising me in the street. By far the great majority of people are fine with this. Some, however, feel they have to act aggressively towards me – as though I'm a champion boxer who needs to be taken down a peg or two. These are usually groups of young men in clapped-out cars who shout, swear and jeer out of the windows as they drive past. There can also be an assumption that if I'm out on the street I must be doing my job. I now just accept it. It goes with the territory.

National newspapers, of course, see anyone in the public eye as public property and their fickleness is legendary – harming or even destroying people far more famous than I shall ever be. One day I can be described in the tabloids as 'The Taped Crusader' or 'Fearless Telly-Sleuth Roger Cook'. The next, I'm an overweight has-been whose career is about to end. I particularly remember one tabloid centre-page spread cataloguing 'Twenty Things You Didn't Know About Roger Cook'. The funny thing was, I didn't know about them either!

For a couple of days there had been one or two telephone calls coming into my colleagues in Birmingham from the *Sun*. They were told that a freelance photographer had taken a picture of me as I left a patisserie in Bristol. Built solely around this location snap, the *Sun* had concocted a whole article about how my weight was seriously worrying my 'telly bosses' and I had been warned to slow down or retire before I gave myself a coronary confronting a villain. This was total nonsense, although I was having real health problems at the time as I recovered from a bout of malaria.

I steeled myself for the story, which was the kind of thing that always upsets Frances. I had come grudgingly to accept that if you are in the public eye, you are going to get turned over by the press from time to time, however unfair you might feel it is.

Then came the call from the police that a hired killer had been caught. The story leaked out from the police in the Southwest and, the next day, gone was the story about my impending demise through my allegedly Olympian cake-eating prowess. Instead, the *Sun* ran a huge story on pages one, two and three about the thwarted shooting of the courageous television investigator who had exposed so many bad people over the years. The story was dressed up with several photographs of professional confrontations which had ended with my being thumped by the interviewee.

I am constantly amazed by the weird rumours that circulate about people the tabloids want to put on their pages. Only a year or two ago, a rather sheepish Daily Mirror reporter arrived on my home doorstep. I answered the door and he asked me whether it was true that my marriage was effectively over and that Frances had left home and was about to divorce me. This information, he added, came from an anonymous 'friend'.

I invited him in, shut the door behind us both, and took him by the elbow round to the back of the house to where Frances was busy hanging out the washing. Eventually persuaded that the anonymous 'friend' was ill-informed and clearly no friend of ours, the reporter beat a retreat accompanied by a very grumpy photographer who had obviously hoped for the shot of a lifetime. Needless to add, no story ever appeared.

A week or so later, however, a story of a real collapsed marriage hit the front pages. The subject, one R. Cook – not me, but the Foreign Secretary!

I have also been the target of other television programmes; twenty-three times in all – mostly affectionate satire in programmes like 'Not the Nine O'clock News', 'Benny Hill' and 'Spitting Image'. But a 'Dispatches' programme screened after our second programme on Arthur Scargill and what had really happened to the money raised for the miners during the strike of 1984 was pure vitriol.

Cudgels were taken up on Scargill's behalf by renowned film director Ken Loach, whose usual work I admire. Mr Loach came up with a mixture of 'explanation', which relied on the selective re-writing of history, 'rationalisation', which relied on thousands of angels dancing on the head of a pin, and personal attack. This approach was echoed in the *Guardian*, which was also involved in the production of the film.

The programme was promoted on the basis that I didn't have the guts to face their questions. The truth was quite the reverse. The producers had twice, in writing, been offered a formal interview with me, subject only to a prior outline of the particular areas they wished to discuss. There was no reply. Their preferred approach seemed to be to doorstep the Great Doorstepper. This they did as I attempted to eat breakfast one morning in the Hyatt Hotel in Birmingham.

There were two cameramen and two interviewers shouting questions at me while Mr Loach, at equivalent volume, urged me to 'Answer the questions, you fat bastard.'

I don't even treat murderers like that.

After nearly half an hour of this, when their film ran out and they had reloaded, I was running late for an appointment, so I left, still offering a proper interview if they cared to do one. On-screen, the episode came across very differently. A few seconds of a discomforted Cook with breakfast egg on his face, a couple of questions, an exchange in a revolving door and an image of my departing back – over which the commentary line implied that I was running away.

The accusations in our programme had been that Scargill had misappropriated union funds and that money intended for the striking miners had never got to them. Our witnesses said that, public donations aside, the funds had come from two main sources: Russian miners showing solidarity with their British brothers, and donations from the coffers of Colonel Gaddaffi in Libya.

After the strike, and our programme, the new freedom in Russia – perestroika – introduced by President Gorbachev, allowed the release of many official documents. Some of these, released to the BBC's former East European correspondent, Tim Sebastian, showed that what we had said about donations from the Russian miners was true. Monies intended to relieve the hardship of striking NUM members had, instead, been diverted to another outfit of which Arthur Scargill also happened to be President – the IMO in Paris. Half a million pounds was later remitted to the NUM from the IMO.

Extracts from those Russian documents – also published in the

Times – were forwarded to the 'Dispatches' production company and to the *Guardian*. Once again, no reply.

As for the Libyan money, there was never any satisfactory explanation as to its final resting place. The NUM's former chief executive, Roger Windsor, had alleged that some of this money, delivered in cash, passed across his desk then through an offshore bank account in the name of a deceased relative, and had been used by Scargill to pay off home loans. This was the key question Scargill would not answer when I had doorstepped him. All he would say – over and over again – was: 'Put it in writing and I'll investigate.' Why he needed notice to investigate his own actions was beyond me.

However, the NUM did eventually appoint Gavin Lightman QC to look into the matter. His report did not substantiate the home loan charge, but was nevertheless sharply critical of Scargill's conduct. Following this, the NUM (President: A. Scargill) sued the IMO (President: A Scargill) for the return of £1.4 million – finally settling out of court for half that amount.

The whole messy business was best summed up by the *Mirror*, normally a staunchly left-wing newspaper – with which we had shared information on the story – in the last lines of a scathing editorial: 'Mr Scargill began the miner's strike with a very large union and a very small house – he ended the strike with a very small union and a very large house.'

But that's not how Ken Loach saw it.

Andy Alan, then the managing director of Central Television, was almost as upset by the 'Dispatches' programme as I was. He said that by the time I had returned from a between series break, a writ for libel would have been issued on the positive advice of a prominent QC.

When I got back, the writ was still unissued. A visibly embarrassed Alan explained that it was now very close to franchise renewal time and Central Television's board didn't want to rock the boat by embarking on a legal action against another independent television contractor. Sorry, but I had broad shoulders, didn't I? From then on, Central's policy seemed to be to rely on those shoulders rather than the laws of libel when the occasion arose.

The tabloids, at least, maintain a simple approach to people like me – it's either love or hate. But the broadsheets can be worse. There, prejudice is compounded with the worst kind of middle-class snobbery masquerading as public concern. In some quarters – particularly where programmes like 'The Cook Report' are perceived as not being 'proper documentaries' – you can find yourself an object of derision. We are an easy target to sneer at, purely because we attract a mass audience.

The *Guardian* displayed the most extraordinary hypocrisy towards us when reporting a programme we had made about the pedlars of outlandish and potentially dangerous 'cures' for serious illnesses.

We had exposed a vet who, as well as treating animals for cancer, gave his liquid treatment to humans in the last throes of the disease. When we had it analysed, the 'cure' he had given us turned out to be orange juice. The vet complained about his treatment by 'The Cook Report' and we were summoned to a hearing before the Broadcasting Complaints Commission.

Along with a lot of people working in my area of television, I had little regard for the BCC. I have no objection to being 'regulated', but here is a body set up to ensure fair play which often didn't play fair itself.

Early on in the life of 'The Cook Report' a prominent member of the Commission told our lawyer, barrister Peter Smith, one of the most experienced practitioners of television law in Britain, that the 'BCC was gunning for "The Cook Report".'

I have no idea why. A few years ago, one of the BCC's committee members, a former trades union boss, told me to my face that it was his job to 'take cowboys like you off the air'. The BCC, and its successor, the Broadcasting Standards Commission, are typical examples of how the British Establishment thinks things should be done when it decides it wants to create a body to rein in rogue programme-makers and adjudicate between members of the public and TV companies. Instead of appointing people who are – or were recently – involved in the industry, the Establishment brings in 'The Great and the Good' – former schoolmasters, clerics and retired civil servants. The BCC people who have ever had hands-on experience of television and its workings are very few indeed. It was particularly ironic that the BCC should view us as they plainly did – in entertaining so many complaints against us – when it was we who had framed so many of the guidelines for how programmes like our own should operate when the genre was effectively created way back in 'Checkpoint' days.

I suppose it was inevitable that this august body and I should fall out in a big way at some stage. The catalyst was that programme on dubious fringe medicine.

When Peter Smith explained to the BCC hearing that vets are not supposed to treat humans, the vet claimed that he could do so because of his acupuncturist qualifications. This came as something of a surprise, since acupuncture had not been mentioned in any of his lengthy prior submissions.

Had any needles been used in his cancer treatment? asked Smith. No – but acupuncturists sometimes used herbal remedies, so it was quite in order to give human patients a 'medicine'. It was preposterous, but the ploy worked. The BCC ruling missed the whole point of the programme.

The vet was probably well-intentioned but eccentric. He was certainly not portrayed as a crook. However, and this was the point, regardless of the guise under which he gave it, he had claimed a ninety-eight per cent success rate for his treatment of cancer. This claim was untested and palpably ridiculous, but nevertheless gave false hope to desperate people.

A woman who had gone to him in the last stages of cancer had been prescribed carrots. Her GP told one of our researchers that she had suffered great pain towards the end of her life, quite needlessly. She could have been getting relief from conventional medicine.

The vet's hearing took place in the morning. The afternoon was taken up with the hearing of a complaint by the parents of a woman who had died of cancer but had sought the vet's treatment in the last weeks of her life. The parents were upset because we had featured their dead daughter – a woman in her forties – in our programme, even though we had been to see them to explain why.

Here, the BCC showed the true intellectual muddle it had got itself into.

Peter Smith had seen that, to judge from the ruling in a couple of earlier cases involving Granada Television, the BCC wanted the notification of relatives if a deceased loved one was to appear on television. It was something that seemed perfectly fair and reasonable.

Smith had asked Howard Foster, who was now a producer, to tell the parents what we were planning to do. But that, it seemed, was no longer the issue for the BCC. They were angry, it eventually transpired, because 'The Cook Report' had not reported the parents' views about the vet in the programme. When Smith tried to explain that he was only trying to adhere to the BCC code as expressed in the Granada cases, and that there was no obligation to include the parents' opinions, he was jumped on instantly. There was no such code, said the chairman, who added that every case was dealt with by the BCC on its individual merits. Quite how programme-makers were to proceed if no previous decision by the BCC could ever be relied upon was beyond me.

Eventually, the BCC was forced to change its rules on the notification issue to accord with what we had argued. The man who made them see sense – Peter Smith. He was given the job of overhauling the whole system.

But we lost both the day's tribunals. Our punishment, if you like, was that we should print and read out the findings on the vet's complaint. There was much anger: we still profoundly disagreed with the ruling and there was no right of appeal.

We decided to rebel. We would broadcast the BCC decision, but I would appear briefly beforehand and say why we felt the BCC was wrong – even perverse. It was a dangerous step, we knew, though there was nothing in the rules to prevent it. Bob Southgate wrote the words, Peter Smith 'legalled' them and I read them on air.

There was uproar. The BCC complained to the Independent Television Commission. They gave Central Television a rocket and, reluctantly, we were forced to broadcast the findings again, without comment.

When those findings became public we were berated by a *Guardian* columnist who sided wholeheartedly with the vet, seemingly on the grounds that we had dared confront such a nice, well-meaning individual – and that his cure might have been a major breakthrough. Howard Foster and Peter Smith wrote a reply to the paper's editor. They pointed out the lack of any evidence that the vet had discovered anything remotely like a cure for cancer; the fact that he had nevertheless boasted to us – during secret filming – that his treatment was ninety-eight per cent successful, and that to give false hope to the terminally ill was morally questionable and certainly a point worth raising in a programme about the value of alternative medicine in general.

They also pointed out to the *Guardian* that the main 'witness' against us in the article had since told Foster that he'd been misrepresented and misquoted to suit their journalist's particular agenda.

The *Guardian* refused pointblank to print our letter as sent. What eventually appeared had been sub-edited to the point of meaninglessness. When we asked why, we were told that it would be completely unfair for them to print a letter like that without giving their journalist the right to reply. The fact that that was exactly what they had done to us didn't seem to make one jot of difference.

Our third appearance before the BCC that year came after another complaint from a person we had exposed in our quacks programme. Elizabeth Marsh, a self-styled but unqualified 'professor' with a conviction for providing a potion related to creosote as a medicine for people dying of cancer, claimed that we had stolen a bottle of her treatment from her. She had also tried to sell us an electrotherapy machine she claimed was good for treating cancer – charging us VAT for it, even though she wasn't registered with the VAT man. The hearing dragged on and on and we weren't believed until Bob Southgate found a piece of secret filming in which Mrs Marsh was pictured pulling a bottle of her brew from her airing cupboard and openly giving it to the 'Cook Report' researchers.

The BCC even gave a hearing to an obnoxious man who for years had systematically stalked a vulnerable woman, writing several letters a day to her and following her. The only time she ever spoke to him was to tell him to leave her alone and we had more than ample filmed evidence of what he was doing. Even the BCC had to admit, grudgingly, that we were right to expose him – but not before allowing the time and expense of a full tribunal.

I took comfort from the fact that after our programme on stalkers, regardless of the machinations of the BCC/BSC, measures were taken by government to have this appalling activity treated as a serious criminal offence.

Fortunately, the mounting of such time-consuming rearguard defences was rarely required. We just concentrated on making the programmes as good as we could make them, and were happy to let the public judge us on that.

*

Long distance international travel combined with some really rough conditions in the field were now wearing my body down. Series Six is one I remember because it brought me the closest I have ever come to being shot – at pointblank range – and I sustained an accidental injury that put me in the consulting rooms of a brain specialist and left me wishing I could lie down in a darkened room for a couple of years.

Townson's confidence in being able to choose the most disparate and unusual subjects and still keep our audience was growing apace. On the slate were programmes on a major building society's disastrously costly advice to some of its more vulnerable customers, the deaths of British soldiers by 'friendly fire' in the Gulf War, the rise and rise in use of the drug Ecstasy, a harrowing story about bullying in the Army and a fascinating tale on the illegal trade in exotic and endangered birds.

Everything started very well. The inquiry into the illegal trade in valuable birds was prompted by a conversation between Steve Warr – recently promoted to producer after a good run of successful programmes as a researcher – with the Royal Society for the Protection of Birds. It was a programme whose storyline grew and grew from quite small beginnings.

The RSPB had some details on a bird dealer called Phil Dobinson who was moving substantial numbers of rare and protected birds around the world and offering them for sale as bred in captivity, which was legal. However, the RSPB had suspicions that Dobinson was somehow cheating the system and passing off rare birds caught in the wild as captive-bred – which was totally illegal.

As with our hot-dogs programme, it was surprising how much money there was in the exotic birds business. And money was all they meant to the corrupt dealers. Birds worth thousands of pounds each were bought for pence from natives of Developing World countries, and shipped round the globe in the most appalling conditions.

More than eighty per cent of such wild-caught birds die before reaching the market, yet such were the colossal profits to be made from the few that survived that the trade continued to boom. And the more that died, the greater the market for replacements – propelling several already endangered species rapidly towards total extinction.

One of Dobinson's former employees had got suspicious about

how his boss was breaking the law and he told us about it. All we had to do was prove what he was doing to get him stopped.

In England, Dobinson had recently received 130 rare birds from what he referred to as his 'captive breeding project' in Zimbabwe. In other words, he was importing birds and claiming it was legal because he had supervised their breeding. The birds were Goffin's Cockatoos, which he was selling in Britain for £450 each. In fact, Goffin's only live in the wild in Indonesia. The experts told us that it would take many years to establish a breeding colony in captivity in Zimbabwe. Our suspicions grew.

Salk and I resumed our globe-trotting partnership of a few years before and caught the flight to Djakarta to find out what Dobinson was really up to. When we arrived, we spent the night in the splendidly neo-colonial Omni-Batavia hotel before picking up our internal onward flight which would island hop across the Arafura Sea to Tanimbar in the South Moluccas. There, we had been told, was most of what remained of the Goffin's Cockatoo population.

We were in for another Developing World airline experience, courtesy of a subsidiary of the then notoriously unreliable national carrier, Garuda. With each island-to-island flight, the aircraft got older and smaller, but there were no significant problems. But the final leg of our journey was a classic. Several passengers joined us, bearing wicker baskets bursting with live chickens bound for market. The birds found this a very stressful procedure and made their feelings plain by clucking furiously as we took off.

We had just got used to the din when we hit a bad patch of turbulence. The crowded and ill-fastened baskets burst open as they crashed against each other and suddenly the cabin was filled with panic-stricken birds, feathers and a generous measure of chicken manure.

Several passengers began to behave like the chickens. It took the rest of the flight to recapture and re-cage the birds and to calm the passengers down, by which time most of us looked as if we had been tarred and feathered.

There were no proper hotels in Tanimbar's largest settlement, Saum Laki. The single main street supported a collection of food shops, hardware stores and pool halls. Halfway down, on the harbour side, was our lodging house. Long, low and timber-built, it came highly recommended as one of the few places on the island with a reliable electricity supply. It had its own generator but, sadly, that failed to benefit the guests because all the power it produced was entirely devoted to running the biggest Karaoke machine I have ever seen – all flashing lights and a sixty-inch screen.

My 'luxury' room had bathing facilities and a lavatory. The former was a brick-built pit half-filled with sea water. The latter, a trapdoor in the wall through which you were supposed to stick your rear end in order to relieve yourself into the stream below.

In the middle of the first night, I woke with a start. There was someone, or something, in the room. I listened, hardly daring to breathe. I could hear the Karaoke machine thumping in the distance. I tried to switch the bedside light on – nothing – the bloody Karaoke machine. I groped in my luggage by the camp bed for the torch I always carry with me and switched it on.

There, caught in the beam, was an enormous, mud-covered pig. I rose from the bed unsteadily, and not a little nervously, wondering what to do. I kept the animal, whose tiny eyes were trained on me unwaveringly, in the glare of the torch until I was upright. I shouted and waved my arms. That did the trick and, with a piercing squeal, the pig shot through the toilet flap from whence, presumably, it had come.

Bizarre incidents like that stick in my memory, and there have been a lot of them. But I tend to forget, or to minimise, the things that often go with a 'Cook Report' investigation. The endless waiting for something to happen, the freezing cold or swelteringly hot stakeouts, the gut-wrenching worry felt by the whole team that something will go wrong, the hundred-hour working weeks . . . Still, I do recall that, apart from the porcine intruder, the remainder of our stay at Saum Laki all went more or less to plan and we were able to recuperate in comparative peace from the strenuous forays we were making from first light till dusk into the steaming, spice-scented jungle.

We were shown how the native people trapped the Goffin's Cockatoos, sneaking up to them at night and firing glue-daubed arrows at the birds as they slept on branches high up in the trees. It was extraordinary to see the birds plopping down to the ground around you, caught in the glare of the lanterns carried by the hunters, who then packed the stunned creatures into string bags.

While we were there, a top level conference of the Convention on International Trade in Endangered Species was taking place in Kyoto, Japan. At the end of it, worried CITES members voted to categorise the Goffin's Cockatoo as Appendix One – along with the elephant, rhino and panda as a species seriously in danger of extinction.

We also discovered that it was from the Indonesian Islands that Dobinson was paying for the Goffin's to be shipped to Singapore and then Zimbabwe where they would be 'laundered' as captive-bred birds before being exported to European countries like the UK. Dobinson could expect to get £900 a pair for the birds he sold. The local trappers got precisely £1 for capturing those same two birds.

Before we left for Singapore and Zimbabwe to confirm at first hand what Dobinson was doing, we made it public that, to stop the birds falling into the wrong hands – literally – we would buy any Goffin's Cockatoo trapped on Tanimbar. Our helpful landlady, who had taken the Goffin's plight to heart, offered to organise this. She also arranged to have the birds kept in a safe holding area until they could be released into the wild, away from danger, under the supervision of the World Parrot Trust.

All this was done with the best of intentions but it had an unplanned and unwanted result. We created an even bigger local market for Goffin's Cockatoos. Our landlady was paying better prices than the dealers and the parrot poachers didn't have the added hassle of smuggling the birds off the island. They worked even harder.

Eventually we were the owners of five hundred of these rare creatures which had almost eaten our landlady out of house and home before the Parrot Trust was able to move the majority of them safely back into their natural habitat.

Several weeks and many thousands of miles later, we had followed the parrot trail through Singapore to Zimbabwe and had gathered enough of the evidence we needed on Dobinson's cruel and illegal bird-laundering activities to be able to confront him back in England. We also discovered that he had thirteen convictions for a variety of offences, including cruelty and selling rare birds with false paperwork.

But the profits far outweighed the fines and Dobinson, instead of going out of business, just kept expanding his markets at home and abroad.

Getting out of Saum Laki was a lot more difficult than getting in. At the local office of Mapati Airlines, the few flights always seemed to be fully booked, whether you had a reservation or not. The staff were giving priority – and free tickets – to their nearest and dearest. As a result, we fell further and further behind schedule.

Depressed and frustrated at having missed yet another flight, Salk and I sat gazing at the tatty advertising posters on the wall of the waiting room. Mapati Airlines. We burst into laughter and then into song simultaneously. Other would-be passengers looked at us uncomprehendingly as we chorused: 'It's Mapati and I'll fly if I want to, fly if I want to . . .'

Shortly afterwards, we got our tickets. Perhaps it was the singing.

We were still giggling intermittently as we approached the ticket desk. When we reached the head of the check-in queue, there was an ominous rumbling sound and the earth started to shake. The ticket clerk's eyes bulged, he flung our tickets down on his desk and executed a near-perfect barrel roll through the window behind him. The wall containing the window shook itself to pieces. We rocked and staggered, clinging to a buckled roof support. The earthquake stopped as quickly as it had started. Nothing life-threatening, but enough to scare the ticket clerk out of his wits.

He reappeared, looking sheepish, twenty minutes later and told his dust-covered audience that although the terminal building was damaged, the airstrip was fine – so the flight back to Djakarta would run, to our enormous relief.

Our trip back was uneventful but, ten days later, that same aircraft crashed into a hill at the end of the runway, killing everyone on board, including seven of our island landlady's relatives.

The last part of the programme was to be filmed in Guyana, where trapping birds in the wild was still legal, despite CITES' efforts. Steve Warr and Salk came with me to see some of the trapping as it happened in the dense Guyanese jungle.

It was hard going. All three of us would go out with our jungle guide and a bird trapper, travelling in dugout canoes and across land, chopping away at the trees and chest-high undergrowth just to make any headway. Cutting your way through the jungle is tiring work. Strangely, Salk, who was then about fifty-three years old, and I, at forty-nine, seemed to be finding it easier going than Steve Warr, who was in his early thirties and claimed to be one of the fittest members of his hockey club. We 'old boys' put it down to stamina born of a lifetime of hard work.

Warr had hired three canoes – one for each of the Cook people. He named them 'The Director's Canoe', 'The Cameraman's Canoe' and 'The Presenter's Canoe'. Mine was the biggest, for some inexplicable reason.

Salk would go ahead in his canoe and set up his camera and tripod on dry land ahead of me. Warr would join Salk and they would film as I paddled past, trying to look reasonably proficient. On about the third 'take', I still hadn't given either of them the shot they wanted – and my bottom was feeling rather damp. I had been concentrating so hard on paddling and steering that I had failed to notice the fact that I was about to sink. I paddled like crazy for the shore, and just made it. There was a bloody great hole in the bottom of my boat. And there were crocodiles and innumerable biting and stinging things in the waters we were travelling on. I shuddered.

To get into the rainforest where we were filming, we had to fly out of the capital, Georgetown. We had very little in the way of supplies, particularly drinking water that we could trust. The local trading stores had only fizzy drinks. Within a couple of days we had drunk the place dry so we commandeered our guide's Land Rover and got him to drive us over the border into Brazil for some more.

If it wasn't for the fact that it was so cruel, and deprived the world of some of its rarest and most beautiful animals, one might admire the patience and ingenuity of the trappers who take the scarlet macaw. They would cut huge fronds of palm leaves and hoist them over their heads and shoulders, and make their way through the jungle looking like giant, shimmering, green beetles.

Then they would climb eighty feet to the top of a tree holding a live macaw as a decoy on a rope. As soon as a free bird heard or saw the decoy, it would fly down and perch on a nearby branch, never suspecting it had landed right next to a human being with evil intent in his mind.

Salk filmed as an arm reached slowly out of the palm fronds and slipped a wire noose over the head of the newly-landed macaw. In seconds, the bird's wing feathers had been clipped and it dropped out of the tree, flapping awkwardly earthwards to be grabbed by the trapper's mate. A quid earned for the trapper. That scarlet macaw would fetch £1,000 in the UK. The native trappers had no qualms about showing us their side of the business – what they were doing wasn't against local law.

A night later, disaster struck. To avoid anything unpleasant that might enter the hut where the three of us were staying, we had hooked up hammocks several feet off the ground for our night's sleep. During the night, the rope holding the head end of my ham-mock worked loose. Fortunately, it did so slowly and I was able to narrowly avoid crashing headfirst to the concrete floor almost six feet below. But what happened was bad enough. I swung, barely awake, towards the ground. My head hit the deck and, still wrapped in the bedding, I swung away like a pendulum to crash back onto the floor a couple more times. My shouts woke the others, who, with some difficulty, dropped down and ran over to see how I was.

I felt sick and dizzy. There was blood all over my head and I was having difficulty walking. I was in a fair amount of pain.

Luckily, we were almost at the end of our shoot and we pulled out of Guyana a day or two later. I floated around with double vision until, when I got home, Frances insisted I went to see a specialist. I had damaged my neck once before and there was concern I might have re-fractured the bones.

I was still on strong painkillers when Howard Foster came to see me in my office to explain what he wanted me to do on his story about Clenbuterol and the IRA.

This drug, although not a hormone, was capable of increasing the weight of beef cattle dramatically. Farmers north and south of the border in Ireland, who were corrupt enough to give it to their ani-mals, could make £200 more than they could usually expect per beast. Cattle were being slaughtered, sometimes at night, to avoid testing by the Ministry of Agriculture, and sold into the massive intervention market. This was the notorious 'beef mountain' dreamt up by the EC to take in surplus cattle and keep up prices for the farmers. Most of the mountain would end up being fed to Eastern European families in times of famine.

But whoever ate the meat ran a serious health risk. In Spain, there had already been two thousand cases of Clenbuterol poisoning.

Farmers were overdosing their animals in the belief they could make them grow even more. The chemical caused huge increases in heart rate – threatening the lives of unborn babies and their mothers, and people with heart conditions.

As quick here to spot a potential profit as they had previously been with the building industry, the IRA moved in on Clenbuterol, ignoring the health risks. By 1991, they were making so much money selling it to farmers that they had virtually ceased robbing banks. Foster had gone to meet one such farmer, who had promised to spill the beans. What he hadn't told Foster was that he had also told 'the boys' that someone from 'The Cook Report' was coming to see him about the Clenbuterol they were supplying him. There was welcoming party for Foster in the Dungannon pub where the meeting had been arranged. Threats were made – fortunately without violence at that stage – to the effect that the consequences of pressing on with the story were likely to be terminal. We pressed on nevertheless.

The Clenbuterol market was frighteningly similar to the more conventional, but equally illegal, narcotics trade. One of the main suppliers of Clenbuterol to the Irish market was a man called Wynand de Bruyn, who ran an outwardly legitimate chemical business near Breda in Holland. Foster had already had de Bruyn watched when he went on a trip to Buenos Aires, Argentina, the world manufacturing capital for Clenbuterol. We knew that his supplies, which were smuggled into Holland, were worth £80 million a year. He had even bought his own island off Curaçao, off the South American coast. He had been arrested and charged by the Dutch authorities for smuggling Clenbuterol a few months before, and the police were expecting de Bruyn to try to skip to his island retreat with his ill-gotten gains.

Foster, Grahame Wickings, sound recordist Keith Conlon, a Dutch researcher called Jos van Dongen and myself had tackled de Bruyn outside his Dutch house in February – two months earlier. We parked our minibus across his electronically-operated gates in case he tried to leave by car. Jos van Dongen pressed the intercom to the house and asked to speak to Mr de Bruyn.

Nothing happened for twenty minutes until the front door opened and two figures came striding towards us. De Bruyn was at least six feet five inches tall and twice as wide as me. He didn't look pleased.

We found out from the police later that the big blue Mercedes which we were blocking in had £300,000 stashed in its boot for deposit in his bank in Zurich.

His son was with him. He wasn't as thickset as his father, but was easily six feet tall.

I started to ask de Bruyn some questions, but he ignored me – why would a Dutchman know who the hell I was anyway? – and made straight for the camera. De Bruyn Junior grabbed Grahame Wickings round the waist and arms. Dad put both huge hands around the camera and pulled it away from the trapped Wickings's grasp.

He lifted £35,000-worth of Sony Betacam above his head and smashed it to the ground. Then he picked the shattered camera up from the road and did it again. Then they turned on the rest of us. I tried to put myself between him and Keith Conlon. I felt my shirt rip as he lashed out. Foster and Conlon were struggling to keep hold of the sound equipment. Conlon's eye and forehead were dripping blood from where de Bruyn Junior had dragged him to the ground. Then the police arrived. Luckily, before the 'red mist' had descended over Mr de Bruyn, he had called the police in order to have us removed from the road outside his home.

While we were at the station giving statements to the police, de Bruyn's lawyer rang. De Bruyn was happy to buy us a brand new camera and pay all our expenses in cash if he could just have the film we had shot of him. The battered 'Cook Report' team answered the relayed request with one voice and a single word – Bollocks.

Our inquiries touched a nerve with the criminals involved in making money from the cattle drug. Now Howard Foster wanted us to confront another of the farmers who had been illegally dosing his cattle. His farm was situated right in the middle of pro-IRA 'bandit country'. Here, the police travelled in pairs and, from past history, Roger Cook didn't advertise his whereabouts to the locals.

We arrived at the farm a couple of days later and found the farmer's son, who was awaiting trial for feeding Clenbuterol to his herd. He seemed quite resigned to talking to us. Then his father arrived and all hell broke loose. He punched Clive Entwistle, sending his glasses flying across the farmyard. I got between the furious farmer and the semi-prone Entwistle, still groping on the ground for his glasses. If the farmer had a problem, I said, he should address it to me.

By way of reply, he began to rain punches down on my neck, head and shoulders. We were clearly not going to get an interview out of him, and I called Entwistle, the sound recordist, cameramen Salk and Wickings back to the car. The farmers hadn't finished with us, however. There was a problem finding the car keys and as our driver fumbled, the son steered the farm's forklift truck, its prongs a few inches above ground level, at the side of the car. He obviously intended to tip the car over with us inside it.

If that wasn't bad enough, his father was now holding a shotgun and was lifting it, aiming to fire directly through the windscreen at my head, about five feet away. I was a sitting target. I ducked as low in the seat as I could go. He squeezed the trigger. Nothing happened, mercifully. It had jammed.

He turned the shotgun round and held it by the barrels. Then he smashed it hard into the windscreen. The glass crazed and buckled, leaving the clear outline of a shotgun butt right across it. He was screaming at us in rage as the engine burst into life and we sped off. Close call.

There was a twist in the tale. Although examples of meat tainted with Clenbuterol had been found in Spain and the Low Countries, where armed gangs were distributing the stuff willy-nilly, no British beef had tested positive for the drug. Foster, stuck in Belfast at Townson's insistence for yet another weekend, did a sample buy from a dozen butchers and supermarket meat counters across Ulster. We had been told to buy ox liver because the liver retained Clenbuterol in its greatest concentration. Foster duly bagged and labelled all his samples and took them to a laboratory for analysis.

Five days later, the results came back. One sample had proved positive. It was from Northern Ireland's leading supermarket chain and it was several times over the recommended safe limit.

When the programme was broadcast, there was uproar in Ulster. The Ministry of Agriculture tried to dismiss the laboratory findings, which annoyed the analysts there, who were put under pressure to retract what they had found. They stood firm. Next, the Ministry issued a statement saying that even though the Clenbuterol levels were high, there wasn't enough to harm the consumer. It was hardly the point – what mattered was that farmers were routinely dosing their cattle with a banned and dangerous substance and the enforcement agency charged with controlling and monitoring the industry wasn't doing its job properly.

Ulster Unionist MP Ken Maginnis had given an interview in the programme about the IRA involvement in Clenbuterol dealing. In the mind of the public, the drug was now firmly associated with terrorism and health issues. After the broadcast, the agriculture ministries both north and south of the border pledged to work together more closely.

Privately, we were told by friendly Customs officers and Ministry of Agriculture officials that there was little that could be done. Farmers would always be susceptible to a substance that helped them eke out a living. The IRA had already opened up new smuggling routes into Dublin Docks from South America, and onwards using time-honoured routes across the unmanned country lanes that criss-cross the Eire/Ulster border.

More worryingly – particularly since the advent of BSE and all that has meant for the British beef industry – there was a problem with the province's abattoirs. Northern Ireland boasts a unique, computerised monitoring system for its cattle. Records are kept of individual animals, the herd they belong to and where they go if they are sold on. Indeed, it is the probity of this system which led to the ban on beef exports being lifted first in Ulster after the terrible impact of BSE and CJD.

What we were told, unofficially, by people we trusted, as well as senior Northern Irish politicians, was that the computer system was being sabotaged by a handful of slaughterhouses. By day, they processed the cattle according to the rules. Then, by night, the bad boys arrived with their truck loads of Clenbuterol-dosed animals. The computer, of course, was switched off while this went on.

Agriculture officials who tried to intervene were attacked if they were discovered watching the illegal operators. One farmer drove his tractor over a surveillance vehicle before speeding off with his cattle to hide them over the border in Eire. Without increasing the resources, it seemed unlikely that much would change.

It is naive to expect much to change as a result of a television programme, but a lot depends on the subject. Sometimes, the medium can make things happen – take Michael Buerk's coverage of the Ethiopian famine, for example. That inspired a huge fund-raising effort which saved many lives. People responded to the moving images of fellow human beings in terrible suffering. There aren't many subjects that lend themselves so readily to this visual treatment.

CHAPTER 7

When Push Comes to Shove

At 'Checkpoint', we had had a fair number of smaller-scale successes. Fly-by-night businesses, fraudsters and con men were exposed and effectively shut down. The public were warned and didn't fall for their tricks again. Sometimes, laws and regulations were changed or tightened up because we showed that there were loopholes. But we also whetted the appetite of the public for bigger-budget investigations that had more bearing on their lives – hence the huge mailbag we used to receive and my desire to move on to television and a wider audience.

'The Cook Report' was usually subject-led, rather than taking issues and examining them. That seemed to be what people wanted to see. We raised the public's awareness by focusing their attention on examples of wrongdoing so that, even if there were no arrests or changes in the law, at least next time a subject like the leadership of the IRA, the conservation of endangered species or the horrors of a new drug arose in conversation, someone might remember a dramatic image or two from one of our programmes and form an opinion.

Townson had already decided that he wanted to start the next series off with an exposé of Triad gangs in Britain, the Chinese secret societies that had infiltrated the lives of their own people and were firmly entrenched in mainstream organised crime. He deputed Howard Foster to find the right location for us to show what the newspaper cuttings and his own populist nose for a good story already told him was out there somewhere.

Sometimes, a subject so compelling arises that we have to move heaven and earth to show it to people. This happened soon after the end of the 1992, sixth series. That we should put ourselves in the way of an extremely arduous – not to say dangerous – undertaking so soon after working ourselves into the ground for eight or nine months says something about how strongly we felt. Even more remarkably, we took on this one-off special project despite knowing that from 1993 onwards our workload would double to fourteen programmes a year, split into two series.

During the summer of 1992, Paul Calverley had been contacted by a group of Moslems who told him about a route between Belgium and Britain used for smuggling in illegal immigrants. One of the men giving the information also mentioned particularly brutal atrocities being committed in Bosnia against the Moslems by a Serbian paramilitary group. The man showed Calverley some gruesome photographs of what appeared to be the genitals of the menfolk of one village, amputated and displayed on trays by the aggressor Serbs. We were all shocked and disturbed by what we saw. Calverley started to investigate who exactly this group of Serbian irregular soldiers were.

To our intense relief, we discovered that the contents of the trays we had seen in the photographs were actually a local meat delicacy, not what we had been told. But by that time we all knew that we were on to a big story. One of the details might not have been quite as advertised, but we were sure that ethnic cleansing was happening on a large scale. For once, the usually anonymous perpetrators of the genocide could be identified. The sinister figure behind these murders was one Zeljko Raznjatovic – nicknamed 'Arkan'.

In 1992, the West had heard many stories about 'ethnic cleansing', an antiseptic-sounding phrase that masks the horror of wholesale genocide. But proof was hard to find. Nailing the individuals responsible for it was unheard of.

Arkan was a man with a fearsome reputation of international proportions. Born in Montenegro in 1953, the son of an army officer, he had started to get into trouble with the police when he was spotted as a potentially useful secret agent. As a young man, he was sent all over the world to spy on the enemies of the Yugoslavian communist regime. He is also believed to have assassinated half a dozen Yugoslav nationals living abroad in safety, or so they thought. This had clearly given him his taste for travel, high living – and extreme violence.

Back in Belgrade, he started to make the fortune he knew he needed to indulge his material desires. As long ago as 1975, when he was just twenty-two years old, he was being described in the Yugoslav press as one of the most dangerous criminals in Europe. Bank robbery, murder, black marketeering – he carried out all these and it made him rich.

By the time the bloody civil war started in the former Yugoslavia in 1992 Arkan was wanted in six countries – Holland, Italy, Finland, Belgium, Croatia and Sweden. He was captured in Sweden after a series of robberies and was arraigned before the courts. Just as the charges against him were being read out, Arkan opened his attaché case and produced a sub-machine gun. He sprayed the court with bullets before escaping to a getaway car outside. He made his way back to Serbia and has never been recaptured.

Apart from making money through crime, Arkan's other great passion in life is football. But not as an ordinary fan. He became the head of the quasi-fascist Red Star Belgrade football supporters club – which was army-run. The Red Star supporters are extreme, even by English soccer hooligan standards. Shaven-headed, they scream taunts at the opposition. Their xenophobia and love for all things Serb is as vocal as it is frightening. Hardly surprising, then, that when Arkan decided to set up his own militia to attack Serbia's 'enemies', he chose his men from the ranks of the Red Star supporters club.

With the blessing of the authorities – Arkan was by now under the patronage of the Yugoslav President Slobodan Milosevic – he formed the Serbian Volunteer Guard, nicknamed The Tigers. He moved freely around Croatia and Eastern Bosnia, toting his Heckler and Koch sub-machine gun at the head of his 1,000-strong army. One report describes him as 'like a man possessed' as he laughed at the massacre of hundreds of innocent Moslem civilians.

Arkan and his men dressed in proper battle fatigues and were videoed for self-promotion on manoeuvres, crawling under netting, firing at targets and spreading camouflage over their armoured vehicles. To complete the image – which would have been preposterous had it not been backed with such murderous intent – Arkan bought a tiger cub which was led on a rope at the head of his ugly band's impromptu parades.

Back in Belgrade, Arkan had robbed and looted from enough of his own people to be able to buy his own football club. His first ambition had been to buy his beloved Red Star Belgrade. This, apparently, was blocked by Milosevic himself, who feared that such a take-over would give Arkan too big a popular power base, threatening Milosevic's own authority into the bargain.

Instead, Arkan bought bottom-of-the-table Obilic and became an object of hero-worship by the club's fans, who called him the 'Commandante'. The chants and songs that come from the terraces are about ethnic cleansing and the purity of Serbia. Before long, through bribery and intimidation, Obilic began to rise through the league, backed by Arkan's huge personal wealth.

Meanwhile, in 1991, Arkan moved The Tigers into Croatia during Serbia's war with the now independent Yugoslav nation. A year later, he led a murderous campaign to drive Croats and Moslems out of the eastern Bosnian town of Bijelina. Calverley's Moslem contacts could give us survivors of Arkan's attacks. A former friend of Arkan, a photographer, had been invited to witness The Tigers at work. He had taken pictures of the Tigers murdering unarmed villagers in Bosnia. What he had seen had so disgusted him that he had moved to New York where he maintained a frightened silence about both the butchery he had seen and the man who was orchestrating it. At least his pictures had come into our hands.

Was there just a chance that this arrogant man, who invited a photographer along to a massacre, might consent to an interview with a British television programme?

Calverley used a variety of intermediaries to get a message through. At first, there was no response. Then, a few weeks after the initial request, word came back that such an interview might be possible. While we waited for the decision, the 'Cook Report' team went into Bosnia to gather evidence with which to confront Arkan if we actually got to meet and film him.

We were carrying several thousand US dollars to buy our way around the devastated countryside and we had bought heavy, blue flak jackets and helmets from a military suppliers in London. At my insistence efforts were made to increase my personal insurance. In places like the former Yugoslavia they don't play by the accepted rules. If anything went wrong in this lawless war zone, I wanted

Frances and Belinda well provided for. Negotiations were still going on when I left.

In late August, Paul Calverley, producer Clive Entwistle and cameraman Mike Garner arrived in the coastal city of Split. Their first filming site was to be the refugee camp of Zenica. Time was tight and there was only a narrow window of opportunity before the first snows rendered the local terrain almost impassable. A battered grey Mercedes diesel saloon was acquired as crew transport. It was cheaper and stronger than a hire car and expendable in case of attack.

By arrangement with the Moslems who first put Calverley onto the Arkan story, they were introduced to a young student who spoke good English and was between terms at college in Zagreb. He was to be our guide around Zenica and then in Lechevo, where it was said there were survivors from a recent massacre who would name Arkan and his Tigers as the killers.

Initially there were surprisingly few outward signs of conflict along the way. The crew were put up and fed by unfailingly generous and hospitable local families, despite an acute shortage of food. Eggs and bread were considered a feast.

As the Merc bounced along the pitted and rutted roads towards Lechevo, they came across an old man chopping wood in a small clearing by the roadside. Paul stopped the car and, through our student interpreter, asked him what he knew of the massacre.

There was plainly no one else around, but he would only respond in a whisper. The fear in his eyes was obvious, and he barely broke off his chopping action as he spoke. In the end his instructions were simple; they needed to travel on another few hundred metres to the first house on the left. The young man there had apparently seen everything.

A few minutes later, this slight seventeen-year-old lad had committed his painful memories to videotape. He had hidden in a ditch as Arkan and his henchmen had mown down most of his fellow villagers with automatic weapons. Later, a sixty-eight-year-old woman recalled how she had been shot three times and left for dead. Her slaughtered family and friends had been heaped on top of her, but she had managed to extricate herself and crawl to safety after the Tigers had gone. There were many more searing stories like theirs.

The crew picked me up a few days later back in Zagreb, 'fresh' from a red-eye flight across the Atlantic. We headed back in to the war zone. Picturesque stucco and terracotta-tiled houses soon gave way to shattered and smouldering ruins, green tress to blackened abstract shapes silhouetted against the cold sky.

Nothing I had seen on television could have prepared me for this. Whole communities had been razed to the ground. Great craters had opened up where once there had been shops, flats and schools. The remnants of families wandered around, dazed and distraught. Bodies lying beside the roadside had not just been shot. They had often been multilated as well.

We stopped in the small town of Vocin. In architecture and ambience it had once resembled an Austrian resort, but now it looked more like a quarry. The Serb paramilitaries had almost blown it to bits. They had marched through plundering, burning, murdering and terrorising as they went.

Vocin apparently used to boast of its happy ethnic mix. Serbs, Croats and Muslims had lived side by side for years, but the Serb paramilitaries had forced neighbour to turn against neighbour at the point of a gun. Many Muslims and Croat men were simply marched off into the woods and shot. Not content with that, the paramilitaries even victimised members of their own ethnic group. One man, we were told, had been forced to attempt the rape of his Muslim next door neighbour's two daughters. He was then made to douse the entire family with petrol, subsequently incinerating them inside their own house. When the paramilitaries left, he committed suicide. By heroic contrast, the local grocer, a Serb, had defied the invaders and risked his life by concealing ten Muslims and Croats in his cellar for the duration.

What had happened in Vocin was a microcosm of what was still happening across the country. It was also beyond comprehension, and certainly beyond the scope of one small television programme, to convey the atrocities anywhere near adequately.

Even on the road out of town, where there were no obvious signs of conflict, there was no room for complacency. Every spinney, tree-clad hillside or isolated farmstead could contain a group of Slivovitz-fuelled, armed men intent on destruction.

It wasn't long before we experienced this at first hand.

We were heading for a place called Slavonski Brod on the Croatian border to see for ourselves what Arkan's Tigers had left behind them there. As we bumped and bounced through the potholed main street of one war-ravaged small town, there was a sharp burst of automatic weapon fire from our right. We saw the bullets ripping lumps out of the concrete of the building in front of us. When we looked behind, the same thing was happening to the walls of the block of flats. Somehow, the strafing had passed in an arc which appeared to have gone right through our car. We were all too shocked to speak for fifteen minutes.

It was dark when we arrived at our hotel in Slavonski Brod that night. We had telephoned ahead to make sure that our information was correct and that it was still able to give us rooms. The English-speaking manager had said there would be no problem – there would even be food available. That was a bonus. For the past couple of days provisions had been extremely scarce. We had stopped whenever we saw anything for sale by the roadside and had subsisted largely on eggs or bread offered up by local people.

Something had happened between our phone call and our arrival, however. Where the hotel restaurant had stood, there was now a smouldering hole in the ground. It had come under mortar attack in the early evening. The manager was very apologetic. There was no food available.

On the reception desk in front of us he placed five sets of keys, two cans of lager each and five black plastic bin liners.

'I can see what these are,' I said, picking up the keys. 'And these cans are probably our dinner. But what are these?' I enquired, indicating the bin liners.

'Your windows, sir.'

In the morning, windows peeled back, came two reminders of how people in the most wretched circumstances cling on to what remains of their previous, normal lives. In the shell of a block of flats opposite, there was one vaguely habitable unit. Over what remained of the balcony and across the twisted steel reinforcing rods jutting from the shattered concrete all around her, a middle-aged lady was hanging out her washing. In the street below, I could hear whistling. An old man in overalls came into view pushing a large, green municipal wheelbarrow. Along the pockmarked pavement, littered with rubble and strewn with the remains of burnt-out cars, this man was carefully sweeping up autumn leaves.

These are images I shall never forget.

Mike Garner, who now shared the camera work with Salk on tougher foreign assignments, was a resolute character who had left his native Zimbabwe a few years before to try his luck as a freelance cameraman in Britain. He had found a natural home at 'The Cook Report'. We had rapidly struck up a rapport – perhaps because of our shared colonial backgrounds. I called Garner 'The Ridgeback', after the tough and robust breed of dog favoured by some of the whites who remain in Zimbabwe.

Garner was a no-nonsense type of fellow who adapted to whichever situation he found himself in and didn't complain. When in mischievous mood, he would refer dismissively to the producers and researchers as 'blowflies' – parasites of dubious worth when compared to the journeyman camera operator.

At our next destination, Podravska Slatina, Garner made a discovery. Our shell-scarred hotel had an adjoining dance hall. There on a small, raised podium stood a splendid dust-covered drum kit, with high-hat and all.

Garner had sidled over to the drum kit and sat himself behind it. He found the sticks and started to beat out a rhythm, dropping in the odd bass beat with a push of his foot. He gained in confidence – this boy had obviously played before – and he let fly with a few drum rolls and cymbal crashes. We sat back and enjoyed the performance. Suddenly, he was silenced by the arrival of angry neighbours. Apparently, we were making too much noise. Quite how Garner's little performance could offend when, that same evening, enemy mortars had destroyed half the building, I couldn't fathom. We said goodnight and went up to bed.

We filmed the most distressing scenes over the next few days. Villagers, still grief-stricken by the carnage of a few weeks before, took us around the houses of the dead.

One man had been murdered by Arkan's thugs as he lay in his bed. All that remained was a pillow soaked in blood, now turned to the colour of the autumn leaves.

Just outside another village, there had been a horrifying discovery. The Tigers had swept in, raping or shooting housewives in aprons and head scarves like so many I had seen over the past week or so, and taking the men away into the nearby woodland. Now a shallow grave had been found. From the recently-turned soil came the dead. Grieving began again with howling and wailing that was truly distressing to witness.

We left war zones with heavy hearts. But, with the prospect of confronting the man responsible for this senseless barbarity, a little iron had entered my soul.

Two days later, our trusty Mercedes had taken us from the Bosnian and Croatian nightmare to the comparative civilisation and security of Serbian Belgrade. We were sitting in one of Arkan's chic little ice-cream parlours, just down the road from the Obilic ground. We had been told to wait there after a series of telephone calls to his 'minders'. It was quiet inside the shop. Outside, there were serried ranks of benches leading down to the football stadium, designed to catch the fans as they left after the game. Whatever else he was, Arkan definitely had an eye for business.

Before we had left our hotel, Mike Garner had put on his jacket camera, in case Arkan decided that he wanted to seize the tapes from his professional Beta camera. My radio mike was sending clean sound into the mini-recorder strapped under Garner's shoulder as well as into the 'official' camera, so even if we lost the Beta tapes we would still have broadcast-quality audio to go with whatever secret filming Garner got with the jacket camera.

Just as we thought we were never going to get our interview, two black Mercedes drew up outside the ice-cream parlour. Four large men in charcoal-grey suits climbed out of each one. They were carrying Czech-made fully automatic weapons and looked warily around them in a way they can only have seen in bad gangster movies. The little gang waited on the pavement outside the shop until another black Merc drove up. The driver got out and opened the back door. A slim, dapper figure climbed out. Arkan.

He was about five foot nine inches tall, in dark glasses and wearing an elegant, grey Armani suit. He was good-looking and had the cocky air of a man who expected to get whatever he wanted. We got up and walked out of the store to meet this ruthless murderer.

He seemed prepared to be affable. He took off his shades and we shook hands. He asked me, in fairly good English, where I should like him to sit for the interview. 'Let's do it outside, just here at this table,' I said, motioning Arkan to a chair facing out over the benches and the football ground.

Arkan lifted both hands in assent, and slid over to the seat. Garner set up the camera and I moved in next to the lens. Arkan looked across to me and squinted. Excellent. I'd got him staring at the sun. He was going to have to put on those villainous-looking shades again. Let no one be in any doubt here – appearances can sometimes be deceptive, but not in this bastard's case.

I started gently, asking him a bit about his past. He glossed over his criminal activity in Western Europe and started to portray himself as a good Serbian patriot fighting to preserve his nation and its culture. I nodded and listened. I thought to myself: 'Here I am, having a civilised conversation with a man I believe to be a genocidal psychopath.' And what was more, we were sitting in an ice-cream parlour with pretty pink tablecloths.

Whatever the consequences, I was going to have to break this cosy atmosphere and take a risk. The whole 'Cook Report' team knew I was going to do it. The reality – that we were surrounded by eight heavily-armed men in a country where law and order held little or no meaning if you disagreed with Serb supremacy – could not affect what we had planned.

I passed Arkan over some still pictures of the villagers he and his men had massacred. He started to get angry. The thin smile he had worn up until now disappeared. 'Keep up the pressure, make him lose his cool,' I thought to myself. I pressed him on the pictures. 'Don't they show that you are guilty of carrying out ethnic cleansing?' I asked.

Arkan's arrogance got the better of him and he began to boast. He was proud, he said, to be a war criminal if that meant that he was getting rid of the Moslems.

What an admission to make, I thought. You might come to regret that later. But I needed to pull things back from outright confrontation. This was a character who machine-gunned defenceless men, women and children with a whoop of delight. I guessed that he didn't have much in the way of self-control once he'd been wound up sufficiently. I backed off and asked a few easy questions. He seemed to relax and, two minutes later, I ended the interview on an easy note, saying that we had another appointment and that we had enjoyed meeting and filming him.

Arkan and his henchmen retired to a back office inside the ice-cream parlour while we dismantled the camera and sound gear. I could tell from the way they were looking at us that they hadn't yet made their minds up about the interview – or whether to let us go.

Arkan was having second thoughts about what he had said in front of the camera. Whether he himself or one of his lieutenants was weighing up the consequences of his boasting, I couldn't be sure. If he did decide that the interview shouldn't ever be shown, there would be nothing we could do to prevent his men from taking the tapes from us. I prayed that Mike Garner had got some usable footage with the jacket camera and that the radio mike had worked properly.

We sat tight and waited, feigning indifference to what was, really, quite a dangerous position. We had no allies. We were at the mercy of a mass murderer.

One of the three black Mercedes pulled away, a passenger wearing dark glasses in the back. Five minutes later, we were allowed to return to our hotel.

The Arkan film went to air at the end of October 1992. We were told that after he had seen the programme he flew into a rage. He came across as exactly the man he was – a posturing, dangerous criminal who murdered innocent and defenceless people – however macho he and his thugs tried to appear with their tiger cub and display of weapons.

Researchers at the International War Crimes Tribunal at The Hague agreed with us. A few months later, they issued ten names of people 'suspected' of war crimes committed during conflict in the former Yugoslavia. What they didn't reveal publicly then was that Arkan had already been secretly indicted for atrocities in Croatia and Serbia. To reveal that at the time, we were told, would have been to close off completely any chance of having Arkan sent to the West if Milosevic ever got fed up with him. If Milosevic had known he had a wanted war criminal in his camp, said our friends at The Hague, he'd make sure that the West never got its hands on him.

The Tigers continued with their murderous outrages – now aware of the threat of indictment for war crimes, they took to wearing IRA-style black balaclavas with slits cut for eyes and mouth. In 1995 they appeared on the battlefields of northern Bosnia, allegedly tying up their fellow countrymen and humiliating them for supposed cowardice in the face of the advancing Croatian forces.

Arkan moved into politics, forming his own party – the Serbian Unity Party – and becoming an MP. He married a glamorous pop star, Svetlana Velickovic, Serbia's leading proponent of nationalist folk song. He had become rich enough to build a huge, bunker-like house for himself and his family adjacent to his beloved Red Star Belgrade football stadium. He was courted by the media who did not dare say a bad word against him, so powerful was he.

Then, in 1999, when the Kosovo conflict blew up into full-scale war, there was Arkan again, offering to send his men into battle against the Kosovans and Albanians. They were to give support to the murderous Serb police as they moved into the province, supposedly to root out the Kosovan Liberation Army but, in truth, to evict the non-Serbian population at gunpoint. I have absolutely no doubt in my mind that it was the prospect of Arkan's Tigers rampaging mercilessly through the countryside that led to the mass exodus of the civilian Albanian population from Kosovo. Arkan's indictment is now public and his rash boast that he was 'proud to be a war criminal' will be key evidence if he ever faces justice in The Hague.

The only satisfaction I can take from my visit to the former Yugoslavia is that 'The Cook Report' was able to warn and alert people about the threat that lay waiting inside Serbia.

We came back, not to enjoy a few days' respite, but to pick up the fast-developing Triad story.

Manchester had one of the worst Triad problems in the country. Triad extortion and violence were escalating out of control in its Chinatown district. The Greater Manchester Police had even established a special Chinese Unit to help the ethnic community which was increasingly in the grip of the gangs. The extent to which the Chinese, historically a reticent and self-dependent race, were prepared to take that offer of assistance remained to be seen.

We had tried for three months to persuade a member of the Chinese community in Britain to go undercover for us in Manchester. We wanted to provide a new target for the Triads and film them in action, but the very real likelihood of reprisals made volunteers for the job of undercover agent impossible to find. Howard Foster spent weeks trying to persuade just one Chinese individual to go under-cover for us. Even men about to join the police force were too cautious to take the job on. 'You don't understand,' they would tell Foster. 'These people don't forget. You can think you are safe for ten or twenty years. Then . . .'

The unspoken ending to the sentence was usually accompanied by a chopping movement made with the outside edge of the hand – directed either at the neck or the back of the legs. If we wanted further proof that the Triads exerted an undue and illegal influence on the lives of the Chinese community in Britain, it was there in spades for the 'Cook Report' team to see in the faces of the men we were trying to get to help us.

Finally, in desperation, we cast our net wider. Clive Entwistle, trusted by Townson to deliver this difficult but potentially explosive story, approached a small, unlisted company in London which specialised in providing close personal protection for wealthy inter-national businessmen. Its boss listened to what Entwistle had to ask him and opened his contacts book at the letter H for Hong Kong.

'Give me a week, I'll find you somebody good,' he said. And we waited.

The operation had been set up in total secrecy. Howard Foster had been delegated to lose himself in Manchester's Chinatown for a few weeks to find out who the main targets and victims were. Foster, who, like me, fancied himself as a *bon viveur*, managed to incorporate several visits to Chinatown's best restaurants in the course of his research. The story soon started to take shape, as Foster started to lose his.

He made contact with one of the Chinese Unit's operational detec-tives, Roy Tildsley, a thoughtful, bearded character in his late thirties, who spoke some Cantonese and knew most of the businessmen in Chinatown. He said it would be extremely difficult to expose what was happening in the Chinese community because of the fear the Triads instilled. In four years his unit had only had one successful prosecution – and that was because Tildsley had actually been the witness to an attack outside one of Chinatown's gang-run restaurants.

He told Foster that he would help 'The Cook Report' if we could persuade his most senior commander to sanction it. Foster, Clive

Entwistle and I arranged to meet the head of Manchester CID, David James, in his office at force HQ in Old Trafford. James, an experienced officer with whom we had worked in the past, had asked Tildsley's immediate boss, Detective Chief Inspector Alan Boardman, to sit in on the meeting.

The policemen wanted to know what we planned to do and who our targets were. Tildsley, who was keen for the operation to go ahead, had confirmed what Foster was hearing about who the principal Manchester Triad leaders were and what crimes they were involved in. Foster repeated this to the senior officers and I added that 'The Cook Report' wanted to expose these people doing what they habitually did by capturing it on film. Anything we got, the police were welcome to after it had been broadcast. If it led to successful prosecutions, then so much the better.

There is always a danger involved here because any police officer worth his salt knows that the evidential requirements of a criminal court of law and that of an investigative television programme, no matter how thorough, can be poles apart. David James turned to Alan Boardman. 'Are you happy to give this a go?' Boardman looked at Tildsley.

'If Roy thinks it stands a chance, yes,' he replied.

Tildsley concealed his relief. 'If this is taken a stage at a time, is planned properly and security is kept in place, we could get somewhere, sir,' he said.

Of the many police forces that 'The Cook Report' has worked with, the Greater Manchester Police is one of the most helpful. The Obscene Publications Squad of the Metropolitan Police, with dedicated men in its ranks such as 'Moose' Donaldson, Michael Hames, Jim Reynolds and Bob MacLachlan, has also seen fit to work with us with mutually beneficial results.

I have no illusions about why policemen decide to aid a television programme like ours. There are many hurdles to clear before a decent working relationship can begin. The first may be to circumvent the force press office. That is something of a generalisation as there are some excellent people working in police press offices, but the vast majority are civilians whose sole purpose in life seems to be to obstruct something which, by common consent, is probably going to do some good.

Next, you have to identify who the detective 'on the ground' is – the person who understands and controls what is going on – and come to an understanding with him. It might come as a surprise that some of the biggest investigations carried out in Britain are in the hands of detective sergeants, constables and – if it really is a major job – detective inspectors. By that, I mean that they are the ranks most likely to be there, on the ground, dealing with the reality of any inquiry. They are the blokes to ask about what is really going on.

The more senior the police officer, the more likely it is that he or she has more than enough on his or her plate handling the day-to-day paperwork. Operations to catch criminals can often hinge on whether or not there is enough money in the kitty to pay for the necessary overtime.

Couple that with the practice of people experienced in a particular specialisation being moved into something totally unrelated to stop them getting stale or – more unlikely – corrupt, and you narrow down even further the chances of finding someone with a mind to help you.

It was with the help of David James, his uniformed opposite number Trevor Barton and Alan Boardman that 'The Cook Report' was able to identify paedophiles using internationally-based computer bulletin boards and the Internet. They seconded one of their most precious assets – the most experienced computer pornography investigator in England – Detective Sergeant John Ashley – to our Birmingham studios for six weeks. The result of this unusual joint operation between the Greater Manchester Police and the Obscene Publications Squad was four successful prosecutions and a mine of useful intelligence for the police. Not to mention a tremendous television programme that informed, involved and, yes, entertained its audience.

Researchers and producers on 'The Cook Report' always know when they have found a policeman worth talking to. They sound like real people. They admit that there are problems in the area of crime they deal with. Otherwise, they would be solving every case they investigate and never have regrets that someone got away with something they shouldn't have.

I am no apologist for the police, and if they fail in their duty they deserve to be put under close scrutiny and censured where necessary. But the reality is that in the battle for supremacy between law and order and the criminal, the latter has so many more resources at his disposal. This is where 'The Cook Report' and programmes like it can help.

No police force has all the resources it wants. With our budget and our limited aim – to expose wrongdoing and to get a television programme out of our endeavours – there is often common ground between us. Ask any decent detective if there is an individual or gang he would like to target, but which he is too busy or understaffed to give his attention to, and he will answer yes. Roy Tildsley was a policeman who recognised that we could achieve something with our resources. Once he received the sanction from his bosses, he was free to help us – and more than happy to do so. They knew we were going to make a programme that would expose the Triads in a way they could not, so why hinder it?

An elaborate and secret operation began. Our target was the feared Wo Shing Wo Triad, which ruled supreme in Manchester and the Northwest. The head of the local Triad was a man called Yau Lap Yuen, known locally as Georgie Pi. The Cantonese word Pi means 'cripple' – a reference to Georgie's limp from a hip injury sustained in a gang fight in Hong Kong. Under Georgie Pi's command, the Wo Shing Wo was raking in a fortune in weekly protection payments made by hundreds of Chinese restaurants and takeaways within a forty-mile radius of Manchester's city centre.

It was a pattern being repeated all over Britain. The Triad gangs had largely carved up the country geographically between them. Another gang, 14K, ruled in London and the Northeast. The Wo On Lok Triad was, and is, the Wo Shing Wo's deadliest rival as it operates in the same geographical areas.

Territorial conflicts between these two exploded from time to time, bringing the inevitable 'choppings' with beef knives. These were an ideal weapon for the Triads because they were so commonly used in Chinese restaurants and were thus easy to explain away if the police discovered one in a suspect's home or in his car.

The extortion from small businesses was carried out according to strictly-observed ritual. The amount each restaurateur or shop owner had to pay was often given in multiples of thirty-six, based on some ancient rule that went back to the time when the Triads were highly-secret Masonic-style societies back in China. The money had to be placed inside a red envelope and handed, once a week, to the collector. Failure to pay would bring a visit from the Triad enforcer. Sometimes, the Triads would use Vietnamese 'foot soldiers' to do their dirty business, either to chop their enemies or to ruin their restaurant businesses by taking over several large tables and sitting there all night, every night, their feet all over the tablecloths, talking loudly and generally making it unpleasant for customers trying to enjoy a meal.

The legendary Chinese love of gambling also caused trouble, either because people got so heavily into debt that they couldn't afford to pay back Triad moneylenders, or because rival gambling dens would use violence to try to put each other out of business. The New Year mah jong marathon planned by a legitimate Chinese club was called off after superglue was poured into the locks of the front door and shutters.

Frustratingly for the British police, it was very rare for a Chinese person to complain. Arrests and convictions were few and far between. Even when someone had been chopped and forced to seek help in hospital, Roy Tildsley would be told by the agonised victim that he had 'slipped onto his own knife' or that a stack of blades had fallen onto him from a kitchen cupboard. It was a difficult cultural adjustment for the British policeman to find that, after the taxman, he was the most loathed person to walk the earth.

As we started to make our programme, a gang of Vietnamese from Liverpool had run amok in the 'I Don't No' club and chopped two innocent Englishmen who ended up in hospital minus several fingers.

Georgie Pi had also been suspected of involvement in a variety of serious criminal offences in the past. All in all, he was a formidable character.

We knew that another of the illegal Triad operations was video piracy. Not the copying of mainstream Hollywood blockbusters but of the dozens of Chinese-language soap operas to which many of the inhabitants of Hong Kong are addicted. Thousands of pounds a week were being made by the wholesale duplication of the latest episodes and their rental through Triad-run outlets in and around Manchester.

'The Cook Report' decided to go into business. Roy Tildsley had noticed that a large, shabby 1930s office block on the edge of Chinatown was almost empty. A 'To Let' sign hung outside the window of a first-floor office. He jotted down the letting agent's telephone number and passed it on to Howard Foster. The landlord, an affable South Korean accountant operating from plush offices in Cheetham Hill, happily took three months' rent in advance and wished Foster luck in his new office furniture venture.

Clive Entwistle, meanwhile, had found a company in London to supply tiny video cameras to fit into the walls of the office. Early one quiet Sunday morning, before the Chinese community awoke and began to fill its shops and restaurants, Entwistle and Foster unlocked their Chinatown office and led in a small team of camera technicians, carpenters and joiners.

The plan was to hide four cameras in the walls. The workmen were to build one false wall into the office complete with a hidden door behind which would sit a bank of video recorders. By leaning on the door, our Chinese manager – once we had found one – could disappear quickly from danger into a long, narrow passageway that led to a fire door and fire escape to the street below.

The final touch was to place a microwave transmitter on the ledge outside the office window, so that live coverage of what was happening inside could be transmitted to a television screen in a hotel room a few hundred yards away in Princess Street, where a member of the team could monitor events. After three days of sneaking cables, video recorders and cameras in with the paint, ladders and plasterboard, the office was ready.

Twenty-four hours later, the personal protection company rang Entwistle and told him our man was on his way from Hong Kong. Joe Tan – not his real name – was a twenty-five-year-old working as a security manager in a commercial bank. He was owed a couple of weeks' leave and was happy to come to the UK to do the job for us.

Entwistle and Foster met Joe at Manchester Airport and took him for a drink in the bar of the Portland Thistle hotel, five hundred yards from the carefully-rigged office. Joe, tall, thin and well-dressed, spoke good English. He knew what we wanted him to do and was in total agreement. He knew all about the Triad reputation and displayed a healthy respect for their power, but he also relished the opportunity to expose them if he could.

The following Sunday – the big day of the week for the Chinese community to meet, eat and mingle around the Dragon Arch of Manchester's Chinatown – Joe and his nephew, a student at London's Imperial College, distributed leaflets all over the area advertising his company, Flying Dragon Video, sticking them through letterboxes, putting them under windscreen-wipers and handing them to Chinese passers-by. The telephone number and address of Flying Dragon Video were clearly printed on the bottom of the flyer.

Meanwhile, we had bought 500 pirate Hong Kong video tapes from a distributor in London. They had been the principal exhibits in a recent court case and each one had an adhesive label marked 'Metropolitan Police Evidence. Do Not Remove' on its case. Over two days, with the aid of white spirit and fingernails, Howard Foster scraped every label off. Roy Tildsley's Chinese secretary checked up on the current soap titles sold on the black market in Britain and wrote the titles down in Chinese on 500 new sticky labels. Attention to detail was going to be crucial when the Triads came to check out Flying Dragon Video.

Howard Foster sat in his room in the Princess Hotel watching Joe and his nephew in their office on the microwave link. An extra camera hidden on the landing outside the door gave Foster a view of the staircase leading up to it. He hadn't long to wait before the action started.

For a full hour, Foster watched as a Chinese cleaner diligently swept the same piece of stair carpet outside the office door. Every few minutes, the cleaner would lean towards the door and peer through the keyhole. He was clearly checking out how many people were inside the office.

Suddenly, a group of men in jeans and bomber jackets appeared in Foster's bottom right-hand TV screen. They had come into the hallway and were moving, single-file, up the stairs. Foster recognized two of them as suspected Triad foot-soldiers. One, Patrick Keung, who was leading the group, ran the Triad pirate video shop in Chinatown. At his shoulder was the athletic figure of Simon Chan.

Chan was suspected by the police of instigating a series of knife attacks by Vietnamese thugs in the area in recent weeks.

Foster counted six men going into the Flying Dragon office. Two more stayed outside. Known as the Look See boys, they would keep an eye out for unexpected visitors or the police.

Patrick Keung walked through the office door. He walked up to Joe, who was sitting at his desk, demanding to know who he and his helper were, and how they dared try to set up in business on his patch. Simon Chan advanced on Joe, the secret escape door hidden by a large movie poster behind his back. Joe's nephew was cut off at the other end of the office.

Simon Chan dialled out on his mobile phone and spoke loudly in Hokkien, the dialect used by Triad members. The later translation told us that he was talking to his brother, Alan Chan. He called Alan 'Big Brother', a Triad term commonly used by junior members to address senior ones. Simon Chan said that the newcomers seemed to have a full stock of up-to-date tapes. He listened, nodded and handed the phone to Patrick Keung, who listened briefly and then shouted an order to the others and all hell broke loose.

One of the gang aimed an accurate karate kick at the piles of videos, sending them crashing to the floor. Another lifted a heavy steel office chair and brought it down on Joe's head. His nephew was punched, kicked and had his glasses smashed and ground into his face. Simon Chan picked up Joe's own mobile telephone and rammed it into Joe's face. Foster, watching the horrific scene unfold in front of him, dialled the police and an ambulance.

At that moment one of the Look See boys rushed into the office and shouted urgently to Patrick Keung. Keung ran out of the room, gesturing to the others to follow. Luckily for Joe and his nephew something had spooked the lookouts and the beating was over – for the time being.

Foster also telephoned Clive Entwistle at his home in Rochdale, about twenty minutes drive from Chinatown. It had been Entwistle's fiftieth birthday the day before and he had hosted a massive fancy-dress party from which he and just about every other member of the Cook team was trying to recover. Entwistle shrugged off his half-century hangover, climbed into his car and headed for Manchester.

I travelled up to Manchester that Sunday night and went straight to the Royal Infirmary. Foster and Entwistle were standing by Joe Tan's bed in a private side ward. Joe was being treated for concussion, deep head wounds and a crushed finger, hit as he tried to protect himself from the chair. His nephew was being treated for cuts to his face.

Joe volunteered to be interviewed in his hospital bed about what had happened. His mobile phone had been taken by Simon Chan, an invitation, Joe believed, to call and talk turkey about protection payments from Flying Dragon Video.

We filmed as he dialled his own number on the hospital telephone. He spoke in Mandarin for about a minute. 'They want me to meet them in the Kwok Man Restaurant tomorrow night,' he said.

'Do you feel like going on with this?' I asked him.

'Of course, I shall see this through,' he answered. We left him to get some sleep and went off to plan how we handled Monday night.

We decided to put Howard Foster and three of our occasional helpers – all burly lads – into the restaurant before Joe arrived. They carried two cameras hidden in briefcases. Once Joe had walked in and sat down, the lenses would be pointed in his direction. He was under strict orders to stay put, whatever happened.

Monday evening came. The 'Cook Report' contingent took up their places in the restaurant and ordered food. They saw Joe arrive and sit down – and waited for something to happen. Twenty minutes went by, then one of the guys who had attacked Joe the night before walked in. He had an urgent, whispered conversation with the manager who pointed towards the solitary figure of Joe Tan. The young gangster sauntered over to Joe's table and leaned towards him.

Foster watched in alarm as Joe stood up and walked with his visitor to the door of the restaurant and out into the street. This was exactly what Joe had been told not to do.

Foster followed as soon as he could without alerting the restaurant staff. Outside, he looked up and down Princess Street. No sign of Joe. He called Entwistle. He was with the cameraman, Grahame Wickings, filming the scene outside the Kwok Man from the manager's office in the Princess Hotel. They had seen Joe leave with the gang member and were already on their way to see what was going on.

Five anxious minutes passed and then Foster saw something that made his pulse-rate leap. There, weaving drunkenly through five lanes of traffic, was the slim figure of Joe Tan. His arms and body were shaking and shuddering. He was screaming and trying to flag down passing motorists. Foster dodged into the traffic and reached Joe just as he passed out. He carried him to the pavement and, for the second time in two days, called an ambulance for him.

Joe came round. 'My legs, my legs!' he screamed. He sat up and pulled both his shoes off. His feet were grotesquely twisted and swollen. He grasped them and moaned. 'They going to kill me – and you. We've got to get out of here,' he shouted, looking over his shoulder in panic. Entwistle arrived and hailed a taxi and the two men lifted poor Joe into the back and went with him to the MRI.

Over the next few days, we got the story out of Joe. When he had left the Kwok Man restaurant he had been taken to another Chinatown restaurant, the Pearl City. The Pearl City was on the second floor of an old office building and was reached by a wide staircase that wound round a deep stairwell. Joe had been placed at a table well away from the other diners. The gang member who took him there assured him that there would be no trouble if he co-operated.

Then several of Joe's attackers from the previous night walked over to Joe and formed a semi-circle around him, shielding him from the rest of the room. One of the men motioned Joe into the toilets.

Joe realised he was in mortal danger and took matters into his own hands. As he was being led to the toilets, he made a lunge for the main entrance of the restaurant and made it through to the top of the staircase. As the Triads came after him, he jumped over the banisters and dropped two floors down into the stairwell, landing awkwardly on his feet at tremendous velocity. He heard a horrible crunch as he landed.

How he managed to struggle out of that building and back down the street for help, he never knew. He was taken straight into an emergency ward and an orthopaedic surgeon was called. He told us that Joe's 'jelly bones' under his feet were both smashed. It would be a long time before he would be able to walk again – and even then it was likely that he would have a limp. In the meantime, he would be confined to a wheelchair.

This was shocking news. Back in the Birmingham office, Joe's plight cast a shadow over everyone as we ran up to the opening of the series.

Townson, quite rightly, decided to run the Triads programme first. We had been busy for days identifying Joe's assailants from still photographs – known as 'grabs' – taken from the video footage we had obtained from the hidden cameras in the Flying Dragon office. We later found out that Patrick Keung, Simon Chan and a couple of others were already known to the police. The remainder, thanks to the help of the few Chinese who informed to the police about Triad activity, were eventually identified.

Part of Joe Tan's cover story had been that he was a member of a small Hong Kong Triad anxious to spread its influence to Britain. He had tried to get this across to the thugs who had marched into the offices of Flying Dragon Video before they attacked him. Proof that he had succeeded came a day or so later.

Howard Foster and sound recordist Dennis Fitch had been told that Alan Chan and his men were using The Pleasure Restaurant for meetings and for lunch. Foster and Fitch had placed themselves as customers at a corner table to see if they could get some secretly-filmed footage of him.

Fitch saw Alan Chan walk in and immediately slid the attaché case with its tiny camera onto a chair, pointing the lens at the short, smiling figure chatting to his men as he stood five yards from the Cook team.

'He looks a bit nervous, don't you think?' murmured Foster.

'He does,' replied Fitch. 'And he keeps fidgeting with his coat sleeves.'

Later, when they watched the tape, they saw what Chan was doing. Clearly visible in the palm of his hand was the handle of a beef knife. The fourteen-inch blade was tucked up the sleeve of his expensive, cashmere overcoat – possibly in case reprisals were launched at him by Joe Tan's imaginary Triad colleagues.

We decided to confront Georgie Pi with what we had on him. We knew that Georgie Pi had, technically, entered the country in breach of a deportation order. A helpful Immigration Department official had shown Foster a file on the man, three inches thick. He had won his spurs as a Triad member in Hong Kong thirty years earlier – befriending, then seducing, an underage girl whom he then launched into a life of prostitution, a common procedure amongst the lower level of Triad.

Years went by and Georgie married Sandy Wai, another Hong Kong national who had obtained the right to live in Britain after she had married – and divorced – a British passport holder. But Georgie's past, and the fact that he had received a criminal conviction in the 1970s, had led to a refusal by the Home Office to allow him into Britain. Nevertheless, on at least two occasions he had been found here and kicked out. Now he was here and allowed to stay while his case was under review. In the meantime, he had to report to Stockport police station every weekend. And that was where we confronted him.

As I walked up to him and asked him what he was doing in Britain and how he earned his living, he turned tail and limped rapidly back up the steps of the police station. We followed him inside, still asking questions. He rang the desk sergeant's bell angrily, shouting that he was being harassed and that we should all be arrested. But the desk staff had conveniently retired to a back room. Pi was on his own and rapidly losing face.

'It's illegal, what you're doing, right,' he shouted.

'No, you're the one that's illegal,' I replied as Georgie Pi stomped furiously away into the night.

For the next few days just before the programme was due for broadcast, we started to hear rumours that Georgie Pi was on the warpath. He had lost an enormous amount of face through my confrontation with him. Almost overnight he had gone from powerful ogre to virtual laughing stock in the eyes of the local Chinese community. His anger was mounting as the prospect of his discomfort being shown to ten million people on their television screens drew near.

There was, according to informants, a contract to be taken out on the lives of Howard Foster and myself. By whom, exactly, wasn't yet clear. Then, a few weeks later, Howard Foster had a telephone call from a senior detective in one of the regional crime squads. A known Wo Shing Wo 'enforcer' had been arrested in London on suspicion of extortion. When he was searched, he had Foster's home and mobile telephone numbers written on a small piece of paper. I didn't tell Frances, trusting that the arrest of the enforcer would deter the Triads from taking matters any further.

On the evening of the broadcast of the Triad programme, Roy Tildsley and a uniformed colleague, Mike Gallagher, arrested as many of the suspects as possible who had been filmed attacking Joe Tan. Tildsley knew where four, possibly five, would be with friends around the restaurants, bars and clubs of Chinatown, and he positioned himself in an observation point overlooking the area. Walkie-talkie in hand, he would move in a squad of uniformed officers to make the arrests.

The programme was due to be broadcast at 8.30 on the evening of 12 January 1993. Just after five o'clock, Central Television's legal department in Birmingham received an urgent phone call from Mishcon de Reya, then the company's London solicitors. Lawyers representing Mr Yau Lap Yuen – Georgie Pi – were about to appear before a judge in the High Court in London seeking to prevent the broadcast of 'The Cook Report' programme on Triad activity in Manchester because they believed it harmed the reputation of their client.

Facing the prospect of losing a programme at the hands of a lawyer inevitably makes me angry, even more so when you know that the person bringing the action is a criminal who merely wants to hide what he has done from the public. Fortunately, High Court judges had taken a fairly consistent line on issues like this for some time. If a libel might be broadcast by a programme-maker, they reasoned that provided the company maintained it could prove what it said it could go ahead, and let the litigant sue afterwards. That's what I, Townson and Bob Southgate, who was always called in when trouble like this loomed, fervently hoped would happen in this case.

Townson had an even more pressing problem on his hands. If, by some horrible mischance, the judge agreed with Georgie Pi's lawyers, what would be broadcast in the place of the Triad programme? Graham Puntis, the videotape editor, was hurriedly cocooned in his room with fifty tapes, and was busily assembling the alternative – a programme on prescription drugs that killed people. Like the Triad programme, it was strong stuff, but needed rather a lot of work on it before it was ready. Townson worked away with Puntis. Southgate and I sat next to the telephone in his office, awaiting the verdict. I crossed my fingers and trusted to British justice.

Six o'clock slipped by, then seven. The phone rang. It was Entwistle and Foster. They were in the bar of the Princess Hotel in Manchester, waiting to see how the evening's arrests went. Roy Tilsdsley was desperate to move in on the suspects but had orders to hold off until the court decision came through. At least one of them had moved out of the immediate area, making his apprehension difficult once the filmed evidence of what he had done was televised.

We couldn't help. It was in the hands of the lawyers and the judge, and they were taking a hell of a time coming to the decision we were praying for.

It was almost 8.10 when Mishcon called us back. The judge had thrown out Georgie Pi's application for an injunction. We were clear to play the tape. Talk about cutting it fine. Over a glass of Sancerre, Bob Southgate and I both agreed we didn't want to go that close to the wire again.

The programme was one of the most successful we had ever done, on a number of levels. Even today, seven years on, people still vividly remember its action: particularly that image of poor Joe Tan weaving painfully through the traffic. The violence of the Triads against him was shocking and brought home the reality that they were a criminal force to be reckoned with.

Joe remained in a wheelchair for almost two years. He flew home to see his parents in Hong Kong and returned, telling us that he was unable to live in his home country again. News of his role in the programme had quickly filtered through. Copies of the show were in the hands of the Triads. He was told he was a marked man and that he had better stay away. The problem was, he told us, that retribution did not have to be swift where the Triads were concerned. They would wait twenty years for revenge if necessary. Central Television paid for Joe's private treatment and for his relocation abroad, where he has since made a full recovery and now works successfully in the computer industry. When last heard of, Joe, a good-looking, single fellow, was enjoying himself with the young ladies of his adopted country.

In between operations and relocating himself, Joe made lengthy statements to the police to help make the prosecutions stick. One or two more gang members were arrested at their homes. Two fled to Hong Kong and were caught months later when they tried to re-enter Britain.

The effect of the programme on life in Chinatown was dramatic. For more than six months, the Triads stopped all illegal activity. Small businesses were left alone. No one came round asking for the red envelopes. Georgie Pi, no longer a power in the Wo Shing Wo, relocated to Cheltenham where he reinvented himself as an honest, hard-working restaurateur in the hope that he would be allowed to stay in Britain. To that end, he instructed his lawyers to sue us for defamation, an action that has lain dormant since 1995. Puzzlingly, he is now legally resident in the UK.

Alan Chan went back to running his restaurant, but was recently convicted of taking part in an affray in a Manchester casino.

Patrick Keung and the rest of the gang appeared at Preston Crown Court to face charges of violent disorder – attacking and threatening Joe Tan. The case came up about a year after the programme had been broadcast and, given how badly injured Joe had been, there was a little concern amongst Roy Tildsley and his colleagues that he might not return from the Far East to give his vital evidence.

We needn't have worried. Joe Tan arrived at Heathrow and was driven to Preston where his testimony helped to get Patrick Keung two years in jail. Three others got between two and a half and eighteen months imprisonment.

The Triad programme had been a violent one, but it hadn't directly affected my health – discounting the death threats from the Chinese gangsters. I finished that series in remarkably good shape, having done relatively little international travel. But the respite was about to end. Two stories were surfacing that would push several of the 'Cook Report' team right to the edge – physically and mentally. Myself included.

I recall the programmes 'The Cook Report' has made for lots of different reasons. We might have helped to get the law changed or perhaps I had been able to visit countries I had never seen before. But the programme we made to expose the illegal fishing habits of the Spanish trawler fleet will remain with me for ever because of the sheer violence we experienced – both from the elements out at sea and from the people of one small Spanish fishing town who objected to us exposing how they broke international law.

The story was one of those that grew out of another, unrelated inquiry, and illustrates perfectly how one can never tell where and when ideas will spring up from. We were prompted to make the programme by a chance remark. Producer Steve Warr had been in Ireland, filming the Irish Rangers searching for an IRA arms cache, which they believed was hidden in woodland outside Dublin. The Provos had been busy in Britain in early 1993 blowing up trains and we were making a programme to show how easy it was to obtain explosives from all manner of sources.

In the regiment's mess one evening, Warr found himself chatting over a drink to the military attaché for the Irish Defence Forces. The day's filming had been eventful. The Irish soldiers had been using a new computer system, housed in a mobile caravan, to trace the arms cache. The power supply for the equipment was provided by a generator which, for some reason, had cut out at a crucial moment. Warr had been outside when the generator was re-started. A freak power surge overloaded the computer, and it exploded.

The operator and his officers came out of the caravan spluttering and coughing, their faces blackened, their eyebrows and hair singed. After chuckling at the humour of the situation, the attaché told Warr that IRA ammunition dumps and faulty computers apart, his biggest headache was controlling the 'Spanish pirates'. Warr asked him what he meant and was told that Ireland's naval patrol vessels were spending most of their time chasing Spanish trawlers, which were either fishing where they weren't supposed to be or catching undersized fish and hiding them in secret holds concealed below decks. Warr was intrigued.

Even more interestingly, the Spanish boats often flew 'flags of convenience', sailing with a token British member of crew to qualify as a British-registered vessel, thus allowing it to operate in British and Irish waters. The Irish clearly saw Spanish trawler activity as a threat to their own fishing industry.

The evening ended with an invitation to Warr to join an Irish naval ship on patrol to see the problem for himself. Townson sanctioned the trip and Warr spent several days at sea. The navy boat was equipped with the latest satellite and radar gear and it wasn't long before he witnessed the crew boarding one of the 'pirates.'

Once on board, the navy crew resorted to less sophisticated but equally effective methods of investigation. The leader of the boarding crew pulled out a tape measure and ordered his men to check the height of the exterior of the upper and lower decks. Two naval ratings then disappeared to measure the interior height of the two decks. There was a discrepancy of five feet. This begged the question of what was filling the five-foot space inside the boat. The Spaniards obviously knew they had been rumbled – they looked sullen and their captain began to argue.

The Irishmen dropped down to the bottom of the hold and began their search. One called out to his skipper five minutes later. He had found a trapdoor hidden under a carpet in the crew's quarters. The door was lifted. Down below, glinting in the torchlight, was box upon box of undersized hake packed in ice – the tiny fish were all about three inches long and a popular delicacy in Spain. But the illegal fishing was a real threat to the survival of the fish stocks of those countries prepared to wait for the fish to grow to the legal length of about a foot.

When he reached dry land, Warr telephoned Townson to tell him what he'd seen. Townson responded in typically blunt fashion: 'Steve, can you find a hidden hold and undersized fish being landed in Spain, and can we film all that?'

'Yes,' Warr replied. He heard the heavy pounding of Townson's thick fingers on his desktop computer keys before the editor hung up. It looked as if 'Spanish Pirates' was going to go ahead.

For the next fortnight, on the advice of the Irish Defence Attaché, Warr visited every Irish coastal town that boasted a courthouse. He took details of every recent conviction of a Spanish trawler for illegal fishing. He then spent a full week cross-referencing the details with those of the trawlers' owners. His research showed that the Spanish had chosen three British centres to register their boats – Cornwall, Wales and Scotland. There were no fewer than 250 Spanish trawlers operating in Irish and British waters. Warr discovered that several had a dozen convictions or more.

The worst offender was a boat called the *Juan Mari*, which had been caught and convicted seventeen times.

'Where's that one registered to?' asked Townson.

Warr checked his paperwork. 'Cornwall.'

'And where does this boat really land its catches?' demanded Townson.

A little port on the Spanish Basque coast called Ondarroa, Warr's records told him.

'Find out what sort of place it is – and are they up to no good?' was Townson's parting shot.

Warr telephoned Nigel Bowden, our 'man on the Costas'.

'It's ETA country,' said Bowden. 'You go in there and show what they are up to and you've got trouble.'

ETA, the violent Basque separatist organisation, had a reputation even more fearsome than that of the IRA. Over the years it had murdered thousands of people it perceived as enemies from all walks of life. Presumably, television presenters who made trouble for their local supporters would fall into their definition of 'enemy'.

Bowden rang Warr back an hour later to tell him that Ondarroa was in that week's headlines. ETA had just blown up the local Customs post there. 'Even the cops don't dare go in there,' he warned. 'I suppose I can expect Roger tomorrow.'

Bowden had performed the dual role of investigator and interpreter for 'The Cook Report' in Spain several times. He knew what to expect, and always accepted the role with enthusiasm disguised as bad grace.

First, we needed to go out on the high seas to film the Spanish trawlermen at work. Warr, Mike Garner, sound recordist Dennis Fitch and I joined the Irish patrol vessel the *Eithne* in Dublin. She was a frigate equipped with sophisticated tracking gear and a reconnaissance helicopter. We were due to be on board her for a week.

Unfortunately, however beautifully appointed a ship may be it still has to go out to sea, which is something I have never been particularly comfortable with. The waters in question were the roughest I have ever seen. As we cruised slowly out of the calm of the harbour, it hit us. Force Ten strengthening to Force Twelve, the captain announced.

Warr and Fitch started taking sea-sickness tablets straightaway. Garner and I held back on the grounds that they did no good anyway.

Filming was impossible for the foreseeable future so I went to my cabin, already feeling unwell.

'You've gone green, Roger,' said Warr as he clung unsteadily to a handrail. 'Are you sure you don't want some of these tablets?'

I stayed below for two full days, alternating between lying in my rocking bunk and throwing up in the heads – the ship's toilets. Every day, some poor crew member had to hose them down. Even the crew was beginning to succumb to seasickness. Only Garner seemed able to withstand the buffeting and keep his food down. I had to admire the constitution of 'The Ridgeback'. He had a stomach of iron.

When the storm finally died down a bit, Garner set up his tripod on the bridge, ready to film my interview with the captain. Then, suddenly, the sea got its revenge. 'I've got to put my camera down,' he announced, before rushing to the side of the ship.

It seems strange to relate that getting up in the air in the ship's helicopter was a calming experience, but it really was marvellous to break free of that awful heeling and rolling and feel the relative stability of flight.

While we were in the air, trying to keep the camera steady, the pilot spotted a Spanish trawler, the *Orlamar*, its nets spread out behind it. It had no licence to be fishing in those waters. The pilot radioed the bridge and the *Eithne*'s skipper decided to take a closer look. When we landed back on the *Eithne*, Garner joined the Irish navy boys in the inflatable Zodiac boarding craft. Dennis Fitch fitted the boarding officer with a microphone and DAT mini-tape recorder so that we could get an audio record of what had happened to go with our film. The prospect of my clambering aboard a rocking and hostile Spanish trawler was still too much for me to contemplate. I stayed behind.

The trawler was stuffed full of tiny hake, which Garner duly filmed, and the Irish prepared to escort the trawler to the nearest harbour at Castletown Bere. Thankfully, the arrest meant that we could, at last, get off the infernal boat. As we stepped off the tender and on to the quayside, we all fell victim to that cruel trick the inner ear plays upon people daft enough to take to the high seas. Terra firma became anything but, and we reeled around the quay like a group of friends returning from a long pub-crawl – flinging our arms around each other for mutual support and giggling in relief at having made it to dry land at last.

The town's only taxi drew up at the end of the quay. Its owner politely asked us if we would like to be taken to our hotel. He seemed to know exactly who we were and what we were doing. There would be no charge for the service, he informed us.

The kind treatment continued after we checked into the small guest house and were told that we were expected at the town's only wine bar for a meal and drinks. The owner greeted us at the door. 'Mr Cook, you're a famous man. Welcome. Come in and enjoy yourself.'

We had the crew of the *Eithne* to thank. They had told the locals about the programme we were making about the 'Spanish Pirates' and, because the town relied upon its own fishing industry for survival, they naturally concluded that we were doing something good.

In court, the Spanish skipper decided to claim that he had been set up by the navy to get a film crew aboard his vessel. He asserted that Garner had forced his way on board illegally. Thanks to Fitch's mini-recorder, however, the court was able to hear the Irish officer telling the trawler that he had a film crew with him and asking if it was all right to bring the camera on board. The Spanish skipper could clearly be heard saying that it was perfectly okay.

The trawler crew was convicted of illegal fishing and was fined £60,000. The trawler was to remain anchored off Castletown Bere until the fine was paid.

Townson also wanted us to film with a British trawler and interview the fishermen about the Spaniards and the 'flagging' that gave them the right to fish in British waters. So, we headed for Newlyn in Cornwall: the same members of the 'Cook Report' team, and exactly the same weather.

Only this time, we weren't in a nice big frigate but in a small trawler that bobbed and dipped around like a cork in the water. It stank of fish and diesel in equal, noxious measure. It didn't seem to bother the skipper one little bit but, ten minutes out of Newlyn harbour, as we headed for the Isles of Scilly, I felt the urgent need to throw up.

Garner couldn't keep the camera steady, and the waves were getting bigger. Warr – and the captain – decided it was time to turn back. I stood at the back of the bridge, hanging on to a handrail and throwing up off the side of the boat. We had just got back to the comparative safety and calm of the outer harbour when we were struck by a massive freak wave that pushed the boat over at ninety degrees. I disappeared completely under water. If I hadn't already been gripping the rail as tightly as I could with both hands, I would have been swept under the boat and God knows what would have happened.

As I surfaced, I heard Warr shout, 'Where's Roger? Oh, shit!' Everyone looked at me. I was soaked from head to toe, and still wanting very much to keep being sick. I was told later that no self-respecting drowned rat would have let itself slip into such a state of dishevelment.

The skipper told us that the weather was now improving and suggested we might like to head out to sea again. Warr told him in no uncertain terms that we were heading home and that that was it for the day.

Over the next few weeks, we filmed a variety of ingenious illegal fishing ruses worked by the 'flagged' Spanish trawlers. Extra holds full either of undersized or illegal quota fish were found hidden in crew quarters, behind wardrobes and in secret tunnels running the length of the boat. The extra storage room increased the catching capacity of these Spanish vessels by as much as fifty per cent. In Gibraltar, we found a boat builder who confessed to building most new trawlers with the hidden compartment already installed.

It was time to head for Ondarroa to get the evidence on the *Juan Mari* and her sister ships. Mindful of the need for caution, Garner, Warr and Bowden arrived in the village and posed as an Australian film crew keen to do some filming about EEC fishing policy. The British and Irish navies kept in touch with us and told us when the known 'pirates' like the *Juan Mari* were about to arrive back in Ondarroa.

Strangely, these boats always landed their catches under cover of darkness. By some miracle, the 'Australian crew' also favoured night-time working and, within two weeks, had filmed the *Juan Mari* landing six tonnes of minuscule hake and ten times its legal quota of cod.

An unsuspecting dockers' union man told us that for every five hundred boxes of fish his members landed for the trawlers, two hundred, at least, were illegal. The trouble with the British, he sneered, was that they were stupid enough to obey all the rules. 'Here, if something doesn't suit you, you just ignore it, don't you?' he said.

He also added that if ever this was exposed, or filmed, Warr, Garner and Fitch would undoubtedly end up in the harbour along with all their equipment.

The EU had recently tried to investigate the crooked fishing at Ondarroa but when the officials had arrived in the village, they had been told that there were no hotel rooms available in the entire region. This blatant untruth delayed the investigation and allowed all the undersized fish to be moved out of the village and off to the wholesalers before any of the officials could see what the fishermen were up to.

It was time to confront the fishermen of Ondarroa. Our team consisted of Garner, Fitch, Bowden, a former British fisheries inspector who had brought along a measure to check the size of the fish being landed that evening on the Ondarroa dockside, Derek Ive, a British photographer based in Madrid, and myself.

As we walked down to the harbour, we were spotted. A cry went up and people streamed out of the fishing sheds and storehouses to see what we were doing.

I led our group up to the owner of one of the trawlers that was openly unloading box upon box of three-inch hake. I started to ask him what he was doing bringing in illegal fish. His response was to grab hold of the camera. He shouted, 'These bastards are trying to shop us. Come on and help me.'

Suddenly, the quayside was full of people. They advanced on us threateningly. Some were carrying bill hooks, others had long wooden poles used for dragging the boxes of fish around. The situation looked ugly. I kept on asking questions but was drowned out by the shouting mob. Suddenly, they were on us. I remember Derek Ive trying to reason with the crowd. It was no use.

They wanted Garner's camera. He and I both grabbed hold of it and held on for dear life. There was no time to think of retreat. This wasn't about being brave, it was about pure survival. There wasn't even fear, just the sense that one had to get on with the job and the consequences would take care of themselves.

About ten Spaniards tried to take the camera from us. There was a brief see-saw tussle and I felt both my elbows click. They had been pulled out of their sockets. I let go and they clicked back in again. Now Garner was being hit with the hooked poles. He was bleeding from an ugly, gaping head wound.

The crowd had the camera and the lighting gear. We had given Derek Ive a Hi–8 camera as a fall-back if something like this happened. But the crowd had taken that as well. Everything was hurled straight off the edge of the dock and into the harbour.

The crowd's blood was up. They rained blows down on all of us. Some threw fish at us. They were all shouting. We could not escape and had to take it. We were all getting hit, but I was really concerned for Mike Garner, who was losing quite a lot of blood. Surely the police must have seen what was going on. There were 600 people after our blood and the forces of law and order were nowhere to be seen.

The back of my legs were being hit with the wooden poles. Our fisheries inspector was trying to defend himself with his plastic measuring board. Empty fish crates crashed down on our heads. A chant rose up.

'What are they saying now?' I asked Bowden.

'String them up, I'm afraid,' he replied. Things weren't looking good.

Then, just as I thought we were about to be thrown in the sea or end up swinging from the nearest lamppost, the crowd seemed to lose interest and started to move away. In five minutes, they were gone.

'They realised we had no evidence because they'd chucked all the gear into the water,' Nigel Bowden explained. 'Good job they don't know what we've filmed here over the past few weeks.'

I reminded him, 'It's only a matter of time before they remember that you're that Australian crew that was here for all those night-time shoots. Then they'll come back and really do for us.'

We were just getting ready to get into our cars and drive as far away from Ondarroa as possible when a police car showed up. The two officers had seen what was going on but had decided it was wiser to stay well away until the danger from the crowd had passed.

The senior officer spoke angrily to Nigel Bowden for two minutes. 'Well?' I asked.

'He's saying that he could arrest us either for causing a riot or breach of the peace,' said Bowden.

We left as quickly as we could, and I have never returned to Ondarroa. We didn't give up on retrieving our tapes and camera gear, though. First, we tried to hire a team of divers locally to go into the harbour waters for us. When we explained the circumstances, the refused to take the job. Eventually Townson agreed that we could fly in a team from Britain. When the locals spotted the two-man team preparing to make their first dive, a delegation was sent over to them. The lead diver later told us that he had been told that whatever 'The Cook Report' was paying to recover the tapes, the people of Ondarroa would double it.

None of us on the quayside on the night of the attack could pinpoint exactly where the tapes and kit had been thrown and, after two or three days, the divers called the search off. Matters were made more difficult because, in their panic at being filmed, the fishermen had thrown a lot of their over-quota and undersized fish over the side of their boats – leaving a putrefying carpet of rotting carcasses all over the sea bed.

As a result of our programme, the Spanish fisheries inspectorate made a face-saving visit to Ondarroa. Another riot broke out immediately and the inspectors were forced to shelter inside a fish shed until the crowd were satisfied that none of their boats was going to be inspected. As far as I know, the situation is still the same.

My legs were black and blue from the beating they'd received. Garner needed half a dozen stitches in his head. Everyone had been badly bruised and shaken.

The programme caused much indignation when it was broadcast. Questions were asked of the Spanish in the European Parliament and, for a while at least, our Fisheries Protection vessels increased their searches of the Spanish 'flagged' trawlers. But, at the end of the day, that British flag entitled them to fish where, perhaps, they morally should not and unless a frigate was to sit by those trawlers day in, day out, the illegal fishing was bound to resume sooner or later.

Back in the Birmingham office, we looked at the still photographs

Derek Ive had managed to take of us all on the Ondarroa quayside just after the attack. I stared at the pictures and felt shocked at what I saw. I looked exhausted, washed out. Mike Garner was battered and bleeding. We could all have been killed. Was it worth it?

The tabloid press seemed to think so. They carried the quayside pictures with bold headlines condemning the 'Spanish Pirates'. The intrepid 'telly supersleuth' had done it again, exposing wrongdoing on an international scale.

For months, there had been occasional newspaper reports, mainly tucked away in the foreign pages, of nuclear material being smuggled out of the former Soviet Union for sale illegally in the West. In just twelve months, the German police had made no fewer than 160 seizures of radioactive chemicals – all of it on its way to, so far, unidentified groups keen to obtain the capability to manufacture nuclear weapons.

The World Trade Center in New York had just been bombed by Moslem extremists. Was it only a matter of time before one of these fanatical organisations got hold of enough plutonium to rig up a small bomb to be detonated in another Western city?

Clive Entwistle and Paul Calverley were on the case. Some friends of Mike Garner worked for Greenpeace. They were in touch with a young Russian journalist who had contacts with the gangs selling weapons-grade plutonium, and much more besides.

Entwistle went to Moscow to meet the reporter – Kyril – to see if he would help. Subject to certain conditions – that neither he nor his contacts would be filmed or identified in any way, he agreed. He reminded Entwistle that the people we would be dealing with were dangerous and that we had to be very careful. I flew out to Moscow to meet him. He was young and, understandably, nervous. We persuaded him that we had the expertise and the resources to carry off a 'sting' on his contacts.

The plan was that I would pose as the representative of a Middle Eastern organisation keen to buy Plutonium 239 – the essential ingredient for putting together a small nuclear bomb. Back in Britain, we hired a consultant nuclear engineer, John Large, to see if it would be possible to make such a weapon. The simple answer was yes. In fact, the prospect of an attack using one had been worrying the experts for some time. It already had a name – a 'dirty bomb' – so called because it would be rudimentary, inefficient but, nonetheless, deadly whether it triggered properly or just dispersed millions of nuclear particles over the immediate, highly-populated area.

John Large built us a replica 'dirty bomb' small enough to fit into a briefcase. It was frightening to click open such a commonplace piece of baggage and see the tubular, pre-assembled nuclear unit inside, complete with plutonium core and battery-operated timing and detonation devices.

Another expert told us in interview that a small terrorist group would quite easily be able to find the necessary components if they were properly funded. In Moscow, we were hoping to prove that he was right.

Mike Garner joined Entwistle and me in Moscow. He and secret filming equipment wizard Alan Harridan had hurriedly created two cameras that were built into clothing, which Garner was to use when meeting the gang. In a series of cloak and dagger meetings at the Slavjanskaya hotel, Kyril helped us to plan our visit to the gang's HQ. He was beginning to have second thoughts about what was about to happen, and was only just holding his nerve.

The following morning, Garner and I were joined by Kyril and two heavy-looking characters with bulges under their coats – Kyril's underworld 'contacts' – and we set off in an impressive-looking hire car for one of Moscow's outer suburbs. Eventually we stopped in front of a gloomy, low-rise, pre-war apartment block in a surprisingly leafy street. Kyril led us to the front door of a scruffy, ground-floor flat and rapped nervously on the frosted glass.

The door opened and a dishevelled man in his thirties waved us quickly inside. He invited us to sit down in a makeshift office, which centred on a rickety desk, bare but for a telephone. Garner sat down last, making sure he could get a good shot of our host with the camera which was built into the breast pocket of his denim jacket.

The man introduced himself as Gennady. He said that he could obtain most nuclear materials from a variety of sources. He pointed to the telephone. We just had to tell him what we needed and he would make the call to his 'business partner', who would arrange delivery. I told him that we wanted twenty-five kilograms of plutonium for our Middle Eastern clients. Gennady didn't bat an eyelid. He picked up the receiver and dialled his friend. They spoke in Russian for a minute, then Gennady put the phone down and talked to Kyril. The journalist translated that weapons-grade plutonium would cost $15 million dollars a kilo but that for a large order such as we were placing, Gennady was prepared to close the deal for $200 million dollars. Had we wanted a uranium/plutonium mixture, we could have had it straight away. As it was, pure plutonium would take a little while to obtain.

He had uranium and plutonium straightaway? I asked.

Gennady smiled and told us to stay where we were. He walked over to a cupboard under his staircase. He reached inside and, with a grimace, hauled something into the room – a lead-covered container about two feet high. Suddenly Garner dropped forward onto his knees. My God, I thought. He's been irradiated. In fact, he was just trying to film the lettering and codes stamped on the outside of the canister with his secret camera, while appearing to want to check out the details for his own professional satisfaction.

Before we left, Gennady gave us a small sample of nuclear material from the container so that 'our people' could have it tested to prove he could deliver what we wanted. I hoped to God that the small container he'd given us was leakproof. Everything seemed so ramshackle and amateur – a scruffy man in a cardigan operating from a shabby flat with weapons-grade nuclear material hidden under his stairs. My blood ran cold. We left Gennady with a handshake and agreed that we would come back to him as soon as we had spoken to our clients in the Middle East.

After the meeting, it was clear that Kyril wasn't happy with what we were doing. It was just about the last time we saw him – and I can't say that I blamed him. We were all very nervous. In his absence, however, we were without an interpreter for our covert meetings with Gennady. We could hardly approach one of the translation agencies and ask for someone to come and tell us when the Mafia man was planning to deliver our plutonium.

In the meantime, our sample had been taken to the Atomic Energy Ministry laboratories in central Moscow. Screened by residential developments, the laboratories were housed in a series of low, cream-painted buildings which, on the inside, reminded me of Dr Who's Tardis. A worried-looking scientist opened the sample with his hands encased in heavy silver gloves built into the side of a radiation-proof cabinet. He emptied the contents of the phial into a glass dish, and we filmed him testing it.

Sure enough, it was exactly what Gennady had said it was. We interviewed a Ministry spokesman. It was obvious that he knew that his country was haemorrhaging nuclear material through the Russian Mafia, but he put a brave face on things and vowed that he would do everything he could to stop it.

Back in Birmingham, programme manager Pat Harris had had a brainwave. Central had just finished filming one of its most successful dramas – 'Sharpe', starring Sean Bean as the swashbuckling soldier hero of the Napoleonic Wars – in Eastern Europe. An English woman who spoke fluent Russian had been working on the production as an interpreter and she was coming back to the UK via Moscow. Would she help?

Surprisingly, given that I had to tell her exactly what we were involved in, she agreed and cheerfully set off with us for our second visit to Gennady. This time, he had brought in his partner, Ilya. They had had an idea. If, as we said, we wanted the plutonium so that we could make a nuclear warhead, why not just buy one ready-made? They had an SS 20 ballistic missile they could provide for us – what did we think?

As our interpreter translated, I felt a sense of unreality wash over me, as I had the first time I had met Gennady. If we were finding it so easy to obtain these things, what the hell was there to stop a genuine terrorist organisation with real money behind it from doing exactly the same?

I obviously wasn't looking keen on the idea, because Gennady and Ilya were now outlining to our interpreter how the original order of weapons-grade plutonium was to be smuggled out to us. It would be coming through Vilnius in Lithuania. When would we like delivery? And would I please take the details of how we should make the payment to their company? Fine, fine. We took down the details and arranged to talk later. We had all the evidence we needed that the fissile material for our 'dirty bomb' could be found here in Moscow. We flew back to Britain to prepare for the final stage of the programme.

We had decided to take our dummy 'dirty bomb' to the United

States. The totally reasonable thinking was that the bomb set off by the Moslem extremists at the World Trade Center could so easily have contained nuclear material. If not this time, maybe next time. We wanted to ask the authorities there if they had contemplated such a threat and, if so, what plans they had to deal with it.

We wanted to carry out our plan sensibly and without causing any panic, so we informed both British and US Customs exactly what we were doing. The briefcase was thoroughly examined at Heathrow Airport and again when we arrived in New York.

Understandably, perhaps, the New York authorities – from the Mayor's office to the civil defence department – refused to meet us. The story of what we had brought with us and our exploits in Moscow were picked up by New York radio stations.

In Washington, however, I interviewed Bob Kupperman, a former US National Security Adviser who looked at the briefcase's contents and said, 'Oh, my God. My worst nightmare is coming true!' A chilling comment from the man who was once the chief scientist for the American side in the SALT Two disarmament talks. He had warned several times that the ready availability of small amounts of nuclear material on the black market would ultimately give the terrorists the power they had wanted for so long.

Here, in theory, was a bomb small enough to fit into a briefcase but big enough to obliterate Manhattan.

When news of our visit to New York was picked up in Britain, we were lambasted by the *Sun*, which accused me of being 'irresponsible and naive' for trying to 'sneak' the 'dirty bomb' into the US with me. This really annoyed me. We had moved heaven and earth to avoid scaring people. We had informed all the relevant authorities in Britain and the USA and, after all, we were making a very valid point, given our Russian findings.

I insisted that Central complained to Kelvin MacKenzie, then the editor of the *Sun*. Our press department advised against it. 'If you cross the *Sun*, they'll never give you publicity again – not good publicity anyway,' they warned.

I insisted, however, and, a couple of weeks later, an apology appeared in the paper, printed as prominently as the original, condemnatory article. And, despite the fears of the Central Television press department, when we broadcast the first programme about the terrorist activities of Martin McGuinness a few weeks after that, the *Sun* described me as a 'national hero'. This was one 'national hero' who was ready to lie down and sleep for a year.

Frances was becoming increasingly unhappy with what I was doing. It was bad enough that we had all been beaten up badly in Spain, but to have been potentially exposed to deadly radiation led to a kind of nagging worry at the back of my mind which never quite went away again. But if I had been in the wars during that series, so had Peter Salkeld. He was hoping to repeat the success of Steve Warr's programme on illegal dealing in endangered species of birds. He had been told by friends at the RSPB about the theft of wild falcon eggs in Scotland by a gang which sold the chicks on to wealthy Arabs who trained them for hunting. There was a widely-held belief in the world of falconry that wild birds made the best hunters. Consequently, they are highly sought after. A single egg can be worth in excess of £1,000.

The RSPB had pinpointed a falcon's nest in the Scottish Highlands that was regularly robbed of its eggs every year. The society tried hard to keep an eye on the location but round-the-clock surveillance was beyond its means. But not beyond Salk's. He and a researcher pitched camp just inside the treeline at 1,500 feet above sea level. From a makeshift hide near their tiny, two-man tent, they could get a good view of the nest, perched high up on a rocky outcrop.

For thirteen days, Salk watched the female falcon sitting on her clutch of eggs, undisturbed. He and the researcher spent the days together and took it in turns to slip quietly back to the local hotel for a comfortable bed and a shower for the night. The pair of them lived mostly on baked beans, tinned meat and whisky.

Just as he was starting to think that this falcon brood would actually hatch and survive in the wild, Salk saw something moving at the top of the rock face. A human figure. Salk moved across to his camera, mounted permanently on its tripod for just such an occasion. He filmed as a man in his twenties with long hair tied in a ponytail clambered carefully down to the nest.

He opened a flap at the front of his jacket and reached down to the nest. He carefully picked up the eggs one by one and placed them in specially-made pockets inside his jacket – to keep them warm until he could get them somewhere safe.

A few days later, after the RSPB and local mountaineers arrived to check the eggs really had all been stolen, Salk tried to film the robbed nest. Disaster struck. One of his fellow climbers accidentally knocked a rock off the edge of the clifftop. It hit Salk, who wasn't wearing a safety helmet, on the top of his skull. He was hauled to safety, his head and clothing soaked in blood.

We eventually traced the eggs to a Belgian dealer who made a fortune selling the hatched birds on to wealthy Arabs. We wanted to expose him, so we arranged a meeting between him and a potential Middle Eastern customer – a fake sheikh, aka Roger Cook.

For four hours, a make-up artist and a wardrobe specialist worked to transform me from an overweight television presenter into an overweight member of the Saudi Arabian Royal Family. By the time they had finished, I hardly recognised myself. My skin looked realistically burnished, I sported a wonderful dark, drooping moustache, exotic beard and was dressed in full headdress and jelebayah. For the first time in the series, I was actually enjoying myself. I suppose it was probably relief that for once it was unlikely that my 'doorstep' would result in a beating from a 600-strong angry crowd or expose me to dangerous nuclear material.

The meeting took place in the penthouse suite of one of London's best hotels. The mood was relaxed, expansive and obviously confidence-building.

Leaning back in his chair, the bird bandit eventually boasted: 'I'm so good at what I do that I'll never be caught, you know.'

'Well, you just have been,' came the inevitable response.

I was right. There was no violence, just shock and disbelief on the man's face when I told him that I wasn't a sheikh, but a television reporter who had captured his every criminal move on film. Six months of painstaking work had come to a very satisfactory end. I felt so good that I was sorely tempted to spend the rest of the day in disguise and have a bit more fun.

CHAPTER 8

=====

In the Can

It is one of life's ironies that, after having so many bones broken, so many blows to the head and other parts of my body – all in the line of duty – that my career was almost ended by a little old lady.

Frank Thorne – an ex-Fleet Street reporter who was spending a year or so with 'The Cook Report' as a researcher – was driving us back to base after a day's filming. I was dozing in the front passenger seat. We had just come to a halt at the rear of the semi-permanent traffic jam on the M6 at Birmingham when there was a terrific thump and a crash at the back of the car. Waking up with a jolt, I knew straight away that something bad had happened to my neck – it was more than whiplash.

I was in agony and phoned the office which, in turn, called an ambulance and the police. Meanwhile, from the stationary queue of cars, a lady in a smart blue uniform presented herself. On the grass by the hard shoulder she proceeded to examine the shocked elderly lady driver whose demolished Ford Fiesta now sat astride the central barrier. She was pronounced unhurt and asked if there was anyone she needed to speak to. The old lady nodded that there was, and my mobile phone was snatched from my hand and given to the old dear, who then had a twenty-minute conversation about how she didn't think she would make it to that weekend's bowls match.

By this time, an ambulance had arrived and one of the paramedics looked at me leaning against a post, head tilted awkwardly to one side. Making a politically incorrect assumption, he said to the lady in blue, 'Nurse, shouldn't you be looking at this chap now?'

'I'm not a bloody nurse, I'm a doctor,' came the sharp reply, as she took umbrage and then her leave, stomping off down the hard shoulder.

My regular production driver, Declan Smythe, had overheard my call to the office, and had now turned up to see if he could help. He drove me gently back to Central TV's headquarters, where the horrified duty sister had him take me straight on to Birmingham General Hospital.

I spent the night sandbagged, unable to move, onto a steel plate in the casualty department. It was a long night enlivened by the kind of strange behaviour you only find in hard-pressed, inner-city hospitals.

A man with a gaping wound in his arm kept coming in to have it stitched and dressed. He would then go out into the car park, undo all the good work and come back in again. A large West Indian lady chased a ginger-headed intern through my cubicle several times, accusing him, surreally, at the top of her voice, of being a cannibal.

In the morning, the CT scanner I was supposed to have been examined under had broken down, so an ambulance was arranged to take me to a sister hospital some miles away in order to use their facilities. For some reason, no ambulance was available. Eventually, strapped into a Meccano neck collar, I went by taxi, only to find that the second scanner was also inoperative due to lack of funds.

I went private.

The specialist at The Priory Hospital got me an MRI scan and, two days later, I was told that it was time to consider retirement – or suffer the consequences. A full examination of the Cook frame had come up with a number of worrying malfunctions. My blood pressure was too high, I had a kidney problem and the latest injury to my neck had aggravated and extended all the previous damage it had suffered over the years. Why, suggested the specialist, didn't I call it a day?

I didn't want to rush into any decisions, so, first things first, I let Townson and Bob Southgate know what the prognosis and advice were. The next series was due to start in production in a few weeks time, and they got it postponed for two months. I went home to Frances and Belinda to rest.

For the next few weeks, I agonised. Frances, I knew, deep down, would rather I called it a day. As I swallowed the painkillers and lay down awkwardly in my bed at night, I saw her point of view. Meanwhile, the rest of the team kept on working and the producers kept me up to date on how the stories were progressing.

As I recovered I was, for once, able to take a detached view of 'The Cook Report'. I thought about what we had achieved, and what we still wanted to achieve. I thought about my fallings out with Mike Townson and, yet, how we still managed to bring out programmes of which we could all usually be proud. Then there was the team, some of whom had stuck with me through thick and thin. They were an amazing bunch of journalists and film-makers. We had our disagreements, but that was only natural given everyone's diverse and individual nature. They worked hard and played hard. There was no such thing as an eight-hour day or a five-day week. Everyone pulled together to get the job done, then they all lay down to recover. But even then, the journalism carried on – contacts would ring in, stories in newspapers sparked new ideas for another series.

If I stopped, so would 'The Cook Report'. It was a simple fact. The team would find other jobs, of course, but there was nothing quite like what we did. We were all comfortable with the format. We knew instinctively what was the right story for 'a Cook' – where the stings and the doorsteps fitted in, why some stories were important and others commonplace.

Six weeks later, the doctors gave me a partial clean bill of health. I had to have intensive physiotherapy, take courses of tablets and, above all, 'take it easy'. Not possible. I told Frances that we needed a plan. What I really meant was – Let's try and work out how much longer I'm going to keep on doing this, then you and I can look forward to riding off into the sunset together. Another three years – maybe four – we agreed. I went back to work – but carefully.

We had made national headlines with the first programme of the autumn series. In it, we had detailed scientific work carried out by a senior chemical analyst on a possible cause of Sudden Infant Death Syndrome (SIDS), otherwise known as cot death. We didn't claim to have found the definitive cause of cot death, but an investigation by the eminent consulting scientist, Dr Barry Richardson, was worth reporting.

In the course of trying to find out how to stop mildew appearing on marquees manufactured by a friend of his, Richardson had found that the fire retardant used in the material could produce nasty gases if it mixed with other elements. He made a lateral jump and looked at infant mattresses – which were impregnated with some rather worrying chemicals – such as antimony and phosphorus. He carried out tests that seemed to show that if urine seeped from a baby's nappy into the fire retardant in the mattress foam, a thin layer of poisonous gas would form. The theory was, if the sleeping infant was lying face down, he or she might well inhale something akin to mustard gas and simply stop breathing.

Our scientific advisers obtained tissue samples taken from babies who had died of SIDS. The levels of antimony in some were several thousand times the normal reading. Similarly, they tested for levels of antimony in the hair of living infants. Again, the readings were generally extremely high.

The public reaction to the first programme was amazing. We received ten thousand calls from worried parents. We hadn't scare-mongered and we made no huge claims to have solved the mystery of SIDS, but what parents everywhere wanted to know was where they could buy mattresses without these dubious fire retardants. Baby bedding manufacturers boosted production of natural fibre mat-tresses to top speed. The big stores sold out of stocks in hours. Interestingly, Mothercare had had reservations about the risks posed by these chemicals and had not used them for some time, despite government advice that they should.

A second, updating programme was required. Townson and Salk, the producer, moved into top gear, giving themselves just a fortnight to put together the follow-up. Two days before broadcast, Graham Puntis sat in his video edit suite to wait for Townson. The boss had been specific – he wanted Puntis in first thing because there was a lot to do. By mid-morning, there was still no sign of Townson. This was unheard of. When the job needed doing in a hurry, he was always there.

Then the telephone call came through to Pat Harris. Mike Townson had been found unconscious in bed that morning. He had suffered a severe brain haemorrhage and was seriously ill. He would undergo a life-saving operation later in the day. The shock was terrific. None of us could imagine 'The Cook Report' without Mike

Townson. He'd been there from the start and, like him or loathe him, he had been instrumental in the programme's success. As we all waited for news from the hospital, the realisation dawned that we still had a programme to produce and broadcast in less than forty-eight hours' time.

The man who stepped into the breach was Mike Morley. A workaholic fast-track manager at Central, his star was in the ascendant and, still only in his mid-thirties, he was head of the Factual Programme Department and was technically Townson's boss. Although a department head, Morley's roots lay in hands-on programme-making. He had made an award-winning film about the kidnap from hospital and safe return of new-born baby Abbie Humphreys earlier in the year. Privately, he told colleagues that he would love to be editor of 'The Cook Report'. Now, although it was none of his making, he had his chance.

Morley looked at the script and tapes Townson had been working on. As was always the case with Townson productions, they made little sense to anyone other than Townson himself. Even Puntis, who was well-versed in this way of working, could shed no light on how the editor had envisaged this second programme on cot death. Morley called in Salk and his researcher, David Alford. It made sense to allow the men who knew the subject best to put things together.

The two men worked right through the night with Puntis, so that when Morley and I arrived in the morning we had a sensible structure available from which to script and fashion a finished programme. We then all worked through the following night and completed the programme, in traditional 'Cook Report' style, barely half an hour before transmission.

Townson had survived his first operation but was still very ill. The surgeons were worried that he might suffer a second haemorrhage. All the years of heavy smoking hadn't helped. We all waited to see how he progressed.

Morley stayed on as a temporary editor, working closely with me, until the end of the series. To his credit, he left Townson's name as editor on the end of every programme.

Slowly, Townson started to get better. There had been embarrassing scenes at the hospital when he was first admitted. Bob Southgate had likened Townson's private life to a French farce in which everybody had to keep picking up their clothes and hiding in a cupboard until the coast was clear. Suffice to say that a number of friends and relatives turned up to see Townson and the resulting encounters led the nursing staff to impose a strict visiting rota to avoid further trouble.

The two cot death programmes provoked something of a storm in the medical and scientific professions. Some of those who preferred different theories as to the cause of SIDS decided to shoot the messenger. We had given a platform to an eminent consulting scientist. We made no case for rejecting any of the other possible causes – parental smoking or babies sleeping on their tummies. But, like Dr Richardson, we did find it strange, and undesirable, that very high levels of the toxic chemicals contained in the fire retardants used in many baby mattresses were being found in the post mortem tissues of cot death victims. They could also be found in hair samples taken from living babies who had also used the suspect mattresses.

After all the fuss, the government invited Lady Limerick to hold an enquiry into the scientific findings we had aired. Two years later, she reported that her scientists had not been able to recreate the conditions under which Barry Richardson had detected the presence of poisonous gasses. But they had not tested post mortem tissue of SIDS victims, where independent scientists – unconnected with Richardson but working for us – had found alarming levels of potentially lethal poisons. So, even if Richardson's theory for the transfer of these substances from mattress to baby was wrong, such a transfer had definitely taken place.

A cynic might say that the government shackled the enquiry. If the antimony theory was upheld, the government could be faced with huge compensation claims. After all, it was on their advice that these chemicals had been used in mattress manufacture in the first place.

However, it remains an undeniable fact that since those programmes, mattresses using suspect fire retardants are no longer sold, and there has been a further significant drop in the numbers of Sudden Infant Death Syndrome victims, over and above that achieved by the very worthwhile 'Back to Sleep' campaign.

As the months went by, it became obvious that Mike Townson would never be fit enough to come back to work – at least, not as editor of

'The Cook Report'. We needed a new editor to hold things together. Speculation mounted amongst the team when it was known that someone had been chosen – but the identity was kept secret. Mike Morley and his boss, Steve Clark, held a rather melodramatic staff meeting to 'unveil' the new editor. And as the portly, silver-haired figure walked into the room, spontaneous applause erupted. It was none other than my old friend Bob Southgate.

On the face of it, Southgate was far too senior a management figure to take the job. He was the man who had written the franchise proposal that won Central Television the right to broadcast for ten years – at a cost of just £2,000 a year. He had retired as deputy managing director a few months before.

Still, as he told me over a drink the first evening of his tenure, he had been involved with 'The Cook Report' from the very start. He had brought me over to Central Television from the BBC nearly a decade earlier. He had hired Townson and had to view every single episode before broadcast to make sure that it complied with the ITC code. He relished the chance to 'play with the train set' for a year or so before finally embracing retirement for real.

Southgate brought an air of gentility and relaxation to the programme that had always been missing in Townson's day. Having come so close to leaving the job for good after my car accident, I appreciated his approach. I no longer felt like a commodity to be freighted wherever I was needed.

The producers appreciated Southgate, too. At last, they were allowed to produce and edit their own programmes. Under Southgate's avuncular guidance they were motivated to bring in good shows because they were fully in charge, and not because they were driven to go and fetch material for Mike Townson.

By the end of 1996, big changes were afoot once more. Central Television had merged with a newer commercial concern – Carlton Television. The change brought with it the closure of the Birmingham studios. 'The Cook Report' was going to move to Carlton's Nottingham studios. We would no longer be in the middle of a thriving city, but marooned on an industrial estate on the edge of town. I loathed the whole idea. We had previously been offered London as an alternative production site, and that had made much more sense to me.

The move coincided with the departure – for good this time – of Bob Southgate. Pat Harris had also decided not to make the move with us. She and her husband went off to retire to Cornwall. It was the end of an era. Peter Salkeld, too, was not coming with us. After all these years, the management had decided not to renew his contract. I felt very badly about this. He was my friend as well as a valued colleague and travelling companion, but there was nothing I could do to change the management's mind. Their view was that he had been there long enough. Time to make way for new blood.

There was certainly going to be new blood at the top. Mike Morley, forbidden categorically by his boss Steve Clark to take over the programme, much though he was tempted, had found us a new editor. David Mannion was a familiar and respected figure in television. The former Head of News at ITN, he had diversified into running his own company, travelling the world to advise foreign television stations how to make themselves more successful.

Morley had persuaded Mannion to take on the job and impose new, more efficient working practices on us all. Mannion had stipulated that he would be at the helm of the programme as much as possible, but that he did have other commitments to fulfil and would at times be away from the Nottingham studios for prolonged periods.

One of the first things Mannion did was to try to plan the programmes more efficiently. While I applauded this intention, it remained an undeniable fact that the villains never read the script. However much you try to be economical by booking your camera crew and other staff members for specific times, it won't alter the fact that your target may not turn up and do what you want him to, and even criminals fall ill or go on holiday.

One story – tailor-made for us – stands out from the first series under David Mannion. It came to us in the form of a piece of amateur filming that exposed a huge illegal industry based on cruelty. The film had been shown to producer Howard Foster by a senior director of a leading animal charity frustrated by the inability, or unwillingness, of the conservation authorities all over Africa to stop a practice known as 'canned hunting' – where big game is captured from the wild and kept in small enclosures, often in a highly-tranquillised state, until a foreign hunter arrives to shoot the animal at close range for an exorbitant fee.

Foster brought the tape into my room and slipped it into the video player. 'This isn't very pleasant, but I think you'll agree it's something we've got to take a look at,' he said, and sat down next to me to watch the tape.

The opening shot showed a lioness standing uncertainly beside a high, wire mesh fence. As the camera pulled shakily away, we could see three small cubs on the other side of the fence looking longingly at her. Then a low, whispered commentary began as the cameraman, obviously afraid he would be discovered, described what we were seeing. The disembodied voice had a strong, South African accent. 'These cubs have been separated from their mother so that she can be shot by an overseas hunter for a lot of money. She's still feeding them milk from her teats every day, but the hunters don't care.'

We watched as the lioness wandered around the small enclosure, unwilling to stray far from her young. Suddenly, the camera jerked violently as the soundtrack crackled and distorted with the sound of rifle fire. We saw the lioness leap at least ten feet into the air, her back arching in pain. She hit the ground, writhed for a few seconds and was still. Three men walked into shot and bent to examine their prize. One lifted her huge head and struck a macho pose. The camcorder's microphone picked up laughter and the sound of congratulations offered in German.

'This is going on all over Africa every day of every week of every year,' the cameraman whispered, and switched off.

We showed the film to David Mannion who agreed that this was something that demanded investigation. Over the next two weeks, the research team headed off to every conservation group it could find with special interests in African big game. The key questions were: how widespread was 'canned hunting' and who were the men most closely involved in it?

A week later, Foster and his researcher, Peter McQuillan, had established that 'canned hunting' was very big business indeed, especially in South Africa where the re-organization of the new republic and the abolition of its old state boundaries had left hunting laws in disarray. Two conservation groups had offered lists of suspect game ranches and hunters, mostly in the old Transvaal area where the authority of the Mandela government held least sway amongst the independently-minded Afrikaners.

Several names appeared on both lists and we decided to concentrate on these, but in such a way that they would never suspect that they were under investigation. After several brainstorming sessions in the office and occasionally over a glass or two of New World Chardonnay in the restaurant of my hotel, we built our cover.

Telephone calls and faxes to the suspect hunting outfits were never going to work. We had to get right up close to them with hidden cameras and tape recorders and get them to hang themselves conclusively without believing for a single second that someone was trying to trap them. We needed to appeal to their greed by dangling a sufficiently succulent series of carrots in front of them.

We decided we had to get into the big game hunting business ourselves. Not at the 'sharp end' like the men we wanted to expose, but as middlemen – 'fixers' – who could put wannabe hunters in touch with our suspects. And we needed to be based somewhere which had the smell of opulence and a big hunting tradition.

Three European nations are crazy about hunting – Italy, Germany and Spain. We decided to set up our stall on the Costa del Sol. Howard Foster and Peter McQuillan flew there and rented space in an office block near the waterfront in Marbella. They installed a telephone and fax and arranged for an office monitoring company to handle all incoming calls once the team had left. Calling itself Jackson & Co., a name used previously by McQuillan in a successful investigation into paedophiles, this front company was to approach every hunting outfit on the list with a business proposition that would be hard to resist.

Faxes began to arrive in the offices of South African hunting companies from Jackson & Co. explaining that it had a portfolio of extremely wealthy clients for whom it provided every possible facility. A rich man in London demands tickets for La Scala in Milan, Jackson & Co. finds the best seats, books the flights, the hotel and arranges for the chauffeur to take him to his favourite restaurant, and so on. Some of these clients were now expressing an interest in big game hunting, an area hitherto unexplored by the sophisticated operators at Jackson & Co., and to please their valuable and cash-laden masters, the company was sending two of its senior representatives to South Africa in the next week or so. By the way, most of these clients couldn't shoot for toffee but would pay handsomely for the chance to bag and boast about a lion, leopard or rhino. Was there enough interest to make it worth a meeting?

Within four days all the suspect outfits had replied to say they would be very pleased to see our representatives and were sure they could help us.

Foster needed a 'business colleague' he could trust. Someone who could manage a jacket camera, had the gift of the gab with the enemy, who could keep his nerve and – if at all possible – film with a Betacam when the opportunity arose. He came to see me and made a suggestion which I wholeheartedly endorsed. Then he went in to see Mike Morley and made his case. He wanted Salk to work with him.

Although Salk had technically left 'The Cook Report', he was still in constant touch with his old colleagues. Morley realised that Foster was talking sense. Salk was the ideal man for the job. Foster could hire him.

Both men took business cards and headed notepaper printed with their front company logo: 'Jackson & Co. – The Complete Service'. It was decided they would use their real names because of the danger of being asked to produce a passport that was clearly at odds with the assumed identity. They also took two Sony DigiCams – small, unobtrusive cameras which would not look out of place in a tourist area. They were useful for secret filming at a distance, for future identification of targets and locations for colleagues and, crucially, as a legitimate tool for open filming of animals, hunters and terrain to show the 'clients' back in Spain or London.

If you want to film professionally with Beta cameras – the kind that are used to make virtually every news, current affairs or documentary programme on television – in South Africa, you need the written permission of the government and they want to know exactly what you plan to film. It was too early to tell the authorities what we were up to, so Beta kit would be hired once we were in the country and we had something worth filming.

Salk, a cameraman by training, but now almost sixty, doubling as a producer and director, also packed his miniaturised tie cameras. We often use them to obtain our secret close-up film. A tiny video camera is sewn into a tie with its lens seeing the outside world through a hole the size of a pinhead burnt through the material three or four inches below the knot. Microphone and camera wires are fed around the neck of the wearer, hidden by the material of the tie until they are dropped through a hole cut into the back of the shirt collar to be connected to batteries and the bulky Sony GVU–5E video recorder.

Salk dismantled both cameras and hid the components in his clothes and with the DigiCams in his suitcases to lessen the chances of detection by the Customs at Johannesburg Airport. If the gear is found by British airport security people, there isn't usually a problem. If I'm flying with the cameraman, one glance at my face and all comes clear to the puzzled baggage checker. 'Who are you after this time, Mr Cook, or shouldn't I ask?' is the usual reaction once they're satisfied you haven't tried to slip a bomb timer through the system.

The night after their departure, I received a call from Foster and Salk. They had got into Jo'burg with no problems and were to make their first meeting, seven hours' drive east of the city, the following day. From then on they would be sleeping under canvas on a remote farm run by a contact of one of the conservation groups that had helped us identify our targets.

'Everyone in this camp's just had cerebral malaria,' Salk cackled down the phone. 'And crocodiles have eaten two of the three servants in the past fortnight. The third one was killed by poachers last month. Shall we book you into the penthouse?'

For the next week I had to put the progress of the investigation in South Africa to the back of my mind because we had just persuaded the fugitive businessman Asil Nadir to give an exclusive, no-holds barred interview. After the collapse of his Polly Peck empire in 1992, he had fled to Turkish Northern Cyprus, fearing he wouldn't get a fair trial on fraud charges involving £56 million.

The dubious behaviour of the Serious Fraud Office gave some credence to these fears – indeed the programme ended up being as much about them as it was about him – but if I was to put his claims to the test, I had to devote all my time to absorbing the exhaustive briefing put together for me by the research team.

By the time we had completed the negotiations with Nadir's advisors and associates, kicked our heels for a while at the Jasmine Court Hotel in Kyrenia and then actually done the interview at his home, two weeks had slipped by. I now had to refocus my mind and update myself on every last detail of the next project in a matter of hours. A difficult feat to pull off, but as 'The Cook Report' often had to juggle several major stories at once, at least I was used to trying.

Back in Nottingham, after a night's sleep, I drove to the studios.

'Any news from South Africa?' I asked as I walked into the office.

'Your tickets are on your desk,' replied Lynne Salkeld, Salk's daughter and our latest long-suffering secretary. 'You leave this evening. Peter and Howard have arranged for you to kill a lion on Monday.'

The pair of them had been busy over the past fortnight visiting a dozen suspect hunting operators and covering several thousand miles in the process. In my hotel room a few miles from Jo'burg airport, they filled me in on what had been filmed and set up for us to do in the next few days.

Four hunting outfits had offered Jackson & Co.'s mythical clients the chance to kill a lion in any circumstances they wanted. What had distinguished the company we had finally chosen from the others was the discovery that it was actually stealing the lions from the Kruger National Park – the jewel in South Africa's conservation crown. It was drugging them and keeping them in small enclosures until the wealthy clients arrived to shoot them.

Sandy McDonald and his wife Tracey ran their own hunting operation from a block of factory buildings next to the control tower of Pietersburg Airport, a four-hour drive from Johannesburg and a couple of hours from Kruger. They boasted to us that they killed more animals a year than any other outfit in their part of the Republic of South Africa. Tracey McDonald, an attractive and enthusiastic saleswoman, swiftly entered into the conspiracy hinted at by Foster and Salk. When they told her how they overcharged their rich clients back in Europe her eyes sparkled. The prospect of a steady stream of gullible millionaires directed her way by these two middlemen excited her – she loved Foster's plummy Home Counties accent – and she happily told them the secrets of the canned hunting business. The fact that the clients were unable to shoot was not a problem.

As she counted out the US$9,000 Foster had given her as a down payment for the hunting of one lion, she explained how the hunters of the area dug beneath the electrified security fences that surround the Kruger National Park and lured their prey across by dragging bait under the fence to the accompaniment of loud tape recordings of lions and hyenas feeding.

'Before you know it, you've got yourself a Kruger lion. You dart it and keep it safe until your client arrives,' she explained. Peter Salkeld leaned attentively towards her, the lens and the microphone in his tie relaying every part of her confession to the tape turning silently in the recorder under his armpit.

For the denouement, Jackson & Co. was to bring over one of its richest clients. His name was Mr James Rogers, he was worth in excess of £100 million, he was used to getting his own way. He was unfit, couldn't possibly last more than half an hour in the fierce South African sun and he was a useless shot.

Tracey McDonald had the very lion for him. Husband Sandy had been out to the edge of the Kruger himself a couple of days before. It was a beautiful specimen, she gushed. He was about ten years old with a magnificent head and long, dark mane. 'Don't worry, we'll make sure he gets his lion,' she said, handing over a receipt for a deposit so large it had required the signature of Carlton Television's chief accountant to authorise it. Howard Foster slipped it into his breast pocket and hoped the budget-busting outlay would be worth it.

We had decided to keep well away from the Kruger area until the day of the hunt and had found ourselves an inn high up in the nearby mountain range that had fabulous views over the Low Veldt and enjoyed complete privacy. Over some sumptuous Thelema Cape Chardonnay the team discussed the best – and safest – way to handle what was to come.

We had been joined by Andy Rex, a white Zimbabwean cameraman under contract to ITN in Jo'burg. A big, bluff man who had operated in some of the world's toughest trouble spots and been under fire countless times in Bosnia and Rwanda, he saw no problem in what we were going to do. 'I don't know why you boys are going to all this planning trouble,' he said, lighting another Marlboro and settling his bulk comfortably down into his creaking chair. 'If they don't like what you're going to do, we'll just tell them to piss off and we'll get on with it.'

Somehow I felt it wasn't going to be that simple.

So far we had maintained control. We had filmed our targets covertly and hidden the results in a safe back at the farm where Foster and Salk had been staying. We would have our own man capturing every cough and spit; an expensive camera filming an expensive vanity video for a very expensive man. But from the moment we were taken on to the killing ground, everything would change.

By midnight we had thrashed out a plan that seemed to afford optimum protection for humans, lion and equipment.

Mr Rogers and his cameraman would obviously be riding up front with the hunters. Foster and Salk would drive an air-conditioned back-up vehicle on the expedition. We added asthma to Mr Rogers' portfolio and insisted that the vehicle be in close attendance in case he needed to sit in cool, dust-free comfort at any time.

Used tapes could then be smuggled across to the support vehicle from time to time, reducing the chances of the aggrieved hunters grabbing them during the confrontation that would inevitably follow. Salk and Foster would film on the tie camera and the DigiCam from the van as we went along. All tapes would be pushed down the back seat of the back-up vehicle.

Crispian Barlow, an eccentric English baronet who ran the farm where the team had initially based themselves, was to follow us discreetly. If we were gone too long he was to call the police. We had also met the local nature conservation rangers – a group of smiling and enthusiastic Kwa-Zulu Africans – who promised to give us a powerful walkie-talkie on which we could either call them as they waited with Crispian, or use the emergency channel to call the police.

We telephoned David Mannion back in Nottingham and told him our plans. 'Just take care of yourselves and I want a call the minute it's all over.' It's an instruction Mannion had given to reporters and crews in tight spots abroad plenty of times before as editor of ITV's news programmes. A kind and compassionate man, we knew he was genuinely concerned for our safety.

The morning of the hunt dawned bright and clear. I was up, showered and dressed by eight o'clock. Shortly, the others joined me, and we ran over the briefing once more.

Above all, I was to establish from the outset that I was in charge of the hunting expedition – to be dogmatic, bad-tempered, bullying if need be – and to try to maintain that atmosphere even after it became clear that James Rogers was Roger Cook. If I could keep the bad guys on the back foot, we might be able to make a getaway with ourselves and the tapes intact.

We left the hotel after breakfast and drove towards the Kruger. It was a glorious day, perfect for filming but already heading for 40 degrees Centrigrade. I was glad of the cool interior of our minibus. We had been told to meet the hunters at a small safari camp a few miles from the western edge of the reserve.

But first, we parked, as arranged, outside the solitary row of shops in the village of Huidspruit and waited for the rangers and their walkie-talkie. After an hour there was still no sign of them. We checked the two side-streets and the car park of the rough-looking hotel across the road. If we left it any longer, we would miss our rendezvous with Mr McDonald. A last, anxious stare through the heat-haze rising from the empty tarmac road and we pulled away towards the camp. We never did learn why they couldn't make that vital rendezvous.

Salk switched the GSM mobile phone on and tried to call Crispian Barlow. He got a signal but couldn't get through. He tried again, and again. He tried ringing our hotel and then the UK without success. We discovered later that a £1,000 limit had been put on our use of the GSM by the Carlton Television accountants. Our lifeline had been cut off.

Five minutes after we arrived at the rendezvous, a lumbering, long-wheelbase Land Cruiser turned into the driveway behind us, raising a thick cloud of dust. The hunters were an hour early. Crispian Barlow, who was supposed to follow us, wasn't due to arrive for another thirty minutes.

Now we really were on our own.

Five men descended from the vehicle and walked towards us. Leading the group was the bear-like figure of Sandy McDonald, already $9,000 richer and clearly looking forward to another $9,000 once the morning's business was completed. McDonald held out a paw and smiled. 'Welcome to South Africa, Mr Rogers, you've picked a fine day to shoot a lion.'

I went into grumpy rich man mode: 'It's too damn hot. I want to get out of this heat and dust.' I stomped back into the air-conditioned oasis of the minibus. The intention was to restrict my contact with McDonald and his hunters until Foster and Salk had established that this lion was to be shot in the controlled circumstances McDonald had promised.

Andy Rex sat with me, checking his camera gear and listening to the progress of the South African test batsmen against Australia on the car radio. Every few minutes he clambered outside to smoke another cigarette.

Foster and Salk took McDonald to the camp's bar and bought him an orange juice. Salk manoeuvred McDonald into the frame of his tie camera. 'We want to be sure our client is kept safe.'

'Don't worry, make no mistake, this is a canned lion. I've drugged him too, so he won't be going anywhere. Your client can get as close as he likes.'

'He won't think he's being conned?'

'We'll make it look good. We'll drive him round for a bit as if we're hunting, but we know where the lion is. Mr Rogers won't suspect a thing.'

They were interrupted by a shout. The driver of the hunting wagon waved them over. It was Mossie Mostert, a mean-looking man in his mid-twenties whose family had been near the top of the British conservationists' lists of suspects. The 'Cook Report' team had been to his farm a few weeks before and been offered canned lion. Mostert had even shown them round the enclosures where his family kept forty or more lions for hunting. He had told us that he had been accused by the South African Professional Hunters' Association of running canned hunts. He had laughed it off, saying his accusers were the same men who came round begging for a spare lion for a foreign client when there was a shortage of big cats in the wild. If the McDonalds hadn't obliged, the Mosterts would have been next on our list. Now we had both in our sights.

McDonald confirmed to Foster that the hunt would be on Mostert land and, pretending to visit the washroom, Foster left a note for Crispian Barlow with the camp owner, telling him where we'd been taken.

At the height of the South African summer the Low Veldt is covered in dense foliage. I wiped the sweat out of my eyes and looked to my left and to my right in the hope of seeing some landmark I could use to guide me when the time came to make a run for it. Nothing – just the same unending pattern of tall grass and dark clumps of thorn trees. Unless you knew the territory, you could drive through the red dust of these dirt tracks for days and never find your way out.

I looked across at my unsuspecting companions. Perched next to me, high up on the observation bench at the back of the customised hunting wagon, was one of the biggest men I had ever seen. Well over six feet tall with a grizzled, blond beard, Sandy McDonald must have weighed in excess of twenty stone. A Remington hunting rifle with telescopic sights rested across his enormous thighs.

In the canvas-covered driving seat, Mossie Mostert struggled with the wheel, the late-morning sun forcing him to pull his peaked hunting cap low over his eyes. As we bounced across the rough terrain, he steered us closer to our quarry. He stared fixedly past a pair of large-bore rifles and a long, wooden gun rest which were clipped across the folded windshield in front of him. A small, wiry figure with a notoriously short temper, his family owned the property we were hunting on.

On the bonnet of the Land Cruiser sat the tracker, a fit, muscular Afrikaner in standard-issue hunting greens and the obligatory camouflaged cap. He gripped the sides of his lookout seat perched over the front bumper. The butt of a Browning 9mm pistol poked out of a holster at his hip.

At my back stood two colossal Africans known in the big game world as 'skinners'. Their job was to use the fearsome array of knives which they carried strapped to their belts as soon as I had done what their bosses expected of me – to shoot and kill a North Transvaal male lion in the most inhumane and illegal way. Once they had removed the animal's skin and cut off its magnificent head and mane, it would be time for me to pay the white hunters their extortionate fee. Then I'd wait for my trophy to arrive a few months later, impressively mounted by a South African taxidermist.

But I wasn't about to do what was expected of me. In a few minutes' time the cosy atmosphere aboard this bouncing, dust-streaked wagon would be destroyed when I told them exactly who I was and that the cameraman who was filming them was not simply making a vanity video for me. I was there to blow apart a huge conspiracy within the worldwide big game hunting industry.

The 'Cook Report' team followed the Land Cruiser along the red-dirt road towards the Mostert reserve. Then, without warning, Mostert swung his vehicle left down a narrow track and stopped in front of a twelve-feet high electrified wire-mesh boundary fence. The two black hunters dropped from the back of their wagon. There was some movement of hands at chest level and we realised they were undoing a hefty padlock which kept two wire gates closed.

'Crispian's going to have a hell of a job finding us here, we're miles from the main entrance,' said Salk.

Foster tucked the first of the tie camera tapes down the back of the rear seat.

I said nothing and concentrated on remembering my briefing. There's nothing you can do when things go wrong except make sure you do your job as well as you can.

Two or three minutes later our little convoy arrived at a small clearing. It was time for Andy Rex to start the vanity video filming. He stood back from us, the camera on his shoulder. McDonald and Mostert took me to the veranda of a thatched hut where a large, stuffed lion stared unseeingly across a manmade waterhole.

I have never been able to fathom what makes some men want to kill another living creature. McDonald pointed to the moth-eaten specimen before us and stressed the need to break one of the big cat's limbs with the first shot. I let his grisly tutorial run uninterrupted for the camera.

The next part of the charade was target practice for Mr Rogers. The muscular Afrikaner tracker turned to me and said quietly, 'It doesn't matter whether you hit that lion or not. We'll be there to shoot it for you.'

This wasn't what I wanted at all. I did not want that lion killed by anyone.

They gave me three practice shots with one of the Remington bolt-action rifles clipped to the Land Cruiser windshield. The target, a piece of paper stuck to a tree trunk fifty yards away. Andy Rex and Salk pointed their lenses at me and, forehead furrowed in concentration, I fired. Mostert went to collect the paper: one bullseye, two inners, almost passing through the same hole. Now, with luck, they would leave the job solely to me.

Andy Rex and I joined the five-strong hunting party aboard their wagon while Foster and Salk followed in the minibus. Before we set off, McDonald gave them a walkie-talkie.

'Once we get near this lion you're going to have to hold back,' he said. 'Wait until I give the order and stay wherever you are. We'll come back and get you when it's all over.'

The Land Cruiser dipped and bucked as the tracker at the front of the vehicle put on a bravura performance for the benefit of Mr Rogers – studying the ground, signalling urgently for Mostert to stop while he jumped down to examine the spoor of the lion and directing us once he'd found its tracks.

I had no idea how to find our way back to those gates, but I knew from looking at the sun that for the past twenty minutes we had been going round in circles. Then McDonald reached for the walkie-talkie that swung from a strap on the rear-view mirror. 'Howard and Peter, you stay back now. We think we are near the lion now. See you later.' Foster replied briefly in the affirmative and we moved slowly on in silence, leaving the dirt track and moving carefully across a swathe of thick bushgrass towards a cluster of dense foliage. Mostert stopped and switched off the engine.

'There he is, under those trees.' McDonald hissed into my right ear and pointed. I looked across to the clump about thirty yards away. Under the low branches of a thorn tree I saw a massive, maned head swaying slightly in the shade. 'I want you to shoot him underneath the mane,' McDonald continued. 'It's hot and he's in a cool place so he doesn't want to move.'

He can't bloody well move, you've got him stoned out of his head, I thought. I told Andy to zoom slowly in on the lion and then pull out until McDonald and I filled his viewfinder. I could taste the tension. I took a deep breath and turned to look McDonald in the eye.

'I'll tell you why I'm not going to shoot that lion – because he doesn't stand a chance and you know it,' I said. 'And I'm not a businessman, I'm a television reporter making a programme about canned hunting and that's what this is, isn't it, a canned hunt?'

I don't know what I expected to happen. People react in so many different ways. I had prepared myself for instant retaliation, physical violence, rapid denial. McDonald registered nothing. 'Just shoot it below the mane,' he said, turning back in the direction of the lion.

I repeated what I had just said and things eventually began to sink in. McDonald started to argue. The other hunters started to get angry. The tracker, now kneeling a few inches behind my head, told me to get out of the wagon and shoot the lion on foot.

'No, we're not going on foot,' I said. 'I'm paying for this. We're not shooting that lion. Let's get out of here.'

Mostert restarted the engine and drove us back to an anxious back-up team. Salk switched on the DigiCam. McDonald was still in shock but Mostert and the tracker were beginning to think more clearly. Mostert decided things had gone too far. He dropped the wagon into gear and headed back to the clearing.

Back at the camp the walkie-talkie crackled into life every thirty seconds or so and Mostert and McDonald launched into vehement streams of Afrikaans in reply. Mostert turned to me. 'I should kill you for what you have done,' he hissed. The tracker moved close to me and said in a lowered voice: 'If you had come on foot I should have put a bullet in your head.'

When we said we wished to leave they refused, saying that there was trouble out on the public road and the police were on their way. This was bad news. We had been warned that we were in an area where farmers and even policemen met together on Sundays at the Dutch Reform Church to remember communally the injustices heaped on their Boer forebears by the hated British.

I decided we should make a run for it. Andy Rex took his gear to the minibus. Howard Foster pushed every tape behind the rear seat and we all climbed into the vehicle. Foster started the engine and we set off. Round the first bend the track forked. Andy Rex's experience of bush survival kicked in. 'Go left here,' he ordered. 'Now right. See that tree there, I remember that. Left once more and we'll be on the right road.'

He was wrong.

We spent a nerve-wracking few minutes looking over our shoulders and passing the same landmarks until, mercifully, Rex picked up the trail again. Another two minutes of bouncing and rocking over the potholes and hummocks and we saw the open gateway three hundred yards ahead of us. 'Howard,' I said, 'put your foot down.'

We lurched forward, clinging on to straps, seatbacks and dashboard as we headed for freedom. Then I saw two clouds of red dust about fifty yards ahead of us. They converged just in front of the gates. As the dust settled we saw two hunting wagons blocking the exit and a swarm of angry-looking figures pulling the gates shut.

We slowed down and stopped ten feet from the wagons. Out on the public road we could see a crowd of onlookers. Farmers with pick-up trucks, three police cars, the tall, bearded figure of Crispian Barlow peering worriedly through the mesh and a group of excited Africans in ranger uniforms. Too late, they had brought us the walkie-talkies they had promised us earlier that day.

Mossie Mostert, two of his brothers and his father, Albert, walked up to the minibus. 'We want your tapes,' said Mostert Senior. 'You did not have permission to film on my land.'

I pointed out to him that his son and McDonald had not objected to the video and, what was more, I had paid to hunt on his reserve.

Howard Foster and Andy Rex got out and started to negotiate with the police. They came back ten minutes later: 'It's looking bad,' Foster said. 'More farmers are arriving by the minute and they're pressurising the police to do what the Mosterts want.'

At least with the police present, the likelihood of being shot had diminished but the prospect of having to hand over our precious film loomed large. Then I had an idea. Crispian Barlow was out on the road. Because he lived locally he didn't want to be associated with us once we had revealed who we really were. His pretext for being in this vicinity was that we had been renting accommodation from him and that we had left without paying. He was here to get what we owed him.

We retrieved every single tape from the back of the minibus and stuffed them into Salk's jacket. He and Howard Foster walked to the gate and explained to one of the more reasonable police officers that we owed the man with the beard for several nights' stay on his farm. The banks closed in twenty minutes and would it be all right if one of us went with Mr Barlow to get his money? Keen to remove any further source of conflict, the officer agreed and Salk slipped out of the gate and walked as nonchalantly as he could to Crispian's car and they sped off almost unnoticed, not stopping, except for fuel, until they reached Johannesburg seven hours later.

An hour later, the gates were finally pulled open for us. A burly Afrikaner cop walked up to the minibus and leaned into the front passenger window. He spoke to me quietly. 'See, we have opened the gates for you, but take this advice. They will not kill you while we are here. If you were still here in a few hours, you could end up with a bullet between your eyes and there would be no witnesses. Go a long way from here, gentlemen.'

It sounded like good advice to me.

Twenty-four hours later, I shook hands with Andy Rex before leaving for Johannesburg airport with the tapes safely stowed in my luggage. He relaxed his crushing grip and smiled. 'We should work together again sometime. I think I understand what you guys do it for now.'

At that moment, I wasn't so sure that *I* did.

What surprised me more than anything was the viewing figure for the programme: just under seven million. To me, it was one of the most dramatic we had made for a couple of years, and it had been broadcast to a nation of animal lovers. The truth of the matter was that the available audience now had more choice. The days of our pulling in ten or twelve million viewers were over. The BBC had got its act together over targeting popular programmes and putting strong shows on in opposition to fight for viewer share. Now, satellite channels abound and if there is Premier League football on, as there had been when the programme on South Africa was aired, up to twelve per cent of your audience is no longer available. Add the arrival of Channel Five into this mix and you begin to see why the figures of a few years ago might not be achievable.

The effect of the programme worldwide was incredible. It was bought immediately for showing on South African television. There was a huge outcry and Nelson Mandela declared that it was time to change and enforce the laws. Ninety professional hunters had their licences suspended, including Sandy McDonald. Roy Plath, the man who allowed the lioness to be shot on his land – and had inadvertently led us to make our programme – suffered the wrath of the South African housewife.

He was a banana grower supplying one of the biggest supermarket chains in the country. When it was realised that his bananas were on sale in their favourite foodstore, the housewives started petitions nationwide urging the supermarkets to boycott his fruit – and he lost his contract.

The programme was eventually broadcast three times in South Africa – where it spawned a couple of follow-up investigations by local television – as well as in Australia and Germany. We also won an award at the 'Animal Oscars' in Los Angeles, sponsored by the Hollywood celebrities of the Ark Trust.

For another year, we produced two series – covering stories as diverse as an exposé of chart-rigging in the record industry, the rise of a new Fascist party in Britain and the control of prostitution by the Russian Mafia.

Then, for a number of different reasons, the retirement I had once contemplated but rejected, was almost thrust upon me.

The programmes that are broadcast on independent television are chosen by a central body called The Network Centre. The people who work there are vulnerable to removal at the drop of a hat – it is just a reflection of the way commercial television is susceptible to market forces.

In autumn 1997, a new regime came into power. Part of its brief was to halt a slide in ITV viewing audiences. Wholesale changes were clearly going to have to be made.

Apart from a vow to push for the moving of the 'News at Ten' to allow feature films and dramas to be shown 'uninterrupted', there was also an understanding that the new people would revamp factual programmes – of which 'The Cook Report', 'The Big Story' and 'World in Action' were the main examples.

A sudden paralysis seemed to overtake Carlton, which made 'The Cook Report' and 'The Big Story'. Rumours of the imminent demise of Granada's 'World in Action' were rife. No one knew what was happening for sure, but it didn't look good. Carlton was already in the wars over a documentary called 'The Connection' which, it turned out, had largely been falsified by its producer, who had roundly abused the trust of his employers. It was a shameful affair and the head of the London-based department that made the programme was heavily criticised. In my view, other senior executives also became sacrificial lambs.

The effect was to create a defensive atmosphere within Carlton, which was threatened with a heavy fine and, an extreme but unlikely measure, the revocation of its licence to broadcast. The fine was duly levied – £2 million – but the company stayed in business. Hardly a situation to encourage the recommissioning of more investigative programmes like ours.

By Christmas, it was obvious that the 'Cook Report' team were not going to have their contracts renewed. I was told that nobody knew what the future of the series was. We knew the Network wanted a couple of hour-long investigative specials, but was that all?

I didn't know what to do, so I called my agent. Always a man with acute antennae, even Jon Roseman had to confess that nobody could tell what was happening at Network Centre.

I decided to take the bull by the horns and end the uncertainty. After twelve years and more than one hundred high-profile programmes, I had long wanted to reduce my workload. So, after discussion with family and colleagues, I took the decision to announce that I was going to quit the series while I was ahead, as I had done in 'Checkpoint' days. Carlton issued a short press release, which included confirmation of the one-hour specials.

There were soon lots of stories circulating about me finally recognising that I could no longer cope with being battered and bruised. One paper, going one better, headlined its story: 'Cook Quits as Ratings Fall and Beatings Rise'. In fact the reverse was true. I hadn't been hit for a couple of years, and the ratings, at around eight million, had actually risen over the previous series. But why let the facts get in the way of a catchy headline?

At the end of the day, the truth was that I, and every other programme-maker in commercial television, was still in the dark about the future.

Christmas and New Year came and went.

Then came news from the Network Centre. They wanted me to work with Yorkshire Television to present ITV's planned competitor for the BBC's 'Watchdog'. I declined this offer. It just wasn't my kind of thing, but I did accept the offer of two one-hour investigative specials from Yorkshire Television to add to the pair already commissioned from Carlton.

It was all very puzzling the way those at the top seemed to be blowing hot and cold. I learnt later that a senior Network Centre executive had been sitting in the back of a London taxi when the driver started to bemoan the ending of 'The Cook Report'. I have the eloquence of the cabbie to thank for renewed interest in us because, apparently, it prompted the executive to review the programme's viewing figures. No doubt he was reminded that we were still by far the most watched *and* the most appreciated current affairs show in the country.

So, back in harness with a new team at Yorkshire Television, we made a programme on a subject I have touched on before – the fugitives from justice whom the authorities refuse to pursue. I enjoyed working with them and the programme was well received.

Back at Carlton, Howard Foster had been kept on to make the two one-hour specials. He and his colleagues Philip Braund and Stephen Scott produced programmes on art theft and car crime – and we ended 1998 with an amazing audience of almost nine and a half million.

And, with a new two-year contract to make four one-hour specials a year, plus a possible further series of six half-hours, the future looks bright.

At last, I think I have reconciled the needs of work and home. When I work, I work full-time. When I am at home, I am a family man wholeheartedly. The two have become separate at last, with the lessening of my workload. But never let it be said that Roger Cook has decided to take life too easy. The big bloke with the tough questions and the TV crew at his shoulder still has something to say to those with something to hide.